Working
without
Weaning

A working mother's
guide to breastfeeding

Working

without

Weaning:

A working mother's guide to breastfeeding

Hale Publishing
1712 N. Forest
Amarillo, TX 79106
www.iBreastfeeding.com
(806)376-9900
(800)378-1317

ISBN: 0-9772268-6-7

ISBN 13 digit: 978-0-9772268-6-3

Library of Congress Number: 2006927741

Printed by Friesens
Printed in Canada

Working *without* Weaning:

A working mother's guide to breastfeeding

Kirsten Berggren, PhD, CLC

Hale Publishing

1712 N. Forest St. ▪ Amarillo, Texas 79106

© Copyright 2006

Table of Contents

Acknowledgements

> *"Writers are vacuum cleaners who suck up other people's lives and weave them into stories like a sparrow builds a nest from scraps."*
>
> –Garrison Keillor; quoted in *Time*, page 92- April 4, 2004

This book has certainly been a weaving together of scraps, and without the contents of the many brains I've hoovered, I never would have been able to do it. My special group of Bosom Buddies deserve the highest accolades – you know who you are, and I never would have been able to do this without you. From the time I joined the group back in 2000, we supported each other, dug up information, figured out what worked, and all pumped and breastfed our babies for the better part of a year. Some of us longer. Some of us *much* longer... I will happily single myself out as the poorest memory in the group, so please accept apologies for any special tips or details that I left out – but I was the one casting about at loose ends looking to be grabbed by a calling, so I got to be the one to write it down. Thanks especially to Emily, who agreed to start this project with me, giving me the kick in the pants I needed to get started. And a huge thanks to those of you who I've quoted in this book – your stories make it real.

Thanks to all the anonymous and not-so-anonymous women who've posted to the various working and pumping message boards where I hang out – your questions were ultimately the inspiration for this book, and I hope I've answered at least a few of them here for the next generation of women who will be pumping and working.

I have to thank my former boss Jack for providing me with a private office and the flexibility to pump whenever I needed to. As this book and my website consumed more and more of my energy, I probably wasn't the best employee – I think I did him a favor by quitting before he had to fire me – but I still give the company high marks for being very breastfeeding friendly.

Thanks to Gregg at the Department of Nursing, who gave me an office with my small teaching appointment – providing a much-needed location for my work on this book and my unfunded research.

Thanks to Kree for inspiring me with your doula work and passion for natural childbirth and breastfeeding. You and Dr. Kennell were my start in this field!

To my parents – all of you – who have been so supportive of my various and sundry careers and efforts – you are my A-Team of support, and I owe you all my deepest thanks. One of these days I'll even figure out what I want to be when I grow up. Thank you Kay for being my breastfeeding role model when I was an impressionable youth. Thanks to my mom for breastfeeding me and supporting everything I've ever done. A special thank you to you and Fran for underwriting the final push to finish the book.

The most important acknowledgement goes to the two little mouths and bellies that needed my pumped milk all those months, Kairos Truth and Talia River, my two babies. Kai and Talia gave me everything I needed to write this book – two babies who proved to me that breast really is best, and that all my efforts to provide them with breastmilk in their first years were really worth it. Of course, now they clamor for lollipops and cheetos, but that's another story.

And finally, thanks to my husband. He's a great dad, and is putting the kids to bed as I write this so that I have time to work. You were the one who agreed that breastfeeding was the way to go, just because Kree and I said so. You tossed the "free gifts" of formula in the trash. You never doubted that breastmilk was just the right food in just the right amounts for our slowish-growing boy and tubbalicious girl. And you gave me the writing weekends I needed, even if it wasn't quite on your schedule! Thanks, Robyn, for everything.

Introduction

Who am I to say?

You may be wondering, who made me the expert on working and pumping? Where do I come up with these recommendations I'm making? First of all, let me be perfectly clear – I am *not* a health care professional. I may be called "Doctor," but that's because I have a PhD in Neurobiology, not because I've been trained to take care of patients. So, nothing in this book should be construed as medical advice. It's one compulsively well-informed mom's experience and opinions. There, disclaimer done.

I do, however, have years of experience working with moms who are breastfeeding after they go back to work. The first one was me! I started back to work when my son was only a few weeks old, and was full time by the time he was three months. I was so lucky – I had an accommodating boss, a private office, a nice breast pump, and yet, even with all the advantages, I had a hard time pumping enough. I joined an online group of working and pumping moms, and as a group, we muddled through. There were no right answers, but we learned from each other, from the occasional well-versed professional one of us would encounter, and from experience. With the help of that group, I was able to meet my goal of pumping for my son for a full year, without ever giving him formula – although it was pretty close for a few weeks there as I struggled to rebuild a diminished supply.

Why write a book?

The support of that group of women made it possible for so many of us to meet our goals – but as time went on, I realized that our collective wisdom was drifting away.

Moms would leave the group when they were finished pumping, and a new bunch would come through – with exactly the same questions I thought we had just answered only weeks or months ago; I realized the knowledge was not being passed on. My first move was to stay with this online group in the capacity of "community leader." But again, I got frustrated with having to answer the same exact questions over and over – with new people on the board being just as clueless as I'd been when I joined. I talked this over with the other moms who I'd pumped with (our "graduating class," as it were), and as a group, we realized that we had more collective knowledge than was in any of the books we had read, and I was the one who decided to write it down.

I had a background in technical writing, so it wasn't such a stretch that I was the one to start to write the new "manual" for working and pumping. I will absolutely admit, however, that I am far from the most organized of the women I pumped with, nor the best notetaker – so I beg forgiveness for any pearls of wisdom given to me that I dropped.

That said, I am also a scientist by training, and feel comfortable reviewing the scientific literature on breastfeeding for information for this book. So when I make a scientific or medical recommendation, I try to base it on scientific fact (for example, the fact that you can leave breastmilk sitting out for 10 hours is based on the fact that it has living immune cells and anti-bacterial enzymes, and someone really did the experiment to confirm that bacteria didn't grow). Sadly, there really is not much literature about the best ways to manage breastfeeding, although we are learning more every day about how important breastfeeding is to women's and childrens' health - see the next upcoming section, "Why Combine Work and Breastfeeding" for more on this. Because there isn't that much research on pumping, I try to be clear when I am basing something I say on research (by putting in citations) versus when I'm basing a recommendation on the collective experience of what I call "The W&P community." This book is also full of my opinion, and lots of it. If you see a recommendation not credited to anyone else, it's probably something I just decided to say – and as a scientist, I probably based it on some kind of fact somewhere along the way, but there's always the chance that I just thought it up.

Mostly, use what works for you. Every mother, every baby, every pumping experience is different. I'm here to give you a lot of ideas to try – take what works and ignore what doesn't. And remember, I am not a medical professional, and nothing in this book should be construed as medical advice, got it?

First, feed the baby

This is the number one rule of lactation consulting. I make a lot of suggestions that involve holding off bottles, making what you pump during the day last till you get there, and other things that could be construed as withholding food. It's important to know that these recommendations are based on the assumption that your baby will have free and unlimited access to the breast for the majority of the hours in a 24-hour-day. Whether those hours are at night or not, this free access is usually enough to guarantee that your baby is getting enough to eat. However, the most important job you have as a mom is to monitor the health of your baby. If your baby seems like she's hungry all the time, if she's not gaining weight, if she looks saggy and dehydrated, remember, First, Feed the Baby. Exclusive breastmilk is a good goal to have, but not at the cost of a malnourished baby. 99.9% of women are able to provide plenty of milk to their babies when they are nursing directly, but adding pumping and bottles to the mix does complicate things. You're still a good mom if you have to rely on Carnation or Similac to provide some portion of your baby's calories when you're at work. I will argue until I'm blue in the face that breastfeeding is absolutely critical to the well-being of a woman and her child. There is no longer any doubt that it is the best choice. And yet, the need to return to work is a significant barrier to breastfeeding. And so I firmly stand by the belief that "mostly breastfeeding" or "as much breastfeeding as possible" are absolutely viable options for working mothers. It depends on your own goals – and only you can decide what is right for you.

A note to lactation consultants

This book is written as a mother-to-mother source of information and support. I would love for lactation consultants and La Leche League leaders to read it so they will be better able to help working mothers – however, just realize that not everything in here is "by the book" breastfeeding advice. I am fully aware of this fact. My role is to help moms think outside the box in the face of some pretty challenging barriers, and so if my advice contradicts what you're teaching, please forgive me! I hope between the two of us, we can provide moms with enough choices that they can figure out a solution that works for them.

My website

The companion to this book is www.workandpump.com, put together by yours truly. I'll refer to documents you can download from my site in this book. I also host message boards for real - time support and community, so be sure to drop by.

Notes on language

Baby gender: In this book, I try to be as inclusive as possible, and hopefully this is reflected in the language. I randomly alternate between "him" and "her" when referring to your baby (easy for me, I have a boy and a girl). I aimed to equally include moms of sons and daughters, but I couldn't abide by calling the baby "it" or "him or her" for a whole book.

Who is this "Partner" person? I know that people have all kinds of family arrangements, so when referring to the person who is living with you who provides most of the parenting help, I chose the word "partner." This could be your husband, same-sex partner, sibling, close friend, parent or grandparent. For those of you living alone and single parenting, my hat is off to you; you are the hardest working person I know. I hope there is someone in your life who you can call on to do some of the chores I assign to the "partner" in this book – parenting is too much work to do entirely alone (it takes a village, you know).

Culturo-centrism: I live in the United States, and you'll see that reflected in my language (like, I don't know how to spell words like "grey" and "realise"). I hope this writing is not too culture-centric for those of you living in other countries. The principles are pretty universal, but if you live in a place enlightened enough to give a proper maternity leave, you don't need this book anyway. (Ahem, US congress, you paying attention? Put me out of business, please!)

The term "pumping": For the most part, I use the words "pump" and "pumping" when I talk about extracting milk from your breasts. Many women use hand expression exclusively, and never hook up to a machine to get the milk out. However, because the majority of you will be using a pump (and because "work and pump" has a better ring to it than "work and express") I say "pumping." Hand expressers unite – y'all rock – just so you don't feel left out.

Who's watching the baby? I usually use the term "care provider" to talk about the person who will take care of your baby when you are at work. This can be a formal daycare center, an in-home center, a relative, or someone who watches your child in your own home. Because my kids went to a (fabulous) daycare center, sometimes I will say "at daycare" to mean the time when I was at work and my kids were with a care provider, but this applies to those of you whose babies are in any other care situation as well.

Why combine work and breastfeeding?

If you're reading this book, you must have some idea that combining breastfeeding with your return to work is a good thing, but if you want to hear my reasons, here they are:

In short, you express milk at work for two reasons. The first is so you can provide the nutrition of breastmilk for your baby when you are apart. The second (one that a lot of people don't think about) is that you pump milk during the day to keep up your milk supply so that you can continue to breastfeed when you are together. This means that you can still have the warmth and closeness of breastfeeding whenever you are with your baby. Nutrition plus bonding, does it get any better? The combination of these two outcomes makes your efforts during the day so worthwhile that I have never, in six years of doing this, heard a mom express any regret for the time she spent pumping at work. You'll find more information on reasons to breastfeed in the next few pages.

You may have heard that dealing with pumping, extracting and storing milk, all the stuff that goes with being a working and breastfeeding mom, is really a pain. And you know what? You're right. It is hard. It is indeed more difficult *during the workday* than switching to formula. But let me tell you about the time when you're home.

One of my favorite times of day when my babies were little was the moment I arrived at daycare to pick them up. I would sit down in the baby-room rocker and latch them on, and we'd nurse right then and there. I got a nice, soothing oxytocin rush from nursing which helped me relax at the end of the day, and I could sit and gloat over the one thing I could give my baby that nobody else had. There's something special about being needed in that way when other people are with your baby most of the day.

And how about the nighttime? I can remember so vividly sitting up at night nursing my son – it was such a special time. The house was quiet, my husband asleep, and it was just me and Kai. He would nurse, reach up and touch my face, look into my eyes or doze off; I loved those hours. With my daughter I had equally special times, but by then we were fully co-sleeping, so the nighttime blessings with her involved the fact that I never had to get out of bed to mix bottles or get anything for her. Often I would nurse her without even waking all the way up (way more on this in the section on "Nighttime parenting" in Chaper 8!), and she was able to get most of her nutrition "straight from the tap."

Weekends were a breeze because we could just walk out the door with a clean diaper or two and be gone most of the day. The food was always with us! And I knew I'd always have something my baby liked, and something to soothe him if he got fussy.

True confessions – I am the ultimate "one-trick pony" of infant parenting. Crying baby? Boob. Fall down go boom? Boob. Sleepy? Boob. Not sure what else to try? Boob. Having the breast as a soother was such a blessing with my colicky son, and no less of one with my easy-going daughter. Nothing wrong with this approach – I learned new tricks when they got older, and my husband got to be really good at soothing when the trusty boob didn't do the trick.

However, I think the most important part of breastfeeding after I went back to work was the feeling of confidence it gave me that I was still a good mom, even if I did have to be away a lot. I was able to feel connected with my baby even when I couldn't be there. I knew I was a good mom, doing the best for my baby. We all go back to work for different reasons, and ultimately, our choices involve doing what we think is best for our families. But there was always that little bit of guilt about being away. I think breastfeeding helped me a lot with that. Even when I was at work, I was doing something for my child! I was making milk all day long, never fully detached from them. I can't imagine doing it any other way.

Why choose breastfeeding?

This is just my personal perspective – if you're breastfeeding, you may already know all of the health reasons to do it, so I won't belabor the point. However, the health benefits of breastfeeding are no longer seen as some kind of "fringe benefit" we give our babies if we want to go above and beyond. Babies who do not receive breastmilk are at increased risk for childhood diseases such as allergies, asthma, ear infections, respiratory infections, and life-threatening bacterial infections. Additionally, many of the benefits of breastmilk are being found to be dose-dependent. This means that the longer a baby is exclusively breastfed, the more protection they receive. I just came across a paper showing that exclusive breastfeeding for four months resulted in significantly lower rates of common respiratory infections - you know, the kind that keep you out of work (Bachrach et al., 2003). It's taken a while for researchers to start to focus on the effects of *exclusive* breastfeeding versus *any* breastfeeding, but now that it is being examined more carefully, exclusive breastfeeding is showing more and more benefits as compared even to mixed feeding. Finally, many of the adult diseases that are major public health issues today can be linked to a lack of breastfeeding. Rates of type 2 diabetes, obesity, digestive diseases like Crohn's disease and irritable bowel disease (IBD), and allergies are all higher in adults who were not breastfed. Rather than list all of the references here (which would take several pages), I'll refer you to two excellent sources of information: Dr. Newman's annotated Risks of Formula Feeding (http://www.kellymom.com/newman/risks_ of_formula_08-02.html) and a more recently updated page on the health benefits of breastfeeding put together by the International Chiropractic Pediatric Association (http://www.icpa4kids.org/ research/children/breastfeeding.htm).

I wasn't breastfed, and I'm fine!

So what if you were formula fed and a healthy Harvard graduate? Remember, this talk about health risk is all statistics. We all know someone who doesn't use a seat belt and has never been hurt in a car, who smoked cigarettes into their healthy nineties, or that skinny person who eats McDonald's every day. But we understand that these activities carry risks, even if each person who does them isn't guaranteed to be any worse off. Statistics doesn't mean that every child who is not breastfed will get ear infections (or whatever other disease) – it just means that if your child is breastfed, they will be *less likely* to get ear infections. You're *reducing the risk* – not eliminating it or signing on for any guarantees. For example, we now know that a baby who is not breastfed is about 20% more likely to die during the newborn period (Chen & Rogan, 2004). Does that mean that 20% of formula-fed babies will die? Of course not. It means that while our incidence of newborn death is very low in this country, it could be 20% lower if all babies were breastfed (which translates to about 700 babies a year. This is a big number, but compared to the number of babies born every year, it's still a very small percentage – less than 1%.)

But I didn't breastfeed my older child

What if you have an older child who was not breastfed – am I trying to make you feel guilty? Of course not! As parents, we all do the best we can with the information we have. You've gotten new information; you can make different choices. If returning to work was the reason you stopped breastfeeding an older child – well, all the more reason to try it again. You've done the hard part – you've figured out what your barriers are. Now you can read on to figure out how to solve them.

Remember your goals and motivations

Once you start back to work, try to remember the reasons you chose breastfeeding in the first place. My incentive was that I was extremely concerned about dairy exposure, since my family has a history of dairy allergies. Soy wasn't an option because I was freaked out about the pesticides used in growing soybeans and exposing my kids to plant hormones. Whenever I questioned my ability to keep pumping, I would think about my childhood of congestion, sinus infections and sore throats from my dairy allergy, and that would help me keep going.

My husband is a real "stick-it-to-the-man" 60's throwback, and his breastfeeding motivation was about keeping our hard-earned dollars out of the pockets of the pharmaceutical industry (formula companies). When my husband felt like it was too much work for me, or I complained about pumping, I would remind him that we weren't supporting Corporate America, and that would be enough to reinvigorate his support and get him through washing those bottles one more time. Write down your initial motivations, and keep them posted where you wash bottles. It may seem too obvious, but really, it does help.

The ProMoM website has a great motivational list called "101 Reasons to Breastfeed Your Baby," if you need any more reminders of why it's so great (www.promom.org/101/).

I've never met a mom who said that pumping at work was the easy thing to do. But every single mom I've ever talked to is proud of the time she spent pumping. The sense of accomplishment is something nobody can ever take away from you – when you reach whatever milestone you've set for yourself, you'll have something you can really feel good about.

Is it really going to be this hard?

Some people spend a great deal of their lives looking for something to go wrong. Call it the "glass half empty" syndrome, pessimism, being "concerned" or anxious – whatever you call it, I think you know who you are. If you are this type of person, listen up! Do Not read this book and think "oh, look at all the things that can go wrong – these will all happen to me, I'll never be able to keep breastfeeding after I go back to work." That's *totally* not the point. I am here to tell you that you CAN breastfeed for as long as you want to, whether you go back to work or not.

Think of this book like the owner's manual for your car. First you use it to find out where the dipstick is and basic stuff like that, and occasionally you look at it for things like how often the tires should be rotated and what kind of oil to put in. But, once you've checked this stuff, mostly you shove your owner's manual in the glovebox in case something goes wrong. The existence of the owner's manual doesn't mean things are going to go wrong – it's just in case. This book contains your basic operating instructions. Every situation may not apply to every mother, just like how my car's manual tells me how to put it in park even though I have a manual transmission. Use this book to get the information you need, and if there's a problem you don't have (similar to the instructions for putting out gas tank fires that are in my car manual – which I certainly hope I never have to deal with), so much the better!

In answering questions online, occasionally I will come across a woman about to go back to work who says "gee, I wasn't worried at all, but after reading this message board, I'm really starting to freak out!" Whoa! That's not supposed to happen! I want you to recognize the difference between being well prepared and freaking out. The difference between these two states is confidence. Believe that you can breastfeed your baby for as long as you want to – because you can! There are virtually zero obstacles that make weaning mandatory, and I'm hoping that with the information in this book, working and pumping can become just a regular part of your daily life. Not a terrible stress or a terrible hassle – just one of the things that you do as a mom. Which is a wonderful thing to be, by the way.

There are a number of common things that women struggle with – and usually the problems arise because of a lack of information and support. My hope is to provide the information and support up front so that you never even run into a problem. But if you do have trouble, if at any point you feel like working and pumping is getting to be too hard, please, turn to this book. The answers are here, and if they're not here, I hope I've pointed you towards enough resources to find the answer on your own.

You there – don't freak out! You can do it, you won't have any problems you can't solve, it won't be too hard, and if you keep freaking out, you're really going to bring me down. C'mon, just smile – it'll be fun!

References:

http://www.kellymom.com/newman/risks_of_formula_08-02.html

http://www.icpa4kids.org/research/children/breastfeeding.htm

www.promom.org/101

Bachrach V, Schwarz, E. et al. 2003. Breastfeeding and the risk of hospitalization for respiratory disease in infancy: a meta-analysis. *Archives of Pediatrics and Adolescent Medicine* **157**(3): 237-243.

Chen A, Rogan WJ. 2004. Breastfeeding and the risk of postneonatal death in the United States. *Pediatrics* **113**(5): e435-439.

Getting ready for breastfeeding

Even if you're worried about your return to work, remember that the most important thing for you to do on your maternity leave is to learn all about your new baby and get breastfeeding well established. The section "Making plans with your employer," discusses how to set things up with your boss. If you haven't had your baby yet, think about making these plans before you go on leave, or as soon as possible. By planning ahead, you will be more able to relax and enjoy your baby during the time that you can be at home. The rest of this chapter discusses how you can best prepare for breastfeeding, so if you already have a nursing baby in your arms, just skip ahead to the chapters that are more specific to your return to work.

I'm not pretending to write a book all about breastfeeding – just about maintaining breastfeeding after you go back to work. But having a good start to your breastfeeding relationship is an essential part of the equation, so I would like to pass on some tips I've picked up over the years. Here's the most important tip: the number of women who are physically unable to breastfeed is so small it's hardly even worth discussing. Our bodies are designed to feed our babies, and if you are able to carry a baby through a healthy pregnancy, you can be 99.9% sure that you can feed your baby from your breasts. A large majority of women never have any trouble at all with breastfeeding, so don't expect that you will have problems – but you should still do whatever you can to insure the best start. Breastfeeding is natural, but it's not always easy in the first few weeks, so it's wise to go into it armed with good information and with good support lined up. You can learn to recognize things that can cause trouble in order to avoid them, but you should expect that everything will work out just fine – why wouldn't it?

Take a breastfeeding class

Everyone takes a childbirth class, and childbirth takes what – a day? Maybe 2? You'll be breastfeeding for a lot longer than that, and quite frankly, breastfeeding has a much bigger impact on your baby's health than the birth. Yet breastfeeding classes are attended by maybe 20% of parents-to-be. This needs to change. Breastfeeding is natural and instinctive for humans, but that doesn't mean that it's necessarily easy. Women have been breastfeeding since there have been women and babies, but never have we been so distanced from the other women in our families and community. A woman learning to breastfeed 100 years ago was surrounded by her family, her mother, aunts, grandmother, cousins and sisters who had all breastfed themselves and were there to help her and offer tips. The collective wisdom of these women was always there, right in your home. These days, most of us don't live in the same town as our mothers (thank goodness, right?) and many of our mothers didn't even breastfeed us. Doctors are not adequately trained in breastfeeding, we may hear contradictory advice, and many of us are surrounded by forces that will try to undermine breastfeeding (think about all those formula ads promising happy quiet babies, free samples delivered to your door, grandmothers questioning if your baby is getting enough… oh, the list goes on and on).

Take a breastfeeding course – it's usually only a couple of hours, and it can really help you know what to expect. You will be learning from a breastfeeding professional, not just hearing what your doctor, mother, partner or neighbor has heard "from friends." You will learn to recognize a good latch, and see the first signs that there is a problem needing to be fixed. In doing so, you will be able to prevent any problem from becoming serious.

Look for an instructor who is certified as a CBE (certified breastfeeding educator), CLC (certified lactation counselor) or IBCLC (International Board Certified Lactation Consultant).

Find a lactation consultant

Just as you interview potential pediatricians before your baby is born, you should find a lactation consultant. You may never need to call her, but I have had more than one friend tell me they put off calling until they were in real trouble because they just didn't have the energy to hunt someone down in the midst of the post-partum chaos.

> The breastfeeding careers were not certified until recently, and anyone can call themselves a "lactation consultant," but those using the letters IBCLC have passed a certification exam and have thousands of hours of experience. There are great lactation consultants who are not certified and bad ones who are, but at least the certification guarantees a consistency in education.

Whether you are being seen by an OB or a midwife during your pregnancy, a midwife's office will usually have the best recommendations for a lactation consultant, as they tend to focus more on the normal processes of pregnancy, childbirth, and infant care.

You can sometimes find a lactation services group in the phone book under Lactation, or ask your doctor's office for a recommendation. Calling your local La Leche League (LLL) leader is another great resource (use the "find a leader" tool on the LLL website at www.llli.org).

You don't need to have a meeting with the lactation consultant before your baby is born; one phone conversation is plenty. Find someone you are comfortable talking with, and someone who has predictable hours and returns calls promptly. Having her number by the phone after the baby is home with you can be the difference between getting help for problems when they are easily resolved or having them escalate into true obstacles.

Your pediatrician may advertise their nursing staff as lactation consultants – this is a very good sign and means that the office is generally breastfeeding friendly, but ask if they are board certified, or IBCLCs. If not, find a board certified lactation consultant or LLL leader just in case. It certainly can't hurt to have a phone number around if the advice coming from your doctor doesn't feel right to you, or they recommend weaning for any reason.

Choose a breastfeeding friendly pediatrician

Many parents-to-be schedule a meeting with their pediatrician before the baby is born. Pediatricians usually do this as a free visit – just an informal "get to know you" session. There are a few questions you can ask when meeting with a pediatrician that tell you a lot about their level of breastfeeding support. Let them know you are planning on breastfeeding, and then ask a few of the following:

Number of breastfeeding patients and duration

Ask how long most of their patients breastfeed, and if it's less than 6 months, ask why they stop. If the doctor says things like "most women encounter difficulty" or "there's no need to breastfeed longer than that" or "it isn't convenient to breastfeed" or "they can't breastfeed after going back to work" – run! This doctor isn't going to be very supportive. However, if they express frustration at the low levels, or say they wish they were higher, there may be hope. Go with your gut feelings. You need to like this person, you'll be spending a fair bit of time together.

What is the protocol when baby doesn't gain on schedule?

It's useful to know what a doctor will do when a breastfed baby doesn't gain weight according to schedule, or loses too much after being born. Normally, babies lose 7-10% of their birthweight in the first few days after being born. This is easy to understand – they go from the all-you-can-eat food bar of the umbilical cord to having to actually exert effort to feed. They are learning the new skill of coordinating sucking and breathing. And they are drying out. Babies are born aquatic animals and have to adjust to living in dry air. Some of the weight loss is just their skin and lungs drying out.

> There is some thought that babies born by cesarean section tend to lose closer to 10% of birth weight because they are born with extra water on board (edema) from the drugs used in the surgery.

Ask your doctor their protocol if more than this is lost.

A good protocol:

The first step should be to assess the baby's nursing – a lactation consultant or the doctor should watch the baby at the breast to be sure he has a good latch and is transferring milk effectively. This first visit and breastfeeding assessment should be within 72 hours of hospital discharge, if not sooner.

If the latch looks good and is comfortable, the doctor may use a high-precision scale to weigh the baby before and after a feed to see how much milk is being transferred.

Sometimes poor milk transfer is caused by a tight frenulum (the strip of skin that attaches the tongue to the bottom of the mouth – this is also called "tongue tie"). This can be easily clipped in the first few days of life with little trauma to the baby, since the thin skin has few blood vessels and nerves at this point. You can ask your doctor if they will clip tongue-tie themselves or if they refer to an oral surgeon. If they have no idea what you're talking about, or say tongue-tie is never a problem for breastfed babies, again – run.

What next? If the latch is good, and the baby seems awake and alert, a breastfeeding-friendly doc will recommend a "wait and see" approach.

Supplementing should never be the first step in addressing weight gain concerns, but sometimes it is needed. Correcting a faulty latch will prevent 90% of weight gain issues, but if supplementing is needed, it can be done with a tube-feeder at the breast, with cups or with syringe feeding. You can ask your doctor what they like to use, remembering that bottles are not the best place to start.

If your doctor is unable to solve breastfeeding problems, do they have lactation support on staff, or an ICBLC to whom they commonly refer?

Red Flags:

If the doctor says they routinely supplement with formula if a baby is not gaining well, and does not have someone on staff to evaluate latch and breastfeeding concerns, remember that these are not the methods supported by lactation professionals. If a doctor wants a mom to pump milk and feed the baby via bottle to "see how much he's getting" – this is also not a good first step. Most moms are so worried at this point about producing enough that it's hard to pump effectively, and a baby is always better at extracting milk from the breast than a pump.

Honest talk about feeding choices

Does your doctor acknowledge that there are health risks to formula feeding? Does he or she encourage breastfeeding to all patients? We have a weird societal issue with breastfeeding, and many health care professionals are leery of making a woman feel "guilty" for choosing not to breastfeed. Instead of worrying about guilt, we should be focused on making sure every woman gets the best breastfeeding support possible. It is clear that breastfeeding is the best health choice for a baby, and mothers need to know this. There are indeed a VERY small number of women who are not able to provide a full milk supply for their children, and another small group who must take medications that are not compatible with breastfeeding. When these women formula feed, they have no reason to feel guilty, and we are lucky that there is a reasonable substitute. If a woman makes an informed choice to formula feed, knowing that she is making a second-best nutrition choice, then she shouldn't feel guilty either. Well, maybe a little. Like when I let my kids have potato chips and pizza dough for dinner – I know it's not the best choice, and I certainly wouldn't complain if a doctor told me that – but sometimes you're just in a hurry, right? A little guilt helps us make the best choices for our kids! But all this concern over making a mother feel guilty for not breastfeeding is getting a little silly. It's the doctor who should feel guilty if he or she hasn't been able to help a mother enough, that much is clear. Anyway – we certainly don't spare the guilt if a mother is smoking while she's pregnant, or drinking alcohol, or not using a carseat. We all know what second-best health choices are, and physicians need to be honest about this with their patients. Some women will always choose to formula feed – that's their prerogative, just like feeding chips for dinner when you're rushing to swim class.

Breastfeeding recommendation

How long does your doctor recommend breastfeeding? The current recommendation of the American Academy of Pediatrics (AAP) is exclusive breastfeeding (no other foods) for about six months, and continued breastfeeding for a year or more. Even if the thought of breastfeeding for a year makes you kind of freak out, and you're hoping to breastfeed for a few months at best, having a doctor who recommends extended breastfeeding means that you will get the best support during whatever period of time you choose to breastfeed.

Be around breastfeeding before your baby is born

Many women have never even seen a baby breastfeed before they have their own child. It's good to demystify the process. If you have friends who are breastfeeding, ask if you can watch them. Watch with the eyes of a child – don't be afraid to get in close and check out the mechanics. A sure way to see breastfeeding in action is to attend a La Leche League (LLL) meeting. They welcome pregnant women to attend, and will be able to answer any questions you may have about breastfeeding. In addition, making contact with a LLL leader before your baby is born gives you one more person to call if you need support.

La Leche League is gradually changing their policies to be more welcoming towards working women; however, you may find some chapters in which your decision to return to work is challenged by the members or even the group leader. If at all possible, try to take what is of value from the group – their expertise in breastfeeding issues – and leave discussions of working mothers for another time. If you can find a chapter that meets in the evening, there are more likely to be working mothers there, who can share their experiences. Remember, there is precious little information out there for working and breastfeeding mothers (hence this book), so don't get discouraged if there are horror stories about how hard it was to work and pump. As the reader of this book, you are armed with more information than has ever before been available in one place for working and breastfeeding mothers (if I do say so myself), so be confident that with information and your body's innate ability to feed your child – you will succeed!

Rally support

Make your plans to breastfeed clear to those around you. Your partner is your most important support person, and must be 100% behind your efforts to breastfeed. I know, I'm making it sound like it's going to be so hard – it's not! Breastfeeding is the easiest way to feed your baby, but there can be small difficulties and frustrations along the way (just like anything worth doing), and if you are being undermined by those around you, it can become way too easy to quit. If you make it through the first two weeks, you will be in the clear – it's just that the first two weeks of being a new parent are hard, so you need people who support your choices around you.

Who is coming to help after the baby is born? Your mother, mother-in-law, an aunt or sister? Did they breastfeed their own children? If you have a choice, get the most supportive person to be there right after the baby is born, and maybe the relative who bottle fed all of her babies ("and they all turned out fine!") can come later to help out. If you have a friend, sister, mother, mother-in-law, or aunt who successfully breastfed and is supportive of you, this is a terrific person to come for the first few days after you get home with the baby. It's hard deciding who to have come right after the baby is born, and whoever is not invited to come first is going to feel insulted, but you'll just have to tell them that you want someone who can give you breastfeeding advice at the beginning, and you would appreciate their help more when you are starting to get back on your feet and will need more help with holding the baby, changing, bathing, and household stuff. Invite the great cook to come later!

A friend just had her grandmother come visit right after her baby was born, and let me tell you, it was crazy like you read about. I think Gran hadn't been there five minutes before she asked when the baby was going to be on a schedule (the baby was 5 days old). Then she ran through the standard list of breastfeeding-discouraging statements – it was like she had a script! "How do you know he's getting enough to eat? Is he eating again – you shouldn't feed him so often. Doesn't that hurt? Why can't I feed him a bottle for you so you can get some sleep? How long are you going to be doing that? Why is he crying? Is there something wrong with him?" I didn't think one person could be so simultaneously loving of her granddaughter and yet so thoroughly undermining. Honestly, it was something to watch. If you have this person in your life, have them wait at least two weeks to visit, then you'll be able to handle it. In the meantime, be sure you have a digital camera and high-speed internet connection so you can hold them off with an hourly stream of baby pictures.

Pitch the formula

Somehow, the formula companies know when you're going to have a baby. About two weeks before your due date, a package of formula will arrive on your doorstep as a "courtesy." A little more will arrive the day you are due to be discharged from the hospital. Isn't this thoughtful of them. How nice to have a premixed bottle of formula "just in case." Well, the companies are counting on that "just in case" – here's how it works (I'm absolutely jaded about this, if you couldn't tell – but read a book called *Milk, Money and Madness* by Naomi Baumslag and Dia Michels if you have any doubts about their intentions):

- ✂ You come home from the hospital with some preliminary breastfeeding instruction.

- ✂ You are alone, just you, your partner and this brand new little creature – needless to say you are a little stressed about being able to take care of it.

- ✂ It's 2:00AM and your baby is crying – you don't know why – she won't nurse, won't sleep, won't settle for anything. Maybe your breasts are hurting. Your post-partum hormones are a little out of whack and you're convinced you're the worst mother ever and you're starving your baby.

- ✂ You give "just one" bottle of formula to get her to settle – she falls asleep, and your confidence is shot. Turns out you really can't feed your baby – she must prefer the formula because look at her – she's sleeping! Maybe you persist in breastfeeding, but with the underlying suspicion that your baby prefers the formula (she slept so well). If it gets at all difficult, your resistance to switching is shot.

Here's my interpretation of these events:

∾ You didn't get enough breastfeeding instruction or help from the hospital. Perhaps you are getting sore nipples from a bad latch and your baby hasn't learned to efficiently transfer milk yet.

∾ Your baby is having a screaming fit because being born is a heck of a lot of hard work, and after 2-3 days of exhaustion and sleeping, she's finally come to the realization that the spa is closed and she can't get back in. She's pissed, but just needs to work through it (read the section "The first night home" in the Chapter 2 for more on this situation).

∾ You keep trying to nurse. In baby language your child is saying "just hold me and keep me comfortable. I used to live in a much warmer place where the kitchen never closed. I can't go back, I'm pissed, and I've got to get this disappointment off my chest. Just hold me and let me know it's OK."

∾ You hit the baby with a huge gut-bomb of sugar and milk and glop (i.e. formula) and she gives up – she's been drugged to sleep like your uncle Albert after Thanksgiving dinner.

∾ In the morning, she's fine, but you're demoralized. She just needs breastmilk, but now her mom (you) is all stressed out. If she could talk she would say "chill out mom, it's all cool now!"

So – take those lovely formula samples and toss 'em. You don't have to waste – any food shelf would be glad to have them, and if you think you'll want them back, give them to a neighbor to hang on to. Just give them to someone you're not willing to call at 2 AM. No child has ever starved in 12 hours, and in the morning you can have the lactation consultant come by if the baby hasn't settled down.

When she's screaming during the night, you may just need to check out for an hour and get some rest. Have your partner put on the baby carrier and take her for a nice long walk. Hold her and tell her you love her. Eventually she'll fall asleep, and you can get everything sorted out in the morning. Better yet, line up a friend who has breastfed successfully and see if she'll be on call for midnight re-assurances. A lot of new moms have this rough night in the first week – be ready for it, and you won't need that formula at all.

Have a good birth

A good birth is a great way to get off to a good start breastfeeding. Write up your birth preferences (aka "birth plan") making it very clear that you are going to breastfeed, and even if you have to have a cesarean or other surgical birth, arrange to have your first breastfeeding session in the first hour after the baby is born. There are a lot of things that you can do to insure a good start to breastfeeding, and most are listed in the WHO/UNICEF guidelines for a Baby Friendly Hospital. The Appendix lists the Ten Steps to Successful Breastfeeding for hospitals – most are directed towards early and effective breastfeeding support.

The most important thing is to get the help you need *when* you need it. For this reason, I cannot recommend highly enough having a doula present at your birth. A doula is a birth support professional whose job is to provide physical and emotional comfort to the mother during the birth process. Well, isn't this the job of the dad or partner? Yes, but how many births has your partner been to before? None? How about having someone with experience on hand? A good doula will not displace your partner as your primary support person, but will greatly facilitate your partner's ability to help you.

Here's my story: During our birth, our doula suggested a lot of things for my husband to do. When it became apparent to her that I was in back labor (what gave it away? The primal screams or the inability to get comfortable *anywhere*??) she suggested he apply some pressure to the small of my back and try sqeezing my hips during contractions. It was amazing how much that helped! When he was fading with exhaustion, she went to get him a sandwich and coffee so he wouldn't have to leave me, and then rubbed my feet while he took 5 minutes to eat. When our natural birth became a C-section, she stayed with me so my husband could go with our son while he was being examined. She didn't leave until she saw us breastfeeding well, checked in on us every day, and visited us at home the day we left the hospital and again the day after that. Marcia is a saint, and made a birth that spiraled out of our control feel manageable and whole.

Maybe you're saying "well, I have a midwife, so I don't need a doula" but the truth is that midwives and doulas work together all the time. In the hospital my midwife had another patient to check in on, but the doula never left the room. When the midwife was tending to the baby, the doula stayed with me. And when my husband descended into despair at the thought of a cesarean, she took him out of the room and told him he'd better put on a brave face for me and get excited because by hook or by crook he was going to be a dad that day. I can't imagine having a birth without her.

And, if you need any more convincing, Drs Klaus and Kennell have performed extensive studies on the benefit of having a doula present at a birth, and have concluded that the mere presence of a doula reduces requests for an epidural by 47% and lowers the C-section rate from 18% to 8% (Klaus & Kennell, 1991).

How to find a doula? www.dona.com has a nationwide listing, or ask your midwife or childbirth educator. Once again, members of your local La Leche League chapter may have recommendations as well. Doulas rule.

Making plans with your employer

This section covers how to make plans with your employer to support your breastfeeding relationship with your baby. For information on starting pumping and bottles before you go back to work, see Chapter 5 on "Starting Pumping and Bottles," and Chapter 6 on "Your First Days Back at Work."

The best time to plan the specifics of your return to work is before you start your maternity leave. Try to set aside time before your baby is born to talk to your employer about what you will need when you come back to work. In order to maintain breastfeeding and provide your baby with breastmilk when you are apart, you really only need two things:

- ೫ a clean and private space to use a few times a day

- ೫ about three flexible breaks of 20 minutes or so when you can pump milk for your baby.

If there have been women at your workplace who have pumped before you, talk to them about what arrangements they made and how it worked for them. Their experience is your most valuable asset. If you are the first, it can be a bit more challenging, but once your employer realizes that your needs are pretty simple, most are willing to help. The information in this chapter will help you put together a good argument for why it is in *their* best interest to be supportive – in business terms. As a brief summary, you can inform your boss that mothers who breastfeed miss less work due to infant illness, show more employee loyalty, and are more likely to stay in their position after the baby is born. So while it may seem like a lot to ask your employer for extra break time and your own private space, you will be providing them with something of value in return – a happier, more loyal employee who misses less work.

You may be concerned about making arrangements if you have never breastfed before and you're not even sure if you'll still be breastfeeding by the time you get back to work. This is a reasonable concern, but in my opinion, it's better to have the plans in place and not need them than to be scrambling at the last minute.

Getting up the nerve

Talking to your boss about anything to do with bodily functions can be mortifying. Especially when you bring the word "breast" into the picture. I think this is the main reason that a lot of women go back to work without a real plan for managing their pumping breaks – it's just too embarrassing to bring up! However, there is now enough research showing the real financial benefits to employers who support their breastfeeding moms that you can present your argument as a financial one, not an emotional appeal. Your boss may be the nicest person in the world, but unless they are extremely progressive, they don't really care that much about the beauty of your attachment to your baby. They are concerned about having an employee who will be reliable and won't cost them anything extra. Here's how to address these concerns.

When you let your boss know that you are pregnant, he or she will eventually ask you about your plans to return to work after maternity leave. When I had this conversation, I told my boss "I'll be back sooner if I can pump milk for my baby during the day." For my boss it became a matter of getting me back to work sooner – I was willing to take a six week maternity leave as long as my breastfeeding would be supported, since there wasn't anyone to cover for me while I was gone. This was a total ploy on my part. I couldn't afford to take any longer than that – but my boss didn't need to know that. And by making the length of my leave a negotiating point, I had gained the upper hand, and could tell him exactly what I needed: flexibility in my schedule so that I could close my door to pump whenever I needed to (I know, lucky dog, I had a private office).

If you're smarter or richer than me, you won't bargain away your maternity leave like that – but you can still have the upper hand by asking something like "how would you like to reduce the amount of sick days I need to take with my baby" or "how would you like to reduce our health care costs?" Only you know the concerns your employer has, but here's a list of financial points you can use to start the conversation (references follow at the end of the chapter):

₨ Parental absenteeism is three times higher for formula-fed infants as compared to breastfed babies (Cohen et al., 1995).

₨ Companies with an employee lactation support program experience less turnover and lower losses of skilled workers after childbirth. Additionally, these companies are rewarded with higher employee satisfaction, loyalty, and morale (US Breastfeeding Committee, 2002).

₨ Excess use of health care services attributable to formula feeding costs between $331 and $475 *per infant* in babies who never receive breastmilk (US Breastfeeding Committee, 2002; Ball & Wright, 1999).

₨ Companies that have adopted breastfeeding support programs have noted cost savings of $3 per $1 invested in breastfeeding support (US Breastfeeding Committee, 2002).

₨ Insurers pay at least $3.6 billion each year to treat diseases and conditions preventable by breastfeeding (US Breastfeeding Committee, 2002).

Government is on your side

If you think that government agencies will have any pull, you can mention that. The U.S. Department of Health and Human Services (HHS) stresses the importance of facilitating the continuation of breastfeeding after mothers return to their jobs (DHHS, 2000; US Breastfeeding Committee 2001; http://4women. gov/breastfeeding). Breastfeeding support is one of many steps employers can take to prevent chronic disease and improve the health of their employees. The Centers for Disease Control and Prevention (CDC) recommend workplace support for breastfeeding as a public health measure to improve health and reduce obesity rates in the population (www.cdc.gov/breastfeeding and http:// www.cdc.gov/nccdphp/dnpa/obesity). The professional health care organizations are recommending that mothers breastfeed exclusively for the first six months, and continue breastfeeding with the addition of complementary foods until the baby is at least one year old (AAP 2005; ACOG, 2007; AAFP, 2001).

Another strategy is to find out if your state has a breastfeeding-friendly employer award. This is also called the Family-friendly designation, Mother-friendly Business, or something along those lines. It's worth calling your state department of health to see if there is any formal recognition for employers who support breastfeeding. These programs generate a lot of publicity for employers who accommodate their breastfeeding moms. Positive PR is something every company wants, and these awards can really help companies with their recruitment. These recognition programs are also a key piece of winning the coveted "100 Best Companies to Work For" award from *Working Mother* magazine.

Public health institutions can be valuable allies in getting the accommodations you need to breastfeed. Breastfeeding is a public health issue because increasing breastfeeding rates can reduce rates of chronic health problems like obesity, asthma, diabetes, respiratory infections, and many other illnesses that have tremendous cost to society – it really does make a difference.

Many state programs can be found online. By late 2007, the CDC will list all state breastfeeding websites at www.cdc.gov/breastfeeding. These websites have information for employers about the benefits of supporting breastfeeding and how to get recognition. They also contain informational pamphlets for mothers and childcare providers about how to support breastfeeding for the working mother, and information on legislation to support working mothers where applicable. To find out if your state has a program, you can search online using your state name and the terms "breastfeeding" and "employment." Here are some examples:

Los Angeles: http://www.breastfeedingworks.org/index.htm

Oregon: http://www.dhs.state.or.us/policy/admin/safety/breastfeeding.htm

Texas: http://www.dshs.state.tx.us/wichd/lactate/mother.shtml

Washington: http://www.hmhbwa.org/forprof/materials/BCW_packet.htm

Wisconsin: http://dhfs.wisconsin.gov/health/Nutrition/Breastfeeding/bffriendlycomm.htm

Vermont (my state!): http://www.breasfeedvermont.info

There oughta be a law!

Some states do have legislation protecting a woman's right to express breastmilk for her baby during the workday. As of this writing (March, 2006), the states which explicitly protect this right or encourage protection are California, Connecticut, Georgia, Hawaii, Illinois, Minnesota, Rhode Island, Tennessee, Texas, and Washington. You can find a current list of breastfeeding legislation for your state at the National Conference of State Legislatures website (http://www.ncsl.org/programs/health/breast50.htm), from La Leche League (http://www.lalecheleague.org/LawBills.html) and from the US Breastfeeding Committee (http://www.usbreastfeeding.org/Publications.html). In addition, national breastfeeding bills (pending and enacted) can be found on Congresswoman Carolyn D. Maloney's website (http://maloney.house.gov). Congresswoman Maloney is really the voice of breastfeeding advocacy on capital hill, so I encourage you to check out her website and write her emails of encouragement! She's doing great work.

Seems time for a real world story of a mom who made pumping work for her in a very unlikely setting.

Nicole's story – corporate pumping

Nicole is a Quality Engineer for the Ford Motor Company. She works in an environment that is about 95% male and full of engineers and metal workers and the like. Not what you'd think of as a breastfeeding-friendly workplace. But not only has Nicole pumped for three babies while working there, she was instrumental in getting a company-wide lactation policy implemented so that other mothers are able to pump as well.

In a lot of ways, Nicole has been very lucky in the breastfeeding support she has found at work. Her first supervisor at Ford was a woman named Kim who was pumping for her eight-month-old son when Nicole started working for her. Nicole recalls:

I can remember thinking 'where is she always disappearing to?' and then she explained to me she was pumping breastmilk. Of course, her son was eight months old then, so my first reaction was 'why on earth is she still breastfeeding a baby that old?' Now, of course, I've nursed two babies past the age of two and am working on the third! But my boss was totally low-key about it – and looking back, seeing her do it was what made me feel like it was possible.

After Nicole returned to work after the birth of her daughter Mackenzie, she ran into Kim at lunch. They knew there were other moms pumping just from seeing them around. "That black pump bag passes for a briefcase if you've never seen one, but among the pumping moms, that 15 pound bag is a badge of courage – we always seek each other out and talk." This conversation inspired Nicole, Kim and some of the other moms to start pushing for a lactation policy. They talked about what they needed and drew up a wish list – the policy now includes the requirements that all moms have access to a hygienic room, separate from a restroom, and with a key-code on the door. Before the policy started, many of the women would pump in empty offices, but there was no way to guarantee they wouldn't be walked in on. Nicole says,

Once the policy went up, people started asking for designated lactation rooms to be set up, so now almost every facility has a lactation room –you can go on the company website and find out for every facility where the pumping room is. I still have instances where I'll pump in the car when I'm going to a meeting in another building and I don't know where the room is, but if I have to spend more time in another building, I'll look up where the room is. Near my office, I have a room where I go to pump. It's a nice little room – I have a chair, a table and an outlet. It's a small room, but it's separate from the restroom, so it's all we need."

Nicole talks about how having a policy in place has made it a lot easier to bring up pumping. Nicole gets moved around the company a lot since she works with divisions introducing new features, so she's had to go through the discussion of pumping with a new supervisor for each of her three children.

When Mackenzie was born six years ago, it was easy to talk to my supervisor about pumping because she'd been really open about the fact that her partner was breastfeeding their baby. But after Christopher was born, it was harder. My supervisor was one of those women who thinks you shouldn't

talk about your kids at work because it will make you look weak, and it was a lot harder to make sure I had the time built into my calendar for pumping. She just wasn't sympathetic. When I came back after Audrey was born, it was awkward to talk to my supervisor, who was male with no kids, but by then the policy was in place, so pumping at work was more widely accepted. It was a lot easier to have the conversation when I could refer to the policy. What's unique about this group I'm in now is that it's 4 men and me, and of the 4 men, 3 have young kids, and all of their wives have breastfed and pumped. My supervisor and former-supervisor's wives have both breastfed and pumped. For me, it's nice to see that a company policy can influence people who don't even work there! Some single, younger women I work with find pumping 'disgusting' to even think about. But I feel like if I act like it's no big deal, maybe when they have kids, they'll remember it and consider breastfeeding.

So if you're the first to pump at your company, remember that you're setting an example for all the moms who will follow after you!

Nicole's experience is also a good reminder that you often find support in unexpected places. When she was pumping for her first baby, before the lactation rooms, she shared an office with a male co-worker. He didn't have kids, but was so understanding of her pumping schedule.

He would just conveniently go for a walk or something when I needed to pump. We called it 'doing my thing' and he would even remind me – 'isn't it time for you to do your thing?' We had an open door policy in the company, so even when he was gone, sometimes guys from the shop would walk in on me. It was probably more embarrassing for them than it was for me, because finally they took a piece of metal and used a laser cutter to make a cow sign, and then they magnetized it so I could just stick it on my door when I was pumping!

Figuring out the details

This section provides some ideas for setting up the logistics of pumping at your workplace.

Location, location location: If your business does not have an established corporate lactation program (meaning 99% of you), you will need to arrange for a clean, private space in which to pump.

If you don't have your own office, you may have to be a little creative, but there are usually a lot of options better than the restroom. I know women who have converted storage rooms or utility closets by adding a chair and a small lamp. There may be a conference room you can use a couple of times a day, or maybe you can use the offices of people who travel. When my friend Emily finished pumping, she volunteered her private office to one of the administrative assistants who was just returning to work. That was very generous of her, but the real truth is that she used the cover of altruism to go for gourmet coffee twice a day, and then vacated her office during lunch. It wasn't such a hardship, so don't be afraid to ask. Here are a few other ideas for places to pump:

- If your business is in a large building, there may be other companies who have a pumping room you could use – ask around with the HR managers or other employees in the building.

- Your own HR manager may be able to help – there may be an available space you haven't thought of.

- A corner of the employee break room can be made private with a screen or blanket and the sound of the pump covered with music from a portable CD player or radio.

- A locker room can be divided with a screen or blanket, or you can lock the door and pump when other employees won't need the room.

- Make your car into a private pumping room with a battery-powered pump and a folding cardboard screen for the front window (the ones that have a goofy design on one side and say "Emergency" on the other). Park at the far end of the lot for more privacy and hang a towel inside the driver-side window by closing the window on the top of it.

As a last resort, you can pump in the restroom. Because breastmilk has many wonderful antibacterial properties and living immune cells, I don't actually worry that much about the germs – but I feel having to pump in the restroom shows a real lack of respect for the importance of breastfeeding to the health of your baby. Would you want to eat food that was prepared in the restroom? If it's all you have, at least it's a private room that every building has, and it's better than not pumping at all. Work with what you've got, right?

And the time to do it: Many employers are worried about the extra time it will take a breastfeeding mother to express her milk (as the smokers sit outside for 15 minutes every other hour). Once you have established your pumping routine, it is usually possible to pump in 20 minutes, start to finish. If you can eat your lunch on a pumping break, that means you will probably need only two extra breaks a day. There are a lot of ways to arrange this. A generous employer will figure that 40 minutes of lost work is the price for having you back and happy, and won't expect you to make up the time. If your employer doesn't cover these breaks, you can offer to come in early or stay late to make up the time, or take a small pay cut. Maybe you can offer to make up the time once you are no longer pumping, and work 40 minutes longer each day in the second year of your baby's life, or in the second six months when you'll have more energy. Most women find that they don't need breaks other than the pumping break (we're an efficient lot), and their productivity is not really affected. Pay attention to how much time other employees spend chit-chatting, smoking, or on long lunches – your pumping breaks are probably not as long as they take, so don't feel guilty about taking as much time as you need. With tricks like Hands-Free Pumping (covered under "Pumping basics" in Chapter 5), you can even do work-related reading, emails, or phone calls while you are pumping, meaning you only miss the time it takes you to set up. Personally, I consider this to be way too much working, and think that your pumping break should be an actual break from work, but again, you work with what you've got.

Scheduling the first weeks back

It is a real luxury to have the first week back at work be a short one. Try to arrange to start back on a Thursday or Friday, so that you're not faced with a full week ahead of you that first day back. The other advantage to starting midweek is that if you have trouble pumping enough, you can pump a bit on the weekend while you re-evaluate your schedule (the section on "Troubleshooting supply issues" in Chapter 8 has *many* suggestions on how you can pump more). You may even be able to arrange for a few short weeks when you first start back. My friend Mary took Wednesdays off for the first month back, so she never had to be gone more than two days in a row. It meant a 20% pay cut that first month, but it saved her sanity. I worked four day weeks until my son was six months old. This was because I'd put off finding daycare and had no coverage for Fridays, not anything as smart as a plan, but it worked out so well for us.

Your first few days will involve a lot of "getting back up to speed" – checking messages, answering emails, learning new equipment or just brushing the dust off your skills. It's nice to have a little extra time to rest until you're back in a routine. Even if you have to start back full-time right away, starting mid-week can at least ease the first few days.

Practice days

It may make you feel more comfortable to have a practice day before your first day of work. You can do this by arranging to take your baby to their care provider for a day or half-day, or arrange to have a friend or relative take your baby for a few hours. Set your alarm (ugh!) for your workday time, and go through the morning routine as if you really had to be somewhere on time. It can help A LOT to pack your pump (and lunch and whatever else you'll need) the night before. Figure out if you have time to shower in the morning, or if you'll need to do it the night before. Get efficient about hair and makeup. Don't skip breakfast, don't drink too much coffee, and leave plenty of time for nursing. (See why you'll want to practice?)

Leave a bottle or two, and find a nice quiet place to go. Remember, you'll need to pump while you're gone, so it's nice to end up at a friend's house. You could drop by work and say hello to people so your first day back isn't lost to socializing (like this is a bad thing?). Go shopping alone, do something just for you. Call and check on your baby only if you want to, although you'll probably feel better if they know where to find you.

It may take a few days to figure out how to get out of the house on time; I'll freely admit I'm still not good at it, but practice makes perfect. You may be surprised at the changes in your routine. I used to think a shower was essential for me in the morning, but a more forgiving hairdo made it possible to shower at night when I found I just didn't have time in the morning. You're a new mom, people will understand if you look a little messier than you used to…

Choosing a child care provider

Choosing a care provider for your baby is a huge task. It was so daunting to me that I put it off when I found out I was pregnant, and by the time I got around to looking, there weren't a lot of options without long waiting lists. I recommend starting this process as early as you can in your pregnancy or in your process of planning to go back to work.

The options

There are three main types of care providers – daycare centers, home care centers, and care providers who come to your home. The type that you choose depends on your situation and budget, their availability, and just finding someone you like. There is no one right answer, so take your time, look around, and find out what feels right for you.

The most important thing about any care arrangement is the person who is doing it. I had heard great things about the daycare center we finally chose, and have to admit I was a little put off when I went in to see the place. There was duct tape holding things together, no fancy new toys, and the director seemed a bit aloof and didn't seem all that interested in showing me around. The woman in the baby room was kind of shy and didn't have a lot to say right away, and I was worried. So I asked some of the other parents, and heard nothing but rave reviews. Jane (in the baby room) is a living treasure when it comes to taking care of babies. The staff in the "big kids" room was always doing projects, and the other Jane in the toddler room, who I had suspected might be insane, was only crazy enough to keep eight toddlers happily entertained for ten hours a day – a real gift. All the parents I talked to said "don't be put off by the director – he's so great with the kids, and just isn't as good at talking to grownups (sorry Tom, but it's true…). So – when in doubt, talk to other parents – check references, ask for numbers – that's how you'll get the real information.

I'll list some of the pros and cons that I've found with different arrangements.

Daycare centers

A daycare center must be licensed to provide childcare, and will be strictly regulated in terms of facility safety and things like infant-to-caregiver ratios. Most don't allow more than four infants for each adult, though the ratio goes up with older children. I used a daycare center, so this is what I know the most about, and I really loved where my kids spent their days. The center had a specific room designed for infants, so you always knew everything there was baby-proofed and toys were age-appropriate.

Illness: There are two issues around illness if you choose a daycare center: their illness policy and the fact that there is more sickness there in the first place. There were a lot of babies at the center we used, and when one got sick they all did. This is the primary disadvantage of a daycare center—due to the large number of kids, it seems like someone will always be sick, and your child will get sick more often in the first year or so. But - with the benefit of breastmilk, these early illnesses act like vaccinations, and now my kids hardly ever get sick.

A daycare center will have strict rules about taking kids who are sick, so I did have to stay home when my kids had a fever. When you're interviewing, ask about the center's sick child policy. Some require a child to be home 24 hours after a fever has resolved, others let you come back as soon as the fever is over. As a scientist, I think it's not necessary to keep kids home 24 hours after the fever is gone. By the time a child looks and acts sick, it's likely that they've already spread their germs to the other kids anyway, so to me it doesn't matter if they're back right after the fever breaks. You'll find that it makes a difference to your work if you can go back right after the fever is over or if you need to find other care or stay home for another day.

I know, I sound like such a heartless mom – take my sick kid off my hands! But you'll see – there are times when you really have to be at work, you know that your child is in good hands at daycare, and you just need to leave them, sniffles or no. Trust me, it happens, and it doesn't make you a bad mom. If you have the luxury to stay home every time your child is sick, that's wonderful, because breastfeeding directly and the comfort of mom's arms are the best things for a sick baby. If you can stay home, appreciate it for the luxury it is.

Socialization: Babies at daycare centers get a *lot* of socialization. There are usually other kids their age, which means that they will have a cohort of kids to progress with. My five-year-old son just spent the day yesterday with the four kids he met in the baby room when they were all six months old – they are still such close friends. Some argue that kids in daycare are more aggressive as older children. This may be true, but a lot depends on how the caregivers manage aggression. Talk to your care provider about discipline and make sure their philosophy meshes with yours. A strict "no physical aggression" rule was very important for our family.

Our daycare also had a lot of mixing between the ages, which I think was really neat for the kids. The babies got to model older children, and the older kids benefited from seeing the babies cared for and helping with little chores, like fetching toys for the babies. Ask when you interview if the babies are kept to themselves, or if they get out with the older kids at all. Due to layout, some can't do any mixing, but our center had a little loft the big kids could climb to when they wanted to check on the babies (also nice for siblings).

Programming: A daycare center will sometimes have more structured programming for the older children. If you plan to keep your child at the same place until they are ready for kindergarten or pre-school, you might want to find out what the older kids do during the day. I chose our daycare largely because they have a "learning through play" philosophy, take the kids (even the babies) outside almost every day, and have no TV or video. Choose what matches your own priorities and lifestyle. Some people left when their kids were older because they wanted more structured learning before kindergarten – for us, more playtime was important.

Hours: A daycare center usually has very strict hours and limited flexibility. For example, our daycare is open from 7:30 to 5:30, and it'll cost you $5 every minute that you're late picking up your child. They will take kids two, three, or five days a week, but not one or four. They only offer full days, so if you're there ½ day, there's no discount, and you pay by the month whether you use all the days or not. Think about this when looking at your summer, vacations, and your own job flexibility.

Reliability: I always know my daycare will be open. Even if staff members are sick, they have substitutes (and always use the same ones, so the kids know them). We live in Vermont, and have had the center close two times for snowstorms in the five years we've been there. To me, this is one of the big advantages of a daycare center, although it is still important to find out their vacation policy. I was very surprised to find out the first summer that every year they close for a week in July and a week over Christmas. Make sure you know the holiday closings and if they take vacations.

Home care providers

Home care providers are usually mothers themselves who are taking in a few more kids to generate some extra income. Sometimes mothers take in younger children while their own older children are in school, or sometimes people without kids run home care centers. Since these centers are most often run by women, I'll use "her" and "she" in this discussion, though there are certainly men who care for children in their home as well—Daddy Daycare with Eddie Murphy, anyone.

Home care providers can cost less than a daycare center, since the provider is in her own home and doesn't have to pay the overhead for a facility. Some home care providers employ helpers during the day, others take only as many children as they can handle by themselves. Home care centers are required to be licensed by most states, although you will always find more casual ones that are not. Many people choose a home care because it provides (obviously) a more "home-like" atmosphere for their children. Others because the cost is less, or there may be more flexible hours.

How is the day spent? Just like in choosing a daycare center, it is important to find out how the children spend their day at a home care center. I found that many of the home care providers near me spent a lot of time with the TV on, but I'm weird about TV, and really didn't want my kids around it. Others may go on outings or do classes with your child.

I've met two home-care providers at my daughter's gymnastics class. They both have daughters in the class, and each has a younger child she brings with her. It took me almost a year to find out that these babies were not their own children! They treat the babies as if they were their own, pay wonderful attention to them, and bring them wherever they go – to the grocery store, gymnastics class, the library. Each of these mothers watches only one child in addition to her own preschooler, and these kids are getting great care. One of these moms even took her own child to the childcare at the YMCA so that she could do a swim class with the baby. If a home care provider has more children in her care, they probably stay home more of the day. Find out what they do to pass the time.

Safety: If you are leaving your child with a home care provider, make sure you feel safe with the surroundings. Since it is her own home, it may be that not every room is baby-proofed, so find out how your baby will be kept safe once she is scooting around and exploring. Find out if the care provider smokes in the home. Be sure you trust her driving if your child will be out doing errands and such with her. This is not to say that safety is guaranteed at a daycare center, but a daycare center will have a more regulated environment (duct tape aside).

Back-up: If a home care provider is ill, what is her policy? Will she be closed for the day, or does she have someone who can provide backup care for you? What if she becomes ill during the day? What is her vacation schedule? Is she available during school vacations when her own children may be out of school? These are important questions to ask when interviewing care providers.

Illness: Just like with a daycare center, you want to find out what the care provider's policy is when your child is sick. Can your child be cared for if she is ill? If she has a fever? Is there a cut-off point when she cannot come in if she has been sick? Also, find out what the care provider will do if your child is injured. Does she have a back-up person she can call if she is alone and your child needs to go to the hospital, or will she need to take the other children with her?

Care in your own home

The hardest part of my day (to this very day) is getting the kids out the door. Even when they were babies, finding everything, putting bottles in the cooler, packing lunches; these are the barriers I face. Because of my lack of early morning consciousness, I always thought having someone come to my home to care for my kids would be the ultimate time- and stress-saver. I could just walk out the door, off to work, the kids are in the security of their own home – what could be better? For many moms who can afford it, this convenience is the reason that they choose a nanny, au pair, babysitter or other in-home care provider. They will usually care for your baby when she is sick, the hours are often flexible, they can take vacation when you do – there are a lot of advantages.

Just so it doesn't seem like total nirvana, here are a few considerations:

Personality: Your child will be with only one person all the time – it's very important that you and your child get along with this person. It can be worth doing a couple of test days just to make sure the personalities mesh.

Socialization: Find out if the caregiver is willing to take your child to play groups, story hours, or other places where there will be other children. This is not such a factor for small babies, but by the time a baby is about six months old, they really enjoy being with other infants.

Extra Duties: Will you come home at the end of your day to a house that looks like a baby's been there all day, or will your care provider do some picking up and dishes along the way? With an in-home care provider, it is essential that you make *very* clear arrangements about what their responsibilities will be. Do you expect them to clean up only what they use or get out during the day? Would you like them to also clean up from breakfast and get dinner started for you? Will they run a load of laundry or two? A lot of bad feelings can be avoided by being really clear about these things from the first interview.

Back-up: What will be your backup plan if your care provider is sick? Do you have other babysitters you can call on short notice, or will you need to stay home? Sometimes moms in the same neighborhood have care providers who can watch each other's children for a few hours in a pinch – it's a good idea to network with other moms who have in-home care.

Driving and safety: Since it's your house, you have more control over the extent of baby-proofing, but safety is still a concern. Be clear if there are rooms (your office and its spider-web of cords and cables, for example) where your baby should not be. You will also need to make arrangements if the care provider will be driving your baby anywhere. Will your baby go in your car or the care provider's car? Have them drive you somewhere and make sure you feel comfortable with their driving and the safety of their car. Talk about where they would like to take your baby during the day.

A note on family members as providers

Having a family member provide your child's care can seem like an ideal solution. Usually it's free, and you know that they will have your baby's best interest at heart all the time. The same considerations apply as I listed for in-home and home-care providers above, but the relationship with family members can also be more complicated. When you hire a care-provider or pay a center to take care of your baby, it's quite clear that you are the boss. They may have their own policies, but you have the last word about your child's care. If you don't want them to eat cheetos or drink juice or watch TV, you can tell them so and they will honor that request. This kind of thing is harder with family members. If your mother has always watched the Montel show every single afternoon and keeps doing it even after you're pretty sure your baby shouldn't be hearing the words "crack whore," this can be a hard discussion to have. Family members also tend to take more liberties with what your baby eats – after all, if apple juice was good enough for you as a baby, then why shouldn't their grandbaby have it? My mother-in-law, like most grandparents, was a notorious overfeeder. No matter how much milk I left her for the day, I could be sure it would be gone when I came home. I'm sure she encouraged my son to finish bottles, and I have good evidence she gave him lasagna when he was two months old. However, I had to finish my dissertation, I had no money, and she came for a week when my husband was out of town. She had dinner ready for me every night, kept my son happy and safe, and never complained or criticized me. Pick your battles. A little lasagna was a small price to pay. Had she been a long-term care provider for me, we probably would have had to have some difficult discussions.

Your relationship with your care provider

Whatever kind of care provider you choose, your relationship with this person is one of the most important ones you have when your baby is young. It is worth it to go the extra mile to cultivate good feelings and good communication. For me, spending time chatting with my care providers while I nursed my baby gave us a great connection. Tipping at the holidays, birthday cards, and baked goods are also good strategies. If a parent is consistently rude or aloof to a care provider, the care given that child is affected. I know, it shouldn't happen, but hey, we're all human, and I've seen it.

If you have any problems with the way someone is caring for your baby, be sure you let them know – but be mindful of how you do it. Sharing your concerns without sounding critical is an art. Asking questions about your baby's day is *always* a better first step than an accusation. For example, imagine hearing "How was Parker's day yesterday? He ate a lot, was he very fussy?" instead of "I told you not to overfeed Parker. If he's fussy, you need to be holding him more." (The first one is the better choice, in case you didn't figure it out.) Through tactful communication you can usually resolve any issues that arise. If there are things that just won't go your way, then it's decision time. Is it really that big a deal? For example, when other parents started bringing in cupcakes for their baby's first birthdays, sometimes my daughter got a piece, even though she'd had no sugar, eggs or milk at home. At first I was upset to find out they hadn't even asked me if she could have any. But then I realized that she was 11 months old, ate a lot of healthy foods, and I decided not to fight that particular battle. However, if your care provider is doing anything that feels unsafe or just not right to you in their care of your baby, and they do not seem receptive to changing, then it's time to start the painful process of looking for someone new.

Your care provider and breastfeeding

It is very important that your care provider knows how important breastfeeding is to you. They may not know how much control they have over your success or failure, so take the time to explain it to them. For example, explain if they overfeed your baby you will need to pump more, or if they don't feed too close to the end of the day, you'll be able to nurse your baby when you get home. The appendix contains a tear-out guide for daycare providers who care for breastfed babies. It stresses the importance of feeding on demand, frequent holding, and feeding in a manner compatible with breastfeeding. You can just tear these pages out and take them to your provider, or make a copy if you're like me and the thought of defacing a book makes you break out in hives. You can also print out a copy from www.workandpump. com/for_providers.pdf.

When you are interviewing care providers, ask them about their experiences taking care of breastfed babies. Did they have any issues with storing milk for the baby? Did they seem to think it was weird? Were they encouraging? If they are parents, were their own children breastfed? If a childcare provider is supportive of breastfeeding, the most important thing they can do is make you feel normal. They will have a place for you to nurse your baby, will store your breastmilk with whatever food the other babies are getting, won't mind keeping a few ounces in their freezer for you, and will be willing to communicate with you on a tediously minute basis about how much your baby eats each day.

A note on care styles

Your care provider doesn't have to do things exactly the way you do. You may think it will be confusing to your baby if they have one set of standards at home and another at daycare, but all care providers are different, even in the same family. Babies are completely able to adjust to this. Think about your own mother and father, or whoever the significant caregivers were in your childhood. Certainly there were things you could get away with when you were with dad that you knew not to even try when mom was around. You figured out these differences before you could even speak, and your baby can do the same. One of the adjustments my children had to make was being used to a pretty intensive parenting style from me and then adjusting to a little more benign neglect at daycare. Because there were other babies, their needs could not be met as immediately and they had to get used to taking turns (even for feedings – the reality of having 6 babies in a room is that sometimes you just have to wait). In spite of this, I had tremendous confidence that they were well taken care of, and both of my kids are still very attached to the care providers they had from infancy and toddlerhood. There's a certain amount of letting go involved, it's true. And it's sad when you realize that your baby is attached to someone other than you and your partner, but believe me, it's much better if they can form a strong attachment with their caregiver – everyone will be healthier for it.

References

Kennell J, Klaus M, McGrath S, Robertson S, Hinkley C. Continuous emotional support during labor in a US hospital. A randomized controlled trial. *JAMA*, Vol. 265 No. 17, May 1, 1991.

United States Breastfeeding Committee. 2002. Workplace Breastfeeding Support [issue paper]. Raleigh, NC: United States Breastfeeding Committee.

United States Breastfeeding Committee. 2002. Economic Benefits of Breastfeeding [issue paper]. Raleigh, NC: United States Breastfeeding Committee.

Cohen R, Mrtek MB, Mrtek RG. 1995. Comparison of maternal absenteeism and infant illness rates among breast-feeding and formula-feeding women in two corporations. *American Journal of Health Promotion*. 10:148-53.

Ball T, Wright A. 1999. Health Care Costs of Formula-feeding in the First Year of Life. *Pediatrics*. 103(4):870-76.

American Academy of Pediatrics Policy Statement. 2005. Breastfeeding and the Use of Human Milk. *Pediatrics.* 97; 100:6.

U.S. Department of Health and Human Services. 2000. HHS Blueprint for Action on Breastfeeding. Washington, D.C. U.S. Department of Health and Human Services, Office on Women's Health.

United States Breastfeeding Committee. 2001. Breastfeeding in the United States: A National Agenda. Rockville MD: U.S. Department of Health and Human Services, Health Resources and Services Administration, Maternal and Child Health Bureau.

American Academy of Family Physicians, Breastfeeding Position Paper. 2001. View at http://www.aafp.org/online/en/home/policy/policies/b/breastfeedingpositionpaper.html.

American College of Obstetrics and Gynecology, 2007. Special Report from ACOG, Breastfeeding: Maternal and Infant Aspects. ACOG Clinical Review Vol. 12, Issue 1 (supplement).

National Business Group on Health, 2000. Family in Health Issue Brief, "Breastfeeding at the Workplace". View at http://www.businessgrouphealth.org/services/breastfeeding.cfm.

Getting off to a good start

Hooray! You have a baby! My first piece of advice is: if you are thinking about your job – stop! You have some number of weeks, or, if you're lucky, months, before you have to go back. You'll have plenty of time to worry about work; your first job is to get acquainted with this new little person in your life and get breastfeeding off to a good start. If you already have breastfeeding well established, go ahead and skip to the next chapter.

The first weeks can be a rollercoaster

The first few weeks are about establishing a good milk supply. Even if you're planning on giving bottles at some point, hold off for now. Your body figures out how much milk to make in these first few weeks, setting the stage for an ample milk supply for as long as you choose to breastfeed. Here's how it works – your body makes a certain amount of milk. If it all gets used up, your body makes more. If your baby is nursing frequently, your body makes more. If your breasts are overly full and not being emptied, your body makes less. (For lots more detail on this concept, be sure to read Chapter 3 - "Demand and Supply.") It generally takes about two weeks for your body to decide if you've had one baby or triplets, so be patient as your supply modulates.

When your baby is first born, it will seem like there is no milk at all – because your baby is just learning how to eat, he gets only a small amount of the most useful, digestable food – colostrum. Colostrum acts as a laxative to help your baby pass that gloppy black and green meconium and get rid of jaundice. Colostrum also has many many live immune cells to help your newborn fend off infections, and is high in protein to provide the ultimate nutrition for your baby. Don't worry if there isn't a lot – just keep breastfeeding often. Your baby is getting all he needs, and is learning how to manage the tasks of simultaneously eating, breathing, and swallowing with nice, small, manageable amounts.

After a few days, your mature milk will come in – and often this means the end of manageable amounts, so it's good your baby has had a few days to practice! Your breasts will swell to previously unimagined dimensions, and you will experience the pleasure of milk leaking everywhere every time you have a passing thought involving a baby. Don't worry, this too shall pass. Once your body gets the message that the triplets it was planning to feed were not actually born, it will down regulate the milk supply to a much more realistic level.

So you can see that the first few weeks are full of ups and downs, but once you get through them, breastfeeding will finally begin to feel like second nature, and your hard work will be rewarded with a readily available, perfectly nutritious food for your baby that you don't even have to get out of bed to heat up!

Breastfeeding basics

I'm going to cover the basics here, but I recommend you buy a comprehensive book of breastfeeding basics to have as a reference – my favorites are listed at the end of this chapter.

Get instruction in the birth setting

For starters, get the best instruction you can from the health care providers who delivered your baby – the nurses, midwives and lactation counselors are there to help you get breastfeeding off to the best start, so take full advantage of their services. Doulas are often fantastic breastfeeding coaches as well. You'll probably be impatient to leave the hospital after your baby arrives (although the cuisine is excellent) – but if you haven't gotten enough help with breastfeeding to feel comfortable going home, be sure you ask for the help you need – and it can even be worth staying an extra day in the hospital if that's what you have to do to see the lactation staff – or call to line up a home visit from a lactation consultant the day you get home.

A review of the basics

I think the best breastfeeding instruction is from a live person sitting next to you watching and helping you feed your baby. But just in case you don't have that person there to help, I've tried to cover the most common problems women run into in the first two weeks. Remember that a lot of women will have no problems at all starting to breastfeed – but it's good to know what to do if something comes up, right?

A good latch

The only breastfeeding basic that you really need to know is this: The Good Latch. Latch describes the way your baby attaches to your nipple, and their mouth movements as they suckle. If your baby is healthy and full term, all you really need for successful breastfeeding is a good latch. Why is latch so important? What if you have a "bad" one? Well, it goes like this – if you have a bad latch, breastfeeding will be painful for you, and your baby won't be able to efficiently transfer enough milk. You won't want to breastfeed often, your baby won't get enough, and the next thing you know your doctor is saying "well, we need to give this baby a little supplemental formula to boost her growth." Let's avoid that, OK?

So - what is a good latch, and how do I know if I have one? The basic biology illustration on the next page shows the anatomy of the lactating breast. Notice that the milk glands are all throughout the breast tissue, and their growth is the reason you finally achieved your life goal of a D cup during pregnancy (or the reason your back is killing you if you started out a D cup). The milk glands are connected to ducts that carry the milk out of the breast - see all the little tubes exiting the nipple? New research now shows us that the sinuses we once thought existed under the areola really don't exist. The milk ducts simply traverse through the breast tissue and end at the nipple. When the infant latches on, the mother's pituitary releases oxytocin which then forces milk out into the ductal system. Each time your baby compresses the breast, it allows him to swallow the milk that was in his mouth and then make a vacuum on the nipple as the tongue drops. When the infant makes a vacuum as the tongue drops again. The vacuum causes milk to spurt out of the nipple and fill the mouth. As a result, if your baby doesn't have the nipple far back in his mouth, he may not make enough vacuum to get the milk out effectively.

If your baby is just sucking on your nipple (which is probably how you imagined breastfeeding worked all these years), he isn't creating a vacuum, he's actually squishing the exit tubes shut with his mouth. This means he isn't transferring milk effectively and is probably causing you a world of hurt on top of all that. Because, in a wonderful coincidence of biology, if your nipple is far enough back that your baby can create a vacuum, it's also well out of the way of your baby's gums, lips, and front of the tongue which can work together to inflict some amazing pain on your delicate nipple tissue. The nipple is safely guarded at the back of the baby's mouth while the stronger alveolar skin is noshed on. Try it, pinch your nipple. Ouch, right? Now pinch the skin behind your nipple, much less sensitive, right?

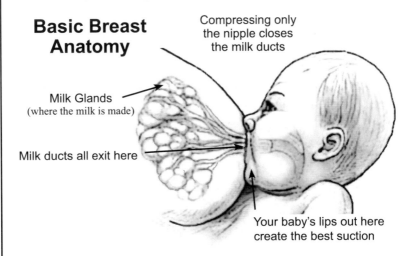

Basic Breast Anatomy

Compressing only the nipple closes the milk ducts

Milk Glands
(where the milk is made)

Milk ducts all exit here

Your baby's lips out here create the best suction

This is why if you were taught correctly how to latch your baby on, you were told that the baby should have a WIDE open mouth before latching, should take in a BIG mouthful of nipple and areola, and should have lips flanged outward. If your baby is well latched, you may be able to see his lips flanged outward, you may hear the distinctive "suck-pause-swallow" rhythm of breastfeeding, but the most important thing is that your baby will be firmly attached to your breast (not just your nipple), and you shouldn't feel discomfort.

If your baby is not correctly latched – this is the hard part – you really need to start over. "But I just got him on there! He's nursing! We're doing it!" I know, you don't want to start over, but trust me, you need to. Stick your pinky finger into the corner of his mouth to break the suction (never pull a latched baby right off

– now that will cause pain!), then gently remove your baby from the breast.

Here's a trick I learned to help with good positioning: position your baby so that he's belly-to-belly with you, and he doesn't have to turn his head to nurse. Support the baby's body with a pillow so your hands are free and his head is right at the level of your nipple. Hold the base of your baby's head (low, near the neck, or high on the shoulders – not the back of the head) with one hand and gently bring his chin against your breast below the nipple, so your nipple points at his nose. That's right, like you're going to shove the nipple in his nose. Hold your breast with your other hand and tickle his upper lip (just below his nose) with your nipple to get him to start rooting, wait for a wide open mouth, then gently snuggle him in closer so his nose comes towards your breast (not your breast towards his head). If you wait until he gapes nice and wide, your nipple will go right into his mouth. Your nipple will be pointed towards the top of the mouth, and he should begin sucking right away. Sit in a relaxed position, don't hunch your shoulders, and remember to breathe. (You'll notice I didn't mention where the baby's body was – this tip works for the cross-cradle hold, the football hold, and any other position you might want to try.) There you go – a perfect latch!

Yeah right, a perfect latch from a book, that's a good one. The real trick is to have someone experienced watching and helping you – but I find that remembering that trick of aiming the nipple towards the baby's nose, not the center of the mouth, does result in a more comfortable latch for a lot of moms. For a great animation of this latching technique, as well as links to many other latch illustrations and videos, check out kellymom's Latching and Positioning Resources page, which can be found at www.kellymom.com/bf/start/basics/latch-resources.html. This page is also linked from my www.workandpump.com/Links.htm page.

You can also assess latch by looking at the condition of your nipple when your baby releases. Your nipple should be pulled out and round. If it is creased across the top (like a brand new lipstick), then your baby is putting too much stress on the nipple, which can cause problems down the road. Usually this creased appearance can be fixed by getting the baby to open wider before latching and by getting the nipple further back into the baby's mouth.

> Remember that breastfeeding, like any other new skill, can take a little while to learn and master. You may be exhausted and emotionally drained in the first several days after your baby is born. Try to remember that after about a week to ten days it gets so much easier, so if you have doubts about your ability to breastfeed – give yourself two weeks. Tell yourself you won't decide to stop before then, make a firm commitment. Just knowing it will get easier is sometimes all you need to get through a few rough days! The first week can stretch to an eternity, but just remind yourself – it's only a few short days.

Doesn't breastfeeding hurt?

A lot of people will tell you that breastfeeding is painful at first, that you should just soldier on through, and it will get better. This is good advice for being in labor, but bad advice for breastfeeding. Labor only lasts a day or two at the outside – you can deal with some pain – but breastfeeding lasts for days and weeks and months. You really shouldn't be forced to suffer through your nipples "toughening up" or any other such nonsense. If you have a good latch, you may wonder, how will I know? What will it feel like? I would like to tell you "It won't hurt a bit," but that may be misleading. As you know (especially now that you've been through childbirth), women define pain in different ways. Beginning to breastfeed comes with a number of strong sensations. Your nipple will be tugged out pretty far, and while it shouldn't feel pinched, it will feel pulled. Is this pain? Only you can decide. But it should feel like something you could get used to, not something where you wince in dread just thinking about it.

In some women, the feeling of the milk letting down (the milk ejection reflex or MER) can also be quite strong. It can feel like the pins and needles you get when your leg falls asleep. This can also be described as "painful," but it should pass rapidly once the milk starts to flow.

If you have always had very sensitive nipples, expect a little more discomfort, but it should be pulling or tingling discomfort, never pinching or a screaming pain. If it hurts, please read the next chapter on what to do if breastfeeding *does* hurt. And even if it doesn't count as "pain" to you, any pinching or raw spots on your nipple deserve a more thorough check by a breastfeeding helper.

Feeding frequency

There are people who tell you that a baby should be fed on a schedule – please don't listen to them! Your baby knows when she is hungry, and if you pay attention, you'll learn her language for telling you this within a couple days. Try not to wait until she's crying to be fed because by that time you'll have to first calm her down. A baby's first signs of hunger include opening and closing her mouth, nuzzling her face from side to side, sticking her tongue out, making little grunting noises, and trying to stick her hands in her mouth. In the first few weeks of a baby's life, you should always respond to these signals by offering the breast. If the baby isn't hungry, she won't nurse, or won't for very long. Don't worry, you can't overfeed a breastfed baby.

Most babies nurse between 8 and 12 times in a 24 hour period, but this is only a rough guideline. Sometimes there can be 3-4 hours between feedings, sometimes babies will "cluster-feed," and nurse on and off for a few hours straight. A feeding can take as little as 15 minutes, or as long as an hour. All of these patterns are normal. As long as your baby is making plenty of wet and poopy diapers (see Feeding Log in the Appendix), you can rest assured she is getting enough to eat, no matter what the feeding pattern. The only time you should be concerned about feeding on a schedule is if your baby is going more than 4-5 hours between feedings more than once a day. If this happens, your baby may not be getting enough to eat. She is going a long time between feedings because her energy levels are dropping. In this case, it is important to wake your baby and try to feed every 3 hours.

I live in Vermont where we have a significant population of African refugees (I know, African refugees going to the coldest, snowiest state. Go figure). These women all tend to breastfeed (at least until they are "Americanized"). One of the funniest things is to ask them how often their baby feeds. They look at you like you're the dimmest bulb in the box. "How often? That's like asking how often you kiss your baby, or how often you stroke their cheek – who would keep track? You just do it when it's time." I find this attitude refreshing, and it reflects the natural pattern of breastfeeding. In our Western society, we're obsessed with time, but if you watch the baby, not the clock, and keep your baby close to you, that's really all you need to know. The only time I recommend watching the clock is if you need to intervene and start waking them up to eat more often. Why don't the African moms have this concern? Because they never put their babies down. They never bundle them and put them in the other room. They don't need to worry about their baby going into a deep enough sleep that they would miss a feeding – it's a cultural thing.

Feeding the sleepy baby

The best way to help a sleepy baby be more interested in nursing is to keep her naked and in direct skin-to-skin contact with one of her parents. The closeness, especially to mom, helps a sleepy baby both conserve energy and be more interested in nursing. It also helps stimulate your milk supply if your baby is not feeding frequently. If your baby has already gotten to a really sleepy state, feeding her can be difficult, but there are tricks to help. Strip your baby to her diaper so she's a little cool – this will help keep her alert. You can rub or pat the soles of her feet to keep her awake, or switch sides when she starts to nod off at the breast. One mom I know stroked her baby's ear to keep her alert. In extreme cases, cool washcloths can be used to rub the baby while she nurses to keep her awake and feeding. Another way to encourage more feeding is to gently squeeze your breast when your baby stops actively sucking – this will express enough milk into her mouth to stimulate more sucking and swallowing. If you consistently have trouble keeping your baby awake to eat, you should see your doctor or call a lactation consultant. Babies tend to get very sleepy when they're not getting enough to eat, but babies also sleep a lot after the ordeal of being born. The diapers will be your best guide.

Supplementing with formula

Sometimes you might hear that you should be supplementing with formula in the first few days of a baby's life. Many of the reasons for this are based on outdated information; there is rarely a medical need for supplementation with artificial baby milk (a.k.a. "formula"). If concerns are addressed early, they can almost always be fixed by working on breastfeeding and feeding more often.

Jaundice: It is normal for all babies to be a little bit jaundiced after being born. Breastmilk and sunlight help the jaundice resolve quickly and naturally. If your baby is more than normally jaundiced, he does not have "breastmilk jaundice," he has "not-enough-breastmilk" jaundice. A jaundiced baby should be fed as frequently as possible, as breastmilk and colostrum help to pass the excess bilirubin (the stuff that makes a baby yellow) through the baby's poops. A jaundiced baby should be awakened to feed every 3 hours until the jaundice is clear. If the jaundice is not resolved within a few days, there are home bili-lights and bili-blankets that can be used to treat the jaundice without supplementing with formula, or a small amount of supplementation can be done at the breast without a bottle. Sometimes babies need to come back to the hospital for more time under the lights, but they should be kept with mom as much as possible during this time. Correcting the baby's latch is usually all that is needed to get the baby more milk, and more milk resolves the jaundice faster. True "breastmilk jaundice" is a rare condition that is only seen after the baby is a few weeks old.

Weight Loss: It is normal for a baby to lose around 7% of his birthweight in the first few days after birth, and some lose up to 10%. Remember, he's been at the all-you-can-eat umbilical food bar for months, and now has to learn to eat. Plus, the air is really dry out here – most babies lose some weight just drying out. If there have been a lot of medical interventions in the birth, a baby can be born with lots of excess fluid (edema), which is also peed out in the first few days. Babies should return to birth weight by the end of the second week of life. As long as your baby is gaining *some* weight by about the 4th or 5th day, there is no need to supplement. If there is a medical concern about weight gain, the *first* step is to assess the breastfeeding situation. This means that someone should watch the baby nursing *for an entire feed*, and assess and improve the latch. You can't tell much about latch just watching a baby who's already on – you need to see how the baby attaches and the condition of the nipple when the baby lets go. If weight gain is a real concern, you can do a pre-and post-feed weigh with a special scale designed for this purpose. Do not begin supplementing until this assessment has taken place, as adding formula to a baby's diet can rapidly decrease your milk supply and put the breastfeeding relationship at risk.

Baby nurses "all the time": A lot of moms think that because their baby is seemingly nursing 24 hours a day, they are not making enough milk, thus they should supplement. While it may be true that the baby is not getting enough at the breast at that exact feeding, the frequent nursing serves to get the baby enough to eat and will bring your milk supply up within a couple of days. If the baby truly seems to be not getting enough, you should have the latch assessed to be sure the baby is really transferring milk effectively. Giving a bottle of formula at this time actually takes away the stimulation your body needs to make more milk, so this is the *opposite* of the solution to not having enough milk.

So mom can sleep: Studies have shown that the mothers of babies who are fully breastfed and kept in the room with mom at the hospital actually get just as much sleep and report being as well rested as the mothers of babies who go to the nursery and get formula during the night (Keefe, 1988). You are not meant to be away from your baby in the first several weeks, and separation itself is stressful for both mom and baby. Breastfeeding through the night, frequent feedings surrounded by naps for mom and baby, and *limiting visitors* are really the way to get more rest. Appoint your partner the "kicker-outer" at the hospital, and allow him or her to gracefully escort guests from the room after a short visit so that you can sleep. Your sleep is sacred, so make liberal use of the "Do Not Disturb" sign for your door. And you *don't* have to answer the phone every time it rings. God invented voice mail for a reason; I think it was so that new moms can rest once in a while.

To give mom a "break": While it is tempting to give a bottle of formula to let a new mom rest, this is a bad idea. A bottle can interfere with the newly developing breastfeeding relationship, and can put mom's milk supply at risk. A better idea is for your loving partner to bring the baby to you in bed and assist you in nursing while you are lying down. If mom is really exhausted, she should be immediately relieved of diaper and burping duties, and all her energy focused on breastfeeding. Be sure to have lots of helpers around to bring water (and more water), prepare nutritious foods, and pitch in with the housework. Mom's only job at this point is to make food for this precious baby – giving a bottle of formula so she has the strength to get up and scrub the toilets is hardly the point. My friend Jenny called me last night – she'd just had her baby at 7AM, was home by noon, and was thinking that she ought to clean up her older son's train set. I said "Jenny, you married Mike for a reason. He's quite capable of picking up a train set. Go lie down!" Anyone who knows me realizes that this is absolutely a case of the pot calling the kettle black, but do as I say not as I do, and get someone to help you with anything not related to taking care of your new baby. Besides, I got a wicked bleed and mastitis from my overexertions. There's a reason mothers were confined to the Red Tent for a month after babies were born in the old days – and it wasn't so they could get their hair done. (Hint: it was so they could rest and be waited on.)

Baby does better on formula: If a baby does get a bottle of formula, many moms are discouraged to see how much "better" their baby does. Maybe some interpretation can help. Think about how you feel after Thanksgiving dinner – turkey, stuffing, potatoes, all the trimmings. Do you feel like helping clean up? Or do you feel like a nap. A big meal makes us tired, and then we fall asleep. Babies are the same way – and formula has more of the sleep-inducing chemicals (like carbohydrates and tryptophan) than breastmilk does. So yes, a baby will sleep better after a meal of formula. And yes, you might get in a nap. But does this mean that it's the best food for your baby? Of course not. Just like we shouldn't have turkey and potatoes and stuffing and pecan pie every single meal. We'd be enormous. And, babies who are fed formula are more likely to be overweight as adults. Eating healthy is not always the easy choice, is it? But hang in there – once breastfeeding is established, it really *really* is the easier way to feed. When you roll over to feed your baby at night instead of going to the kitchen for a bottle, you'll see what I mean.

Who to see for help

Most moms see their baby's pediatrician for help with breastfeeding issues. Some doctors have extensive breastfeeding knowledge and experience, and can be very helpful to a new mom. But it's important to remember that they have gained all of this breastfeeding knowledge on their own. There is no standard breastfeeding curriculum in medical school (in fact, many medical schools don't teach it at all), there is no requirement for doctors to take breastfeeding courses, and much of what they know they have learned from colleagues and other breastfeeding mothers (a lot of "here's what worked for me").

On the other hand, a certified lactation consultant (IBCLC) is required to study many hours of evidence-based breastfeeding practices and pass a certifying exam on breastfeeding-related issues. She is also required to have hundreds of hours of experience directly helping breastfeeding mothers and babies, which your doctor may or may not have. So if you are getting advice from your doctor that doesn't quite feel right, or your doctor is recommending weaning or supplementing, ask for a referral to a lactation consultant. Your doctor is an expert in infant health and disease, but is not necessarily an expert in resolving breastfeeding problems. If you broke your leg, maybe the emergency room doctor could set the bone or maybe they couldn't, but wouldn't you rather wait for the orthopedist? A pediatrician can help with basic breastfeeding advice, but for the tough problems, they should refer to a specialist – a certified lactation consultant.

Please read the next chapter for much more information on why it's perfectly natural to need some help in the early days of breastfeeding.

The first night home – or "What's wrong with my baby?"

Finally, you got your baby home from the hospital, breastfeeding is off to a decent start, you are feeling well cared for and like you might just be able to manage this mothering business.

Then suddenly the night from hell hits. Your baby just won't stop crying. While the breast has soothed her so well up till now, tonight she will have none of it. You try diaper changes, burping, swaddling – maybe she's hungry now – try the breast – no, she's wet, change her, no – it must be gas…

You and your partner are totally sleep deprived, your hormones have your emotions in a twist, you decide in despair that your baby is starving and something must be wrong with your milk. You're probably thinking "Darn it, why did we throw out that formula? What can we feed her? Can I pump a bottle for her? Oh poor dear, starving to death and only 3 days old…"

Stop! Take heart! It's not you – really. Your milk is fine, your baby is fine – let's just try to see things from her perspective for a minute. Imagine you've only ever known a nice warm, dark, quiet, soothing home. Your every need is met without you having to do a thing. You have never known thirst or hunger or fear or pain. Well kiss that life goodbye, sister! Boom – out into a bright room, the air is freezing cold and dry, there are all these strangers around. Suddenly you have to do work to get food. You have wet, cold diapers on your bum all the time, which is only slightly better than the iced sandpaper they use to clean it up with. And just when you feel like you've gotten it under control, there's that crazy ache in your belly *again*! I think most babies struggle through this for about 3 or 4 days just to try out this new world and see how it's going to work for them. Then, one day, out of the blue – they've had enough. Your baby's cries at this point mean "I want back in!" I believe that at some point in the first few days your baby realizes that the good life of the womb is gone for good, and she just needs to be upset about it for a little while.

So what can you do for this inconsolable baby? It breaks your heart to hear her cry, and even more to have her refuse your comforting breast. At this point, all you can really do is hold her and talk to her. Tell her how much you love her, and how this outside world is really not so bad. Tell her that you and the rest of her new family are here to love her and take care of her. Snuggle her in a carrier and take her outside for a nighttime walk if it's not too cold. Have your partner talk to her and carry her and assure her all is well. Snuggle her naked against your bare chest and just let her wail. At some point, she will collapse into sleep from sheer exhaustion. When she wakes up, if you can catch her right at that threshold of sleep and wakefulness, she will probably nurse again, and realize this outside world might just be OK. But certainly you can sympathize with her loss – it's deep inside all of us, somewhere, and it's so fresh for her, she just has to cry. It will get better, and no baby has ever starved to death overnight. As long as she was nursing well before this crazy night, she'll be fine. She just needs to be held and told how much you love her (even if she doesn't hear you over the screaming, she'll get the idea).

> Skin-to-skin contact is the closest you can get to recreating the security of the womb for your baby, so don't be afraid to wrap her in with you and just let her get used to life on the outside slowly.

Your emotions

There is a wonderful elation that comes with having a baby. Even after a surgical birth, most moms feel a rush of energy when that baby is placed in their arms. All is well in the world, the baby is here! But don't be surprised if this elation fades in a couple days, and even if a feeling of weepiness and despair sets in. It sounds so cliché, but your hormones are all over the map after you have a baby, and you can't expect to be at your best until they behave themselves and settle down a bit. You may find yourself incredibly frustrated and in tears after a feeding that didn't go well. Certainly the mention that your baby might not be getting enough to eat is enough to cast you to the depths of self-doubt – is my body letting me down? Am I unable to feed my child? Especially if you have had a birth full of interventions, you may be feeling like your body is just not on board for this whole parenting gig, and it's absolutely normal to feel a lot of doubt.

I think that just knowing this is normal, that you're not alone in these feelings, can be enough to help you get through. It's great if you can let your partner know that you're not at your most confident, and you just need a lot of reassurance right now. I remember after the birth of my daughter (my second child, when I should have been so sure of myself) I had a whole day where I just couldn't imagine how I was going to take care of two children without losing my job and all my friends. I didn't see how it would be possible.

Actually, I'm lying, I don't remember this at all, but my husband swears it happened. That's why your friends haven't warned you about feeling this way – as soon as it's passed, you miraculously forget about it, but trust me, everyone you know with a baby has had at least one hour in the first few days of feeling totally pathetic and inept. If she says she didn't, she's either a total earth-mother goddess, or just doesn't remember it.

I do know one remedy for this feeling – it's a special drug available only to new mothers, and you can make it yourself. It's called Oxytocin, or "the mothering hormone." Oxytocin is released when you nurse your baby, and as it flows through your body, feelings of relaxation and all-is-right-with-the-world will flow to your hormone-addled brain. Get the nursing right, and the mood will follow – being able to feed your baby is absolutely empowering, and the hormonal boost is just icing on the cake.

When you're feeling all out of whack, just repeat "my hormones are making me crazy, they will level out, and I will feel better soon."

Baby blues or depression?

Those feelings of weepiness and discouragement are the legendary "baby blues" – very normal and very common. And it will go away on its own. Postpartum depression (PPD), on the other hand, is not normal, won't go away on its own, and needs medical attention as soon as possible. You can take breastfeeding-safe anti-depressants to get you through this time, so please don't put off getting help. So how do you know the difference?

  ɞ Are you able to ask for help from those around you?

  ɞ Can you share your weepiness and confused feelings with people close to you?

  ɞ Do you take joy in your baby?

  ɞ Do you feel like you can take care of your baby?

If you answered "yes" to these four questions, it means you

are taking important steps towards taking care of yourself, and it's probably just baby blues. If you are finding feelings of hopelessness taking you to a place where you don't even want to ask for help, because, well, what good would it do anyway – you should have been at the doctor's yesterday. Sadly, one of the hallmarks of depression is the inability to ask for help – but if you are feeling anything close to despair, if you lose interest in your baby – just know that there is help available, there are things that will make you better, and please, ask someone you love to help you.

My partner wants to feed the baby

Feeding is a huge challenge if you and your partner are trying to be equal partners in parenting. What a wonderful dad your baby has – he wants to be involved in every aspect of her care – he is a gem, is he not? But just like he couldn't be pregnant, now that the baby is finally here, he can't feed her. And now she's on the outside, and cute and cuddly – it was a lot easier not to be jealous when you were vomiting for 3 months and had swollen ankles. Now you look like a normal person again, and this baby loves you the most – no fair! This can be really frustrating for new dads, especially if they only have a short leave to be home with the baby. Dad comes home from work, and the baby only wants mom, only wants that boob – what can be done? (This doesn't just apply to dads – often the non-birthing mom in a same-sex partnership has these same feelings of being left out.)

For breastfeeding to work in the long run, your partner really has to be on board. You have to agree that the benefits of breastfeeding really are best for the baby, and also realize that parenting is not just about feeding. Your baby has so many needs – eating is just one of them.

When my first baby was born, we had a wonderful division of labor – I did the input, my partner did the outflow. That meant that I would feed our son, while he handled all diaper changes and burping (and believe me, in those first few weeks the burping and spitting up seemed to be the major source of outflow from that child!). Sounds like dad got a raw deal, doesn't it? But really, diaper changing is a wonderful time. Your baby has to be looking up at you when you do it (well, except for those big blowouts up the back…), and it can be such a fun time to tickle those little tummies, play with those chubby little thighs, and really enjoy your baby. The same with burping – this brings so much comfort to a baby; it's a perfect job for your partner to take on.

I had a C-section with my first, and my husband would take him in the front pack for long walks around the neighborhood before I was allowed out and about. Dad introduced our son to trees, birds, and the sky. If your partner is male, babies often find his low voice to be so much more soothing to them when they are tired, so you can nurse the baby, then pass her off to your partner for lullabies.

If dad really wants to give an occasional bottle, wait at least 2 weeks – you and your baby need time to really learn to breastfeed as a team before adding any confusion. After 2 weeks (or even better, wait a month), go ahead and pump a bottle for dad to feed. But remember, breastfeeding is a mom's job, and that's just the way it is. It may not feel "fair" or equal, but as much as men and women are equal in their abilities, it doesn't mean you have to do the exact same jobs. You can find other ways to have an equal relationship, with your partner taking on many of the other parenting roles, without compromising the importance of breastfeeding for your baby's health and well-being. To this day, my husband is much better at baths and bedtime stories than I am, and while I feel little pangs of jealousy when my story is deemed "not good enough," I have to accept that we both have our parenting strengths.

Giving your partner a field of expertise

The most important relationship your baby has is with you, the mother. But the second-most important is with your partner – who is generally the parent of the baby as well. This other parent needs to develop their own parenting style, and their own parenting expertise. It is hard to be a parent if you are criticized for everything you do. I think we have all seen the typical response to this – which is for the criticized person to say "here, you do it." Sure, it's satisfying to be the world's expert on your baby for a week or two – but after a while it starts to feel less like "world's expert" and more like "world's doormat." As in "honey, you've got it all under control here, I'm going to go out for a bit. You and the baby have fun!"

So – how to avoid the parent who drifts away from their parenting responsibilities? Let them be in charge! Let them feel competent! This is a gift you can bestow just by shutting up. Honestly, does it really matter if your baby's dear papa puts her in a pink plaid dress with orange striped pants? No, it doesn't matter – in any real, danger-to-my-baby way, it just doesn't matter. So let it go. Does is matter if the dishes aren't put away just where you keep them? Nope – and you get the dishes put away for you every single time grandma is in town if you don't complain about where they end up.

My husband has had two areas of expertise ever since our first child was born – diapers and bathtubs. After my C-section, he had to do all the diaper changes until I could get around better, and he became the expert. According to him, I never really mastered the right way to fold a cloth diaper, the right way to wipe, or the knowledge of when to use rash cream. I'm pleased to let him be the master of poop, and he has a sense of ownership of the job. He's also the #1 bath-guy. Honestly, I don't enjoy doing baths that much. The leaning over hurts my shoulders, and I got tired of the fact that every time the kids see me naked they want to latch on. Again, it's great for my husband to be the expert. I have no idea what temperature to run a bath, and when he's out of town, the kids always complain that the bath is too cold, and that's OK with me (I mean, I do make it warmer, but it's been good to give away the responsibility for keeping that knowledge of bath temperature). I'm the expert on feeding, when we need new clothes or shoes, doctor's appointments and a few other things, so it's not like I run out of things to do, and he's a more involved parent because I was able to let go and let him be the boss of some areas. Now that the kids are older, he's also the master of packing ski equipment, having warm hats and socks, and setting up play structures, indoors and out. He's a great dad.

A lot of women say they want to start pumping and giving bottles soon so that dad can help with the feedings and "bond" with the baby – as if feeding were the only way to bond. True, it's an easy way to feel attached, but it's certainly possible to bond without feeding. First let me say that a lot of moms who want to pump and have dad give a bottle to "help" soon realize that the setting up of the pump, getting a bottle ready, cleaning the pump, and then feeding is not so much of a help as they'd thought. Just feeding the baby can be a lot easier, and dad can be involved by bringing you the baby when he's hungry, being sure that you have something to eat or drink while you are nursing, then taking the baby to burp, change, or walk after the feeding time is over. Babies love the fuzzy warmth of dad's chest and the low tones of a father's singing. There is a unique role for fathers that doesn't need to involve feeding. Dr. William Sears writes eloquently about father-bonding in *The Baby Book* – a reference well worth owning for all new parents.

Pick your battles

How do you decide where to take a stand? The obvious first choices involve your baby's safety. No, it's not OK for your father to put the baby in the tub and go watch the news – you can put your foot down on that one. But is it OK for your baby to watch the violence of the evening news with his grandfather? Is your dad holding your baby and getting in some cuddle time? I would probably opt for the news+cuddle rather than shutting grandpa out of the care circle just because he wants to watch TV while you're cooking dinner.

Other places to take a stand involve protecting your breastfeeding relationship. Giving a pacifier during daycare is probably OK, but having your sister give the baby a bottle while you're in the shower and will be out in two minutes is not. I think it's possible to let people have their own styles while holding firm that feeding the baby is your job as long as you're there. Once people accept that you'll be the one doing the feeding, they'll start to get more creative about other ways to soothe and play with your baby. Some people are hung up on feeding as the only way to bond with a baby. Denying them this can be hard – but it can help to give them a specific job – like diapers, taking the baby for a walk, choosing outfits, and when the baby is older, feeding the first solid foods.

My mother-in-law is a classic "food-nurturer" – she loves to have people eat what she's prepared for them. She came to stay with us when my son was about 10 weeks old, and loved giving him a bottle when I was at work. But when I was home, she was able to feel like she was feeding my son by cooking for me! She would make these wonderful soups, then watch while Kai was nursing and say "how's that good ham soup coming through, baby? Are you getting good healthy milk from it?" I think she really felt involved in the family affair of nurturing and feeding our baby.

Breastfeeding reference books:

Bestfeeding by Mary Renfro, Chloe FIsher, Susanne Arms

So That's What They're For! by Janet Tamaro

The Womanly Art of Breastfeeding by La Leche League Intl.

The Breastfeeding Book by Martha and William Sears

The Ultimate Breastfeeding Book of Answers by Jack Newman and Teresa Pitman

Mothering Your Nursing Toddler by Norma Jean Baumgarmer

The Nursing Mother's Guide to Weaning by Kathleen Huggins

Breastfeeding Made Simple by Nancy Mohrbacher

There is an extensive list of other titles at www.parentbooks.ca/breastfeeding.html

Troubleshooting breastfeeding problems – the early days

This part is divided into two sections – the first discusses why it's perfectly normal to need help when you are starting to breastfeed – even if breastfeeding is supposed to be natural. The second section gives some solutions for common problems – but is not meant to substitute for in-person help and support.

What if breastfeeding *does* hurt?

If breastfeeding is uncomfortable for you to the point that the word "pain" comes to mind and stays there, something needs to be fixed. There are a lot of reasons it might hurt, and all of them are curable. This is the most important thing – they're curable – with the correct help and a good attitude. Most likely, you need to make a small adjustment to the latch. It's also possible you have candida or maybe your baby is tongue-tied. These require a little medical intervention, but again – fixable.

So how do you know what's wrong, and how do you fix it? One answer – a lactation consultant. For some reason, almost every woman I've ever talked to has this huge resistance to calling a lactation consultant. Is it the cost? A home consult runs about $50-$100, and is often not covered by insurance, so yes, it is expensive. But what if you don't get one and you end up weaning? How much formula does $100 buy? Not much, really, especially once you factor in the additional health care costs.

> Conservative estimates put the cost of one year's worth of formula at $2000-$2500. And this isn't covered by *any* insurance! Even if you are on WIC, they only provide enough formula for a 10 pound baby, so once your baby is bigger than that, you'll still be buying formula every month.

A woman I worked with recently told me she didn't want to put the money into a lactation consultant since breastfeeding probably wouldn't work out for them anyway… Hello? To me, this is like saying "I have this infection in my foot, but I don't want to spend the money on an antibiotic, since I might have to have it amputated anyway if the infection gets worse…". Right – but the antibiotic will *keep* the infection from getting worse, just like the lactation consultant will insure that breastfeeding *will* work out for you.

There are a lot of ways to find a lactation consultant. Many lactation consultants are members of their professional organization, ILCA. Their website, www.ilca.org, has a feature called "Find a Lactation Consultant" that will pull up all members within a 100 mile radius of your zip code. The La Leche League website, www.llli.org, also has a "find a leader" feature, which you can use to get in contact with someone nearby. Other options are to check "Lactation" in the yellow pages, or call a midwife office or your childbirth educator to see if they can refer you. And, last but not least, your pediatrician's office may have either a lactation consultant on staff or someone they frequently refer to.

I thought it was supposed to be natural!

Maybe you just feel like you can work through this on your own. Maybe you feel like women should just *know* how to breastfeed, and if you don't, there's something wrong with you… well, there's not. Let me share my theory of the lost breastfeeding generation. It's not really so off-topic, and I think this perspective can help you feel better if breastfeeding has been a struggle for you.

The lost generation or "When did breastfeeding get to be so hard?"

"Women have always known these things. We just forgot to tell each other for a while."- *author unknown*

If you run into trouble with breastfeeding, you may be wondering what on earth is wrong with you. Women have been breastfeeding since there were first women and babies on the earth, what seems to be your problem? Isn't it supposed to be natural? Well, let's put this in a little cultural perspective. Imagine life 100 years ago. Families were larger, and most babies were born at home. That meant that from your earliest consciousness, you were surrounded by breastfeeding. You saw your younger siblings breastfed, or if you were the youngest, your older siblings were old enough that you saw them nurse their own babies. You watched breastfeeding with the boldness of a child – you put your head right by the mother's breast, you watched the baby's mouth, you absorbed breastfeeding into your knowledge of how the world worked. Skip ahead to the 21st century – did you ever see a baby breastfed as a child? Do you remember it? Were you told not to look? And think about the last 10-15 years of your life. Most of us stop seeing many babies by the time we're teenagers, and most don't see babies through high school, college, our first jobs, and well through our 20s. Had you ever watched a mother breastfeed before you tried it on your own? I know I had only seen it from a distance.

Just like riding a bike

Let's take a walk in the land of analogy. (Humor me, it's my book.) Imagine that you've heard of this great thing called a bicycle. It's great exercise, saves fuel – what a neat thing, maybe I'll try it! The only problem is you've never actually seen a bicycle being ridden, and nobody you know has ever ridden one either. You have one friend who tried to ride one once, but she fell off a lot and you can still remember the awful scabs on her legs. But, you know there are a lot of places you could get to on a bicycle, and you like the idea of a healthier transportation choice, so you go out and buy a bicycle, the funny shorts, a helmet and shoes and a bunch of books on how to ride a bicycle, determined to learn on your own. Yes, this is a blazingly obvious metaphor – but have you noticed what's missing? The person who runs alongside you, holding up the bicycle as you take your first tentative pedal strokes.

All through history, women have had these teachers running alongside them as they learned to breastfeed. When you nursed your first baby, you were supported by your mother, your grandmother, your aunts, cousins and sisters, all of whom had breastfed their babies. They were there to show you how, to provide encouragement, to run alongside you holding you up. There was a wealth of information that had been passed down from generation to generation about how to make breastfeeding work for every woman. The collective breastfeeding knowledge was vast, and we knew how to hold each other up as we learned!

Jump to today – if your mother is with you, maybe she breastfed, maybe she didn't. If she did, she was likely alone in her endeavor, and doesn't have a role model for supporting breastfeeding. There are those around you telling you why it will be hard and why you will fail. This never happened when breastfeeding was necessary for survival! And, to milk this analogy for all it's worth (pun intended), have you ever heard a parent tell a child learning to ride a bike, "don't worry, if you don't figure it out I'll just drive you everywhere?"

Getting the help you need

So what does this have to do with lactation consultants and professional breastfeeding help? Here in the beginning of the 21st century, the collective knowledge of millennia of breastfeeding women has been lost to the formula generation, and we're having to start over from scratch. So – if you need to call in some professional help – do it! We don't have the resources of the women who breastfed "naturally" in the past – we have to find those resources on our own, and there's no shame in it. Would you pay someone to teach you to ski if you'd never tried it before? Sure! Would you expect to fall down a few times as you learned? Sure! It's the same idea. We are rebuilding the collective knowledge, and everything you learn now from a lactation consultant, experienced breastfeeding friend or doula, you will be able to pass on to your friends, nieces, and daughters.

So – find and call a good lactation consultant, La Leche League leader, or other breastfeeding helper. She will usually be able to see you within one or two days, and if she can't, find someone who can.

If you have a lactation consultant visit you and you don't like how she treats you — maybe she grabs your breasts a little too casually, maybe she puts down your birth choices, maybe you just don't click — that's OK — not everyone gets along. Go back to the phone book and find another. If you didn't like your therapist or dentist or hairdresser, you'd find another, right? Remember your power as a medical consumer — you can choose not to get care that you don't like.

If you get conflicting advice, remember, we're having to start over, and many people are just sharing what has worked for them in the past. If breastfeeding hurts, keep seeking help. If your baby cries every afternoon, find other moms to hang out with during that time who will reassure you that it's normal. If you're trying to do it all alone – reach out. The collective wisdom of women only works if we let ourselves get together.

And now for some practical advice.

Breast and nipple pain

Sore spots

In the first days of breastfeeding, when your milk first comes in and your supply is regulating, probably the most common problem is breast lumps or sore spots. Generally these are caused by plugged ducts – when a particular group of milk glands are not fully emptied, the milk can clog the duct and cause milk behind the plug to back up – causing pain, lumps and sore spots. Pay close attention to these spots and treat them immediately. If untreated, a plugged duct can rapidly develop into mastitis – *especially* if you are not resting enough and your immune system is dragging a bit.

How to treat a plugged duct

This is the good part – the first thing you should do is get in a hot shower. Let very warm water run over your breast and begin massaging gently over the sore spot – from "behind" the plug towards the nipple. Sometimes this is all you need to do to release the plug – it's kind of like popping a pimple – you'll feel the plug come loose and milk will begin to spray from the formerly plugged duct – and you'll feel better very quickly. Or you may need to repeat the shower treatment a few times. You can also try applying moist heat to your breast before nursing to soften the plug. But while you are treating the plugged duct, the most important thing is to keep nursing on both sides. You can start on the sore side to be sure it's as fully emptied as possible, and if your breast is very tender, it's safe to take Tylenol or Advil about 30 minutes before nursing to reduce the discomfort. There are a few old wives tales about how to clear a plugged duct – not scientifically proven, but here they are.

ဢ Drink tons of water: It can't hurt, and could help the plug clear more quickly. If nothing else, good hydration insures that your immune cells can get to the problem area rapidly.

ဢ Chin to the sore spot: Some people swear that by placing the baby's chin by the sore spot when nursing, the plug clears the fastest. This can involve some yoga moves, and be sure you're maintaining a good latch as you nurse with your baby draped over your shoulder or lying on top of you.

ဢ Nurse like a cow: Another suggested solution is to nurse like a cow – get on hands and knees over your baby, and nurse with your breast hanging down. And make sure your partner can't find the camera.

Watch for mastitis

If a sore spot begins to turn red, the pain gets a lot worse, or if you develop any flu-like symptoms, mastitis is starting. Mastitis is an infection of the milk caught behind the plug, or anywhere it is not being emptied from the breast. Unfortunately, mastitis is an illness that wipes out your whole body, and it needs to be taken seriously. If you start any kind of a fever, you really should be on antibiotics to clear the infection as quickly as possible. I managed to evade mastitis a couple of times by taking the following approach at the very first hint of fever or body aches – I stopped all unneeded activity, laid around and nursed as frequently as possible, repeated the hot shower-massage technique 3-4 times a day, took zinc, vitamin C and Echinacea, and drank buckets of water. It's hard for any illness to survive a flood, in my view, so I hydrated like crazy. But I was soundly scolded by my usually naturopathic midwife for not getting it treated right away with antibiotics – so take mastitis seriously!

Antibiotics and breastfeeding

So, you let the plugged duct go, you got mastitis, and now you're on antibiotics. The good news is that the mastitis should clear rapidly. The bad news is that you're killing off all of the good little bugs in your gut and your baby's gut, and you're both at risk for an overgrowth of *Candida* – also known as a yeast infection or thrush. In this case, an ounce of prevention is definitely worth a pound of cure, so take steps to avoid thrush.

ဢ Keep your nipples clean and dry – don't keep damp breastpads on – allow your nipples to air dry after each feeding, and wear clean bras and breastpads.

ဢ Go easy on the sugar – it's possible that lots of sugar in the diet contributes to the overgrowth of yeast, so try to ease off on high sugar foods while you're on antibiotics.

ဢ Take Acidophilus – Acidophilus is the active culture in yogurt, and a beneficial organism to have in your digestive system. You can get acidophilus tablets at any health food store, and often in the natural foods section of a big grocery store. Take the recommended dosage for as long as you're on antibiotics. You should also protect your baby from getting thrush – a very painful mouth and diaper rash that can spread to your nipples, causing a great deal of nursing pain. There is acidophilus powder specially formulated for babies – for this you will probably have to go to a health food store. The brand I find around here is called Baby Jarro-dophilus. You can put a little of the powder on your finger and just have your baby suck it off two or three times a day. My babies had nothing but breastmilk cross their lips for at least 5 months, with the exception of acidophilus – and we were lucky enough to avoid any major outbreaks of yeast.

If you do get thrush, there is more information on treating it in the section in Chapter 11 on "Troubleshooting later breastfeeding problems."

Sore nipples

There are a lot of reasons nipples can be sore – but most of them involve latch. If it is painful to nurse your baby, you really need to see a professional. I know a lot of women just try to tough through it, but why not get some help? However, if it's going to be a few days until someone can see you, here are some things you can try.

Make sure your baby is latching on with a wide open mouth. Some babies love to purse their lips like they're sucking from a straw, and it can take time to help these babies learn to open wider. Wait to latch until your baby's mouth is r-e-a-l-l-y big, and undo the latch if there's any pain at all.

Try nursing in a lot of positions. If you have less pain using the football (clutch) hold, then by all means, use it. Try nursing lying down, on your back, sitting up, reclining, and using different holds. Then use what keeps you comfortable. My friend Katie read from a book to keep changing positions when her nipples were hurting, so she felt compelled to keep returning to the position that was causing the most damage. No need. You can start on the side that is less sore if that helps; sometimes a baby will nurse less vigorously on the second side.

Keep nursing both sides until you can get the issue resolved. You may find that your nipple hurts at the beginning of a feeding, but then less as the feeding goes on – this is typically a good sign, and the soreness may resolve on its own in a few days.

Nurse frequently, and try to anticipate your baby's hunger cues. A baby who is not ravenously hungry may go a little easier on your nipples.

After nursing, you can express a little milk and rub it on your nipples – the antibacterial properties of breastmilk will speed healing and prevent infection of any open sores.

Between feedings, keep your nipples as dry as possible. Go topless if you can, or sleep without a bra. Topless sunbathing is sometimes recommended if it's warm where you live. If you need to keep a bra on for comfort, be sure it stays clean and dry, and change breast pads frequently.

Many moms swear by creams and ointments for nipple healing, but there's not really any evidence that they make a difference. A better latch makes a difference. If you do use a cream, purified lanolin is usually recommended, but again, it may or may not help. It can't hurt to try, and you probably have a free sample from the hospital lying around. There are gel pads called "Soothies" that may provide some relief – but again remember, they may make your nipples more comfortable between feedings, but they're not really fixing the underlying problem.

I recently read an article in which a new mom was bemoaning her breastfeeding difficulties. She said she finally went to a lactation consultant who was able to get her baby latched on pain-free, but then when she went home, it hurt again. And then she just went on with the pain. Why did she not go back to the lactation consultant, who had obviously been able to help? She needed my essay from the beginning of this chapter.

Is my nipple actually...*bleeding*???

Yes, it does happen. In the first days of breastfeeding, nipples can crack and bleed. It hurts as much as you would imagine it does, and you're right, it's totally gross. The natural instinct looking at something chewed to shreds by your baby's mouth is to not ever put it back in there, but put it back in you must. If you stop nursing when you have cracks, they won't necessarily heal any faster, but you will put yourself at risk for plugged ducts and mastitis, a nasty proposition. So what to do – my breasts are falling apart!! First, you have to fix the problem – usually a faulty latch is the cause of the cracks, so refer to the section above about calling a lactation consultant – go on now, pick up the phone!

In the meantime, breastmilk itself speeds healing, so put a little expressed milk on your nipples after each feeding and let them air-dry. Use lanolin if this gives you some relief. You can even put some bacitracin ointment on your nipples after feeding, but this you should wipe off before starting the next feeding.

Note also that the small amount of blood coming from your nipple will not harm your baby at all. You may see a slight upset tummy if there is a lot of blood, but it won't do any damage to your baby.

However, if you just cannot stand the thought of bringing baby to breast, if the pain is that bad, you can give yourself a little break by pumping and having someone else feed the baby once or twice a day. The better choice is to just keep on nursing as you fix the latch or other problem, but I've got to be realistic – sometimes given the choice of nursing just one more time right now, or totally throwing in the towel, an overtired, hormonal new mom will choose to quit if the pain is bad enough. Pumping and feeding expressed milk for the feeding that you are dreading the most can offer an alternative to quitting, and can sometimes be the relief that gives you the strength to keep going. So call the lactation consultant first – then, while you're working on fixing the underlying problem, go ahead and pump.

Any pain serious enough to cause you to pump needs an in-person evaluation. It could be your baby has something easily fixable, like tongue-tie, but you'll never know if you just sit home and suffer.

Can I give a bottle?

There are several ways to feed a baby expressed breastmilk, and one of them is a bottle. If you have decided that you have to pump and give your baby milk in some other way – think about using one of the other methods. There is some debate over whether "nipple confusion" exists (where a baby "forgets" how to breastfeed after using artificial nipples), but on the off chance that it does – better safe than sorry. Your baby is learning a new skill – how to eat. It's the most important skill for him to learn in the first month of life, and it's important that he get it right. If he's been practicing on one nipple (yours) and you throw in another from time to time, he's going to have a little more trouble learning.

What else can you do? Babies can drink from a spoon or tiny little cup – they are able to sort of "lap" up the milk like a cat, or you can tilt a tiny bit into their mouths. You can use a medicine syringe or eye dropper to put milk in his mouth. Finger feeding is a feeding method in which a small gauge medical tubing is used to bring milk to the baby's mouth while he sucks on your finger. A lactation consultant can suggest more options. If you do use a bottle, just be sure it has the slowest flow nipple possible. Babies, while young, immature, and nonverbal, are not stupid. They'll opt for whatever feeding choice involves the least effort.

Websites:

www.kellymom.com - a clearinghouse of all things breastfeeding. Run by Kelly Bonyata, IBCLC. Kellymom is always up to date, and draws on the most accurate scientific information. The Latch Resources page URL is given above in the text.

www.breastfeeding.com - a great source of inspirational stories from real moms, including a section for working moms. It also has breastfeeding art, breastfeeding cartoons, and message boards.

Jack Newman's handouts: Can be found at: www nursingbaby.com/nursing/index.htm,www.bflrc.com/newman/articles.htm, www. breastfeedingonline.com/newman.shtml, and www.kellymom.com/handouts/index.html.

Diane Weissinger's handouts: http://people.clarityconnect.com/webpages3/wiessinger/bfing/index.html

Reference:

Keefe MR. 1988. The impact of infant rooming-in on maternal sleep at night. J Obstet Gynecol Neonatal Nurs. Mar-Apr;17(2):122-6.

Demand and Supply

Understanding the basics of how milk is made

This is the most important chapter in this book, so I'll try to keep it short. The basic concept is that your body makes as much milk as your baby needs. Simple, right? But your body, while amazingly proficient, is not telepathic and needs to be told how much milk to make. How do you tell it? In a word, sucking. The more the baby sucks at the breast, the more milk the breast will make. The sucking is the demand, and your body responds with a supply of milk. By spending time at your breast, your baby "places the order" for more milk to be made. Your body fills the order, providing as much milk as your baby needs.

In order to keep up a good supply when you're away from your baby, you have to understand these basic principles. Once you do, you can start to navigate the world of pumping on your own; making smart choices to preserve the best possible breastfeeding relationship with your baby.

Here are a couple of examples of how your body regulates your milk supply:

Too much milk

As a first example, let's say mom has an overabundant supply – too much milk. The baby easily gets enough to eat every nursing; in fact, the baby is full while the breast still has some milk in it, and so the breast is not emptied at every feeding. That unused milk sitting in the breast sends a message saying "Whoa! Too much milk! Slow down!" and the body tones down production until the baby is able to completely empty the breasts at a feeding. Another factor that helps slow milk production is that this baby doesn't feed as often as one whose mom has less supply, since he's getting really full at each feeding. That means that there's more time between the sucking stimulation – when the milk that is sitting there tells your body to slow down a bit. This is what happens when your milk first comes in and you have watermelons on your chest for a few days. You baby isn't used to so much milk, nurses less often and isn't emptying the breasts at each feeding, then thankfully the engorgement starts to decrease as your supply changes to match what your baby needs.

Not enough milk

Now consider a mom who isn't producing quite enough milk. In a stay-home full-time breastfeeding situation, this mom's breasts are drained at every feeding – a strong signal to make more milk. In addition, this baby feeds more often, meaning more sucking stimulation – yet another signal to make more milk. If mom and baby are left on their own to work this out and no supplements are used, this natural signaling will cause the mom's milk supply to increase to where it needs to be. The trick is to let the baby nurse as often as he wants to – he's sending orders to the kitchen to make him some more grub, and if the kitchen is able to listen, it'll comply on the double with milk a la carte. Usually increasing supply (with mom and baby together full time and no supplements) only takes one or two days.

Why is supply low?

Sometimes a low supply is a good signal to mom to relax, take care of herself, and take some of the pressure off. If mom's body doesn't have enough nourishment for itself, it's going to have a hard time making enough high-quality milk. It's your job to be sure your body is a well-fed, well-rested, milk making machine. Believe me, it does take rest to make milk. Resting means not going up and down the stairs ten times a day, taking a nap when the baby goes down – these are the common sense self-care measures you take right after your baby is born. But how many of us are still taking such good care of ourselves after two months, six months, or a year? I'm betting, oh, maybe... no-one? But listen up – as long as you're making milk, you need extra nutrition and extra rest. I am, technically, a doctor, so you can tell people it's "doctor's orders" when you lie down on the couch after dinner.

What about supplements?

Here's a situation that is incredibly common – you probably know someone who's been through it, or maybe you have yourself.

A mother decides or is told, for some reason (usually wrong, but I'm biased…) that she's not making enough milk for her baby.

> If the baby honestly isn't getting enough milk, the reason is usually a poor latch. The latch is the first thing to be checked and corrected any time low supply is suspected. If true low supply is diagnosed, a lactation professional can help you pump and feed your own expressed milk to increase your milk supply, or supplement at the breast to keep up nipple stimulation.

Somehow this baby is thought to be at risk of starving to death before mom can get her supply back up, so supplements must be started immediately (note the tone of sarcasm…). The worried mother begins giving the baby a bottle of formula after each feeding at the breast, or maybe even just once or twice a day.

Based on the concept of demand and supply – let's play this one out (hang with me, it's a worthwhile exercise). The baby getting supplements goes a longer time between feedings, since he's getting full on the formula. The sucking signal comes much less often – a powerful signal to the body that there is already plenty of milk, or even too much. The doctor or other "helpful" advisor says mom will just need to supplement for a few days, then she can stop. But what happens when she stops? With less nursing, this poor mom's supply really *has* gone down. Suddenly the baby is hungry all the time! He must be starving! So, it's back to the supplements, and poor mom's supply just can't seem to keep up. Hmmm, wonder why, right? Does it make sense now how supplementing can actually decrease your milk supply?

Weaning off of supplements is hard, and takes a lot of confidence from mom. There's also a fair amount of dealing with a fussy baby who has become used to the stupefying effects of a belly full of cow's milk (which makes babies feel more full than human milk). The way out is to gradually decrease the amount of supplement and increase the time the baby spends at the breast (or pump to add extra stimulation), knowing that the more the baby nurses, the more milk your wonderful and responsive breasts will make. And, of course, make sure the baby has a good latch.

How this applies to pumping

For a lot of moms, the pump is just not as good at giving that sucking stimulation as the baby is. You may find that even if your baby would have only nursed three times between 8:30 and 5:30, you have to pump four times to keep up with the amount that he's eating. The supply (the amount you get from the pump) must be equal to the demand (the amount your baby eats while you're away). As long as these things stay in balance, you can keep pumping and providing exclusive breastmilk for as long as you want to!

> You don't necessarily need to have exact balance every single day, but aim for having a balance between demand and supply over any given week.

If you start supplementing – whether it's with formula or your own milk from your freezer stash, this means two things – 1) your baby is getting more milk than you are making, and 2) your body is not getting the signal to start making more. A lot of moms supplement – there's nothing wrong with it, and you can certainly supplement and keep breastfeeding for as long as you want to. Some moms can use formula during the day, and still have an ample milk supply when they are together with their baby. Others need to keep pumping to keep their supply up. But – before you start supplementing, it's important that you understand the effects it can have on your milk supply and why.

If you're having trouble pumping enough, a lot of techniques for pumping more milk are addressed in the section in Chapter 8 called "Troubleshooting supply issues." These are almost all based on the principles of Demand and Supply. How do you let your body know you need more milk? More sucking, plain and simple. This sucking can come from more pumping or more frequent nursing, or both. But you have to let your body know it should be making more milk – and you and your baby are the only ones who can communicate that message.

Storage capacity

How sensitive your supply is to slight fluctuations in demand depends a lot on your milk storage capacity. Different breasts have different storage capacities, and it doesn't seem to correlate very well at all with breast size. If you have a large storage capacity, you can generally go longer between feedings (letting your breasts get "more full") without sending a signal to decrease production. If you have a small storage capacity, you'll feel engorged sooner after a missed feeding or pumping session, and your body will send a signal sooner to decrease production. What you can and can't get away with in terms of your pumping schedule has a lot to do with your storage capacity. If it's large, you can go longer between pumping sessions – and you may be one of those women who can pump 10 ounces in a sitting. With a smaller capacity (like me), you'll find that even one missed session can impact your supply the next day, and you need to stick right to your pumping schedule or you start leaking. Don't be discouraged if another woman in your office pumps plenty in one session and you're in the pump room every other hour – you both are making plenty of milk for your baby – your bodies are just different. And both babies are getting the benefits of as much healthy breastmilk as they need.

Choosing a plan that's realistic for you

Goals are an important part of your decision to work and pump. Having a goal gives you a reason to sit and wash those pump parts one more time because you're striving towards something. However, unrealistic goals are worse than none at all because you tend to recognize them as unrealistic pretty early on, and feel like since you're not going to meet the goal anyway, you might as well throw in the towel now.

I tell new moms who are breastfeeding for the first time to set 2 weeks as an initial goal. If you can make it to two weeks, you will be over most of the initial difficulties, and you will be seeing how easy breastfeeding can really be. Imagine if you had to decide the second day home if you were going to breastfeed for a year or not at all – that's an impossible decision, you just don't have the information. Those first few days can be so difficult, you wouldn't sign up for a year of any of it! But after 2 weeks, you at least have a sense of whether you can go another 2 weeks, and you take it from there.

The same applies to setting goals for pumping. Figure out the minimum time you want to provide your baby with nothing but breastmilk, or a majority of breastmilk in his diet, and see how that feels as a goal. (Just be sure it's a long enough time to work out any initial kinks you may run into.) Since a lot of moms go back to work when the baby is around 8 weeks, it seems that pumping till the baby is 3 months old is a reasonable first goal. As this goal approaches, you can decide if 6 months feels like a reasonable next goal. At 6 months, you can decide if you want to try for 9 months or a year. Achieving your goals along the way is a lot more satisfying than striving for a goal that's way off on the horizon – we all need some short-term gratification, and meeting short-term goals is a wonderful way to do it. And – if you do decide that it's not working out for you at some point, you have the satisfaction of being able to say "I met a goal!" instead of feeling that you've let yourself down.

How long does breastfeeding need to be exclusive?

In setting goals, another important thing to think about is using supplemental formula. Based on the research, I think it's very important that a baby be exclusively breastfed until at least 4 months of age. This early exclusivity protects your baby against respiratory and ear infections, protects the delicate lining of their digestive system, and may increase protection against adult diseases like obesity and diabetes. However, I know that not everyone can meet this goal – and if you can't, you can't. Some breastmilk is better than none at all at any age. After a baby is closer to six months old, you can start adding some solid foods, depending on what your doctor recommends, and depending on your own personal goals.

For me, it was really important to avoid any dairy products, including formula, because of my own history of dairy allergies. For you, it might not matter as much. I know that for a lot of families, exclusive breastfeeding to six months and never giving formula is extremely important, and they never question that it's what they are going to do. For others, it may be that getting to six months with any breastmilk at all is a huge accomplishment. Set your own goals based on your own reality – nobody can define that but you.

My feelings about infant formula

Let's get one thing straight – I think the way infant formula is marketed is appalling. They go right for the sucker-punch of a vulnerable new mom's emotions – Look at how well your baby could sleep with some formula! – Hey, get some rest, let someone else do the feeding! – Don't forget your free sample, "just in case"! – This one's "just like breastmilk"! Losers. They piss me off.

In my perfect world, we would never need formula. Every mother would feed her baby the way nature intended, straight from the breast. We wouldn't talk about feeling "tied down" to our babies, because being with a baby would just seem so normal. Did you know that when people from other cultures see our advertisements for baby stuff (adorable baby alone on a snuggly blanket or a similar image) they always ask "where's the mother?"

In many cultures, it's just not normal to see a baby without its mother. But – this is not my perfect world. This is the United States, the 21st century, and mothers are expected to get back to work. Mothers are also expected to "get out," away from their babies, and re-establish an independent identity. Other family members can't imagine having a nurturing relationship with the baby if they're not doing some of the feeding. The pressures to formula feed are strong. And, not every mother has a work situation in which pumping is possible for her. So – we're lucky that we have an alternative food available, instead of feeding our babies concoctions of evaporated milk and karo syrup the way they used to. Formula is a fine food – especially for the older baby. Never as good as breastmilk, mind you, but absolutism in the face of an imperfect reality does nothing but turn people off. And so, on to…

My recommendations

Birth to six weeks: This is the most critical period for exclusive breastfeeding – no other foods if at all possible. This gives your baby valuable immune protection when they are most vulnerable, while insuring you have an ample milk supply. This early period of exclusive breastfeeding may also provide protection against chronic disease in a way that mixed feeding can't do.

Six weeks to four months: This is a time when exclusive breastmilk is being shown to have a significant health impact, especially in preventing respiratory infections. However, this is also a time when many mothers struggle with their return to work. Try to keep your baby on exclusive breastmilk for as much of this time as you can.

Four to six months: Breastmilk is still very important to your baby. Depending on your baby and your doctor, some babies start to take supplemental foods or some formula during this time, while others remain exclusively breastfed. This depends on your goals, although the American Academy of Pediatrics does recommend nothing but breastmilk until about six months. Many babies are wrongly supplemented for "falling off their growth curve" even though they are growing normally for a breastfed baby (see the section "Do I need to supplement" in Chapter 8 for more information on growth curves). This is a time that can be hard for working moms, as your baby's intake may be quite high as they become more active – but keep in mind that it does get easier once your baby starts taking more solid foods.

Six to nine months: Your baby is learning to eat other foods besides breastmilk. These foods do not substitute for the nutrition of breastmilk in your baby's diet, but do give you some increased flexibility, as a feeding at the breast can be delayed with a "snack" of food from time to time. Some working moms begin to cut back their pumping and routinely supplement with formula at this time, while still exclusively breastfeeding when they are home. Others stick to breastmilk as the base while new foods are added to the diet. My opinion is that formula can be used as a supplemental food after six months with much less health impact than if it is introduced earlier. Supplementing too much can decrease your milk supply, so it should be done with caution, as I discuss at length later in this book.

Nine months to a year: By nine months, many babies are eating a variety of nutritious foods, and some of these foods begin to substitute more significantly for breastmilk in your baby's diet. If you have been using formula, you may be able to decrease the amount as more foods are offered, while still keeping breastmilk as an important part of your baby's diet. Babies continue to enjoy nursing in the mornings and evenings, and often still at night, but may be too busy to nurse without reminders during their waking hours. It's OK to remind your older baby to nurse when you are home – "nursing on demand" isn't meant as a limitation; feel free to offer before they ask.

After a year: Most moms wean from pumping at around a year, but this doesn't mean that breastfeeding needs to stop. Nutritious foods and drinks can substitute for breastmilk (or formula) during the day, but your baby may enjoy nursing in the mornings and evenings for many months to come. Breastfeeding beyond a year still provides your baby with a healthy food, valuable immune protection, and a special closeness with you. This can be the most pleasant time for a working mother – the hassle of pumping is gone, and only the joy of breastfeeding remains.

Starting Pumping and Bottles

Choosing a pump

A good quality pump is the difference between an easy working and pumping experience, and one that is fraught with worries. There are many many breastpumps on the market, but as of this writing (early 2006), there are only a few that are good choices for a working mom. If you are going to be pumping on a regular basis, you will need a good double-electric pump. The most well-known brands are Medela (the Pump In Style is their most popular pump) and Ameda (makers of the Purely Yours pump). The best non-electric or single-sided pumps for working mothers are the Avent Isis (the greatest manual pump ever made in my opinion) and the Medela Harmony. In my experience, other manual, battery-powered, or single electric pumps are just not strong enough to maintain a milk supply. Realize that this is my opinion, and some women with a strong milk supply have pumped for as long as they wanted with less powerful pumps, but why risk it?

No matter what pump you decide to use, be sure to read the next section on hand expression. Try hand expressing before you buy any pump – some women become so good at it that they decide not to purchase a pump at all. Even if you are committed to electric pumping, hand expression is an essential skill. You can use it in power outages, if you're caught away from your baby for longer than you expect, or if you forget an essential part of your pump. You can hand express in airplane restrooms, in utility closets, in your car, with a fox, in a box, on a train or in the rain (apologies to Dr. Seuss).

Hand expression

I don't personally know anyone who's used only hand expression while working, but it certainly can be done. Hand expression is also an essential skill that everyone should know, and it can really save you in a pinch. The skill of hand expression can spell relief at things like concert intermissions, long plane rides, quick trips to the porta-potty, etc. You can hand express enough milk to stop leaking or get comfortable until you can pump – just spray the milk into some bunched up paper towels and you're good to go. You can learn to hand express into a bottle or wide-mouthed jar if you want to save the milk.

To learn hand expression, get into a hot shower and let the warm water run on your breasts for a little bit. Next place your hand on the same-side breast with the thumb at the top, fingers wrapped below the nipple. Place your fingers and thumb about an inch outside of the areola (not on the areola or touching the nipple) and gently press in towards your chest wall. Now slide or roll your fingers towards the nipple, ending with a squeeze right *behind* the nipple. You don't want to actually squeeze your nipple while doing this, because that will close off the ducts. This is a terrible analogy, but it's a little like squeezing a zit – the way you want to get behind the pimple and squeeze towards the surface. But on a larger scale (I would assume, unless you have really small breasts and extremely large pimples, but let's not go there), after 3-4 repetitions of this motion, you should see some milk start to come out. Admire the way all of the ducts seem to point in totally different directions! (Now you know why you're doing this in the shower the first time.) I find that during a manual expression session, I'll switch my hand position around quite a bit, trying to put pressure on the different duct systems and avoid making a sore spot. Be gentle. It doesn't take too much pressure to get the milk flowing, and you want to be careful not to damage any of the breast tissue, or wear red spots or abrasions in your skin. Practice until you feel comfortable, then keep it as a skill held in reserve. If you forget your pump, you can usually find a bottle to express into, and it's a huge relief to have an alternative that's always handy! Now that my daughter is only nursing in the morning and evening, I can use hand expression as my only pump when I'm away from her for a day or two – just express as much as possible in the shower twice a day, and that's enough to maintain my milk supply.

Advantages: Free, available everywhere

Web Information: Nice animations of hand expression are provided in a language that I absolutely do not understand at http://users.iptelecom.net.ua/~vylkas/expressanim.html. The top animation shows effective manual expression, the lower shows why you don't get any milk if you are just squeezing the nipple.

Reviewing the pumps

Electric pump basics

All electric pumps have a few basic features in common. There is a motor that creates suction, tubing attaching the motor to the flanges or horns (the cone-like pieces that fit over your breasts), some sort of valve, and collection bottles or bags. The motors can run off electricity or batteries or the plug in your car. The motor unit has adjustments for both the speed of the sucking (cycling rate) and the intensity of the suction. The carrying cases for the pumps range from very simple (Ameda's shoulder bag) to pretty complex (the Medela backpack or the Playtex bag). You can also buy some pumps without a case to save money. The case will usually have a cooler compartment to store pumped milk and a place to keep the accessories neatly stored. If you're lucky, there'll be room to throw your lunch in as well.

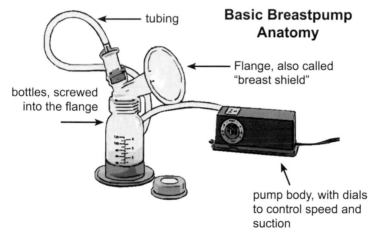

tubing

Basic Breastpump Anatomy

Flange, also called "breast shield"

bottles, screwed into the flange

pump body, with dials to control speed and suction

Medela

Medela really has cornered the working and pumping market – they advertise heavily in mother's magazines, and are readily available in most stores. There are a few different models, and they range in price from about $200 to $300. Now before you balk about the price, go to the grocery store and look at that formula with the added DHA and other beneficial fats claimed to make formula more like breastmilk. That stuff ain't cheap! Usually it takes about 6 weeks of pumping until you are paying less for pumping than you would for formula, and then after that 6 weeks, you get free food for your baby for as long as you continue pumping! If you want to see how much money you will save by breastfeeding, there is a calculator online that will figure out how much you can save for every ounce you breastfeed – it is found at www.kellymom.com/bf/start/prepare/bfcostbenefits.html.

Pump in Style

When I was first pumping, there were 2 models of the Medela pump – the Pump in Style and the Lactina. The Pump in Style is the pump sold for working moms. It is designed to be a single user item, and has a motor that can be expected to last for about a year of full time pumping. It comes in several "working-mother-friendly" styles, which means that the same pump is packaged in different carrying cases depending on if you are a lawyer (briefcase style) or a hip urbanite (backpack style). The carrying case has a cooler compartment where you keep pumped milk cold with little ice packs, a storage compartment for the flanges and tubing, and a motor unit. This pump can be run off a direct plug-in (cord and plug included) or with a battery or car adapter (both extra). For a little extra money, the newer models (the Pump In Style Advanced) have what they call the "2-Phase Expression" let-down stimulator. This feature is designed to imitate the way your baby sucks a little faster until she gets the milk flowing. I have heard mixed reviews about whether this is worth the money, it probably depends on the individual. Some people swear it gets them a faster letdown, others are having to override it every time. The Medela pumps all have adjustable settings for cycling speed and suction strength that are sufficient for the majority of users.

This is a good reliable pump. I've never heard anyone say they didn't like the Pump in Style. The flanges are available in a variety of sizes, so if you have large breasts or large nipples, be sure that you get the correct size.

Disadvantages: - The only downside to this pump is that Medela has strict pricing policies, so you will almost never see it for a discount. You can do better buying it from Canadian companies online if you are in the US and there is a favorable exchange rate, but other than that, expect to pay full price.

Web Information: Homepage is www.medela.com. For an instruction booklet that shows the assembly and operation of the pump, see www.medela.com/NewFiles/PNSA_eng.html.

Lactina and Symphony

The Lactina and Symphony models are Medela's hospital grade pumps. This means that they are certified as multi-user, and have motors built to withstand the next world war. The Symphony has the 2-Phase Expression feature seen in the newer Pump In Style models and a more attractive housing than the Lactina. These are absolute workhorse pumps, and as such, are so expensive that nobody buys them for individual use. These pumps can be rented from your hospital or a lactation consultant, and can be a real blessing if you need them. This pump, in addition to having a die-hard motor, also has more settings for cycling speed and suction strength than the Pump in Style, which can help women who have a very hard time responding to a pump.

These pumps usually rent for between $40 and $60 per month. You will probably have to buy your own "kit" to go with it (flanges, bottles and tubing) since these are not reusable.

Why rent when you can buy?? Reasons to rent: if you're not sure pumping will work with your work situation and want to give it a try for a month before buying; if you have doubts about the effectiveness of your current pump, and want to see how a good pump is supposed to feel; or if you are having a supply dip and want to switch to a different pump for a month to boost your output.

Disadvantages: There's no slick carrying case, and most rental stations still have the old blue plastic box for toting the Lactina around. No pretending it's just a new briefcase, this thing is ugly! But, you can just leave it at work, and carry the kit and bottles back and forth in a cooler, and then you eliminate the ugliness issue, or there is a new stylish nylon carrying case for the Lactina that you can buy with the flange kit. The Symphony is very large, so it's really not meant to be carried around. The cost is the major disadvantage of these otherwise faultless pumps, as even renting them can be pricey.

Ameda

The Ameda Purely Yours is the runner up in the pump popularity contest. It has advantages and disadvantages when compared to the Medela. I have used both pumps, and didn't see a difference in the performance. The Ameda is usually available brand new for quite a bit less than the Medela pumps, and there are a number of reputable sellers on ebay or elsewhere online who sell brand new Ameda pumps for about $150. The Purely Yours can be run on batteries or plugged in (no battery converter needed), and an additional car adapter can be purchased. The carrying case is more basic than that of the Pump in Style, but it still has a cooler compartment for bottles and storage space for the flanges and tubing. The Ameda used to have an advantage over the Pump in Style in that the motor unit could be removed and carried in a separate bag if desired, while the Pump in Style had the pump built into the carrier. However, the newer Pump in Style models have changed to a removable motor as well. Just like the Medela pumps, there are several flange sizes available to go with the Ameda pumps, so be sure that you have the right size to assure the most efficient pumping. The Ameda and Medela flange sizes are slightly different, but both cover a range of sizes.

Disadvantages: There is an audible motor noise with the Purely Yours. It is not very loud, but there is a slight chirping sound with each cycle of the pump. I used to put mine in my desk drawer with the tubing coming out, or you can cover it with a towel if the noise bothers you. Another disadvantage is that it can be hard to find local retailers who carry the Ameda pumps, a potential problem if you lose a part or have warrantee problems. However, most replacement parts can be ordered online so you can get them in a day or two.

Web Information: Ameda's website (www.ameda.com) doesn't have much information on it, but nice diagrams of the pump assembly and instructions can be found at: www.mybirthcare.com/py_instructions.asp and www.mybirthcare.com/py_3_using_hygienikit.asp.

Whittlestone

This pump is marketing itself as the new Mercedes of breastpumps. It comes in at the top of the price levels (around $300), but is also the only successful pump to have a dramatically different approach to milk extraction. The flanges are noticeably different from the plastic shells of the other pumps on the market – the Whittlestone has padded flanges that are designed to massage the breast more like the action of a baby nursing. I have not had the opportunity to try this pump, but online reviews that I have read have been generally very positive. Reviewers describe the pumping action as "gentle," "natural," and "the most like my baby." I have read some reviews that this pump may take longer than the Medela or Ameda – but this could also be a reflection of the learning curve of users accustomed to the more traditional pumps. The Whittlestone was tested on a small group of mothers experiencing engorgement, with good results. However, a later clinical trial found that the Whittlestone was not as good as other pumps at maintaining milk supply over the long term.

When I first started writing this book, the Whittlestone was significantly more expensive than any other pump on the market. However, there are now several pumps at comparable price points, including the PIS Advanced, the Playtex Embrace, and the new Avent Isis iQ Duo, so cost is not as much of a barrier for this pump as it used to be. I think that for moms who have had trouble with discomfort from other pumps, the Whittlestone could be a good choice.

I don't know how difficult the Whittlestone is to assemble or clean, however, I have read one review that says it is "easy to assemble." The Whittlestone also comes with a three-year warrantee on the motor – while most other pumps only warrantee the motor for one year.

Disadvantages: Expensive, not widely available to purchase in person, may not provide sufficient stimulation to maintain milk supply.

Web Information: homepage: www.whittlestone.com. Information on clinical trials is found at www.whittlestone. com/clinicaltrials.cfm. There are also many testimonials on the website.

Whisper-Wear

This pump seems like it would be ideal on first glance, and is marketed as the only true "Hands Free" pump. The flanges look like a half a tennis ball that you put in your bra, put your clothes back on, and pump away. The ultimate in discretion, right? The collection bags hang down from the bottom of the flanges, also discretely tucked beneath your shirt. I have heard a few reviews of this pump, and at this point, the results are still somewhat mixed. The pump was redesigned in 2004 with many improvements, including fixing problems with the milk leaking out from the bottom of the flanges, trouble keeping the flanges in place, and loss of suction if the tubing connecting the flanges to the collection bags is kinked at all. Keep this in mind if you look at reviews online – any before 2004 will refer to the unimproved version. However, I have heard complaints about even the newer version having inadequate suction, and that the pump is too loud. It is not absolutely silent, and the audible motor noise might not be suitable in a very quiet cube farm. However, if you work in a cubicle or factory floor or other busy and public environment and really can't find a room to use for pumping, this pump could mean the difference between pumping and not pumping, so it's great to have available. I have heard of a busy emergency room nurse who used to hook it up on a restroom break, let it run for 20 minutes or so as she worked, turn the pump off and then just take it off at her next break. If you have a long commute, this pump can also be used on your drive, which adds a valuable pumping session during your usual down time. If you look at your work situation and pumping *while* you work or in a public setting is the only way you'll be able to pump at all, this pump is certainly the way to go. The price is about average, running about $200 for the double pump. The single pump (which is just one half of the double – there are separate units for each side) costs about $100 if you want to try it before committing.

Disadvantages: May not be as effective or efficient as other double electric pumps. Reported to run better when plugged in with the optional AC adapter – but then you're tied down.

Web Information: homepage: www.whisperwear.com. Usage demonstration movies are found at www.whisperwear.

com/usagedemo.html. There are also many testimonials on the website from people who absolutely love this pump.

Avent Isis

I adore this pump! Honestly, I think every nursing mom should have one. And at about $50, it's a terrific value. The Isis is a manual pump, so it has no adjustments for cycling speed or suction strength beyond what you provide with your hand. However, it is the only manual pump with suction and efficiency that compares to a good quality double electric pump. This is the only pump you need in your first weeks at home with a baby (if you need a pump at all, which most moms don't) – it can handle bouts of engorgement or pumping to deal with plugged ducts, it's totally portable, oh, I could go on and on. So why all this fuss about a double electric for work? Well, you can only pump one side at a time with the Isis, and you have to use your hands, which eliminates the ability to do other work while you're pumping. I do know women who have successfully worked and pumped with only an Isis (or two), but for me, the convenience of the double electric was worth the extra money. Whenever I travel for work, my electric pump goes in my checked bag, and the Isis is in my carry-on, in case of travel delays or the need to pump in the airport or airplane restroom.

Disadvantage: The only real disadvantage to the Isis is that you can only pump into Avent bottles or storage bags – while there is a converter to pump from other pumps into Avent bottles, there is not yet an adapter to pump from the Isis into other brands of bottles. Another possible disadvantage is the fact that you can only pump one side at a time, which is only a disadvantage if you are pressed for time when pumping or want to use your hands to do something else.

Web Information: Homepage www.aventamerica.com. Cinical trials describing the effectiveness of this pump as compared to a double-electric can be found at www.aventamerica. com/about/news/clinicalstudies/breastpump1.asp.

Medela Harmony

The Medela Harmony is Medela's answer to the Avent Isis. It is a very efficient manual pump that fits on standard bottles. I have heard from one woman who used both that she felt that the Harmony was not quite as efficient as the Isis, but I don't have extensive experience with it. It also claims to have the "let-down" simulator – this is really just a smaller lever at the top of the pumping handle that creates smaller suction. You can do this manually with the Isis; I'm going out on a limb and calling this a gimmick.

The Playtex Embrace

The newest competitor in the world of electric breastpumps is the Playtex Embrace. I had one to try last year, and had several pumping moms test it. First let me say, this pump is a stroke of genius in terms of style. The tote bag is something I would buy for regular use, and it comes with the cutest little inner bags (labeled A, B, and C for Accessories, Bottles, and Cups). The pump body is sleek and flat and is housed in a drop-down compartment of the bag. The big advantage to this pump is that it is extremely comfortable. The flanges have a unique design meant to massage the breast around the areola more than applying direct suction. The flanges are soft plastic and mold to your breast shape. For women who have very large nipples or have had a hard time getting comfortable with other pumps, this one could make a difference. However, because of the disadvantages listed below, I can't wholeheartedly recommend this pump.

Disadvantages: Most testers found this pump to be less efficient than the Medela or Ameda pumps. Most testers found that it took longer to pump with this pump than what they were used to with other pumps. This lack of efficient suction could compromise your milk supply if you are pumping for a full time job. Additionally, this pump is loud. I mean, like, cover-it-with-a-pillow loud. When I tested it, I found the noise to be so annoying it really distracted me from pumping. The nice thing about this pump is that they did an extensive evaluation study right after it was released, and you can look at the study outcomes yourself on their website.

Web Information: Homepage for Playtex breastpumps is found at www.playtexbaby.com/bottlesnadpacifiers/products/breastfeeding.asp. From this page you can select a demonstration video of the pump. Results of the professional evaluation conducted in 2005 can be found at www.professionalevaluationstudy.com/results.html. Keep in mind that these results have been spun by Playtex. For example, you may note that this pump receives its highest ratings in the category of "Attractive and Stylish" and much lower in "efficient," "effective," and "quick letdown." But it also rated highly in "Comfortable" and "Natural Action."

Avent Isis iQ Duo

This is the newest pump on the market, debuting in late 2005. Initial reviews are very very good, although this pump has a price tag to match, with a suggested retail of $350. The pump is based on the design of the manual pump, which makes it very comfortable. The way the pump works is that you pump manually for a few cycles, then press a button and the motor keeps going at the rate and suction intensity that you set manually. It is easy to override this and change suction at any time – there is a data cable that runs from the pump flanges to the motor that sends the information back and forth. The assembly on this pump has quite a learning curve – the parts look more complicated than the more traditional pumps at first glance, but I have heard that once you get used to them it's not bad at all. If you are considering this pump, I highly recommend that you read as many online reviews as you can. Because this pump is so new, information about durability, ease of replacing parts, and ease of use in a workplace setting is sparse. However, Avent has an excellent reputation for customer service, and I expect they will support this pump very well in the early years as it becomes established.

Disadvantages: This is the most expensive pump on the market. It is not yet extensively tested. One report complains of overly stiff tubing that knocks the bottles over too easily.

Web Information: A very detailed video of the pump in use can be found at www.aventamerica.com/products/breastfeeding/breastfeeding_iqduo.asp. Click the "See it in Action!" button below the picture of the pump.

The Bailey Nurture III

This pump is a lower-cost alternative to the Pump In Style and the Purely Yours. This pump uses a manual control for cycling speed, in which you place your finger over a hole in the suction tubing to turn the suction on and off. This pump costs significantly less than the Pump In Style and Purely Yours, but is able to generate about the same amount of suction and is a very good quality pump. One of their company representatives tells me that once you get used to it, the manual cycle control is very easy and natural to use. However, if you've been used to a fully automatic pump, it does take some getting used to. This pump costs just over $100 for a double-electric without the carrying case, about $150 with the case and accessories – by far the best price available. This pump is also approved as a multi-user device, the only pump other than the rental pumps to be so approved. This means you can pass it on to a friend when you're through with it, and it has a five-year warrantee – the longest in the business. This pump also has a small and lightweight motor unit, so it is very convenient to cart around. This pump has been a workhorse of many WIC programs because of its low cost and durability.

Disadvantages: Manual suction control means you can't pump "hands-free" (although there is a foot-pedal control available). It also takes a few seconds for the suction to build up with each cycle, which could make pumping take a little longer, but most moms have reported good outcomes with it.

Web Information: Homepage at www.baileymed.com.

The rest

If you go into a baby supply store, you will see many more pumps than these on the shelves. Think of these as the "stay at home mom" pumps. They are fine for occasional pumping so you can get out for an evening, but they just don't hold up through day after day use. In addition, a lot of them are pretty expensive, $50 and up. If anyone knows of a pump not listed here that is really suitable for a full time working mom, I'd be thrilled to hear about it, but at this point, I have to relegate the rest of the pumps on the shelves to also-rans for the working mom who is serious about pumping.

Here's an overview of the also-rans:

Single-sided electric pumps - overpriced for what you get. These pumps tend to be of lower quality, and are not designed to be used full time. Medela makes one called the Mini-electric (now called the Single-Ease). Medela also makes a double electric designed for occasional use, called the DoubleEase. This pump is NOT meant to be used full-time.

Battery-powered pumps: A pump designed to run solely on batteries does not generate enough suction to extract enough milk or maintain your milk supply (this is not true of electric pumps that have the option of running on batteries).

Plunger-type manual pumps: These pumps are often given out as freebies at the hospital, and come with some of the Medela pumps. Keep it in your bag for emergencies, but this is not a pump that you can use long term. It is awkward and tiring to use, and does not generate enough suction to maintain your milk supply.

Getting a good fit

If your nipples are anything other than absolutely average sized (and how many of us even know what that means?), you may need flanges other than the ones that come with your pump. Even though all pumps come with a "standard" size flange, this doesn't mean that they are one-size-fits-all. Many moms find pumping painful until they get the right size flange, and others find that they can't get a good output from the pump if the flanges are too big or too small. If you buy your pump from ToysRUs or order online, you have to take the size flange that comes with it and order new ones at extra cost. If you buy or rent your pump from a Lactation Consultant, you can have a fitting before making the purchase to be sure you have the right size.

If you have flanges that are too small and rub on the sides of your nipples, you can try lubricating with some lanolin or olive oil, but your nipples shouldn't rub when you're pumping. Many women also report that even if their nipples don't rub, they get a greater milk output with a slightly larger flange size. I think it depends on the location of the milk ducts inside your breast. If the milk collects very close to your nipple, you'll probably do better with a smaller flange, while if the milk collection site is buried deeper in the breast, it will take a larger flange to put pressure in the right place for extracting the milk. However, flanges that are too large reduce efficiency as well, so fit really is important.

Flange Inserts: If you can't find the right size flanges, there is a new product on the market that can help. A company called "Pumpin' Pal" makes a plastic flange insert called the "Super Shield" (sells for about $13). This insert has a gradual slope where the cone part of the flange meets what we call the "tunnel" – the tube that goes to the bottle. Because there's not a sharp angle, these inserts are more forgiving when it comes to size. They are also angled so that you can sit back a bit more when pumping. If you're not getting a good fit, they are inexpensive enough to be worth a try.

Where to get a pump

New pumps

There are lots of retail stores where you can buy a pump, BabiesRUs and ToysRUs carry breastpumps, as do many other retail outlets. If you are having trouble finding pumps in your area, there are only about a billion online sites selling them, allowing you to shop around for best price, added extras like free bottles and cheap shipping.

Check around to see if you can find a lactation consultant who sells pumps in your area. The advantage of buying locally is that you can get help in determining if the flanges are the right size for you, and you will always have that person available to troubleshoot any problems that might arise with the pump. It may cost a few dollars more, but there's no substitute for good service in my book.

As I mentioned in discussing the Ameda pumps, there are a number of good sellers at any given time selling brand new pumps on ebay. When looking at buying a pump on ebay, check out other items in the seller's store, or information about their store. Sometimes lactation consultants and nurses sell on ebay offering phone support and pumping advice – this seems like a good deal.

Others are medical supply houses, also generally a safe bet. When buying from an individual, be sure to find out if the box is sealed or if the pump has ever been used – see below.

Used pumps

When browsing ebay for a pump you will see lots of people selling used pumps – but that kind of creeps me out. There are several concerns with buying a used pump, especially from someone you don't know. First is the health issue, which merits some more explanation about the difference between pump models. The Pump in Style, like most pumps, is designated as a single-user medical device. This means that it is not possible to totally sterilize the motor parts that could contact the milk. Because there is no barrier between the milk collection area and the tubing, there is a remote possibility that milk can back up the tubing and contaminate the motor. The Purely Yours has a protective barrier between the milk collection area and the tubing, so while it is not formally rated as such, I consider it to be a safe multi-user device. Because of the design, it is virtually impossible for milk to back up into the motor. You will need to sterilize the collection kit (flanges, valves and tubing) if you have a used Purely Yours, or buy a new kit for the pump. The Bailey Nurture III is the only pump officially approved as a multi-user device, so if you buy a new collection kit, you don't have to worry about contamination.

However, there are other concerns with buying a used pump. For one, you don't really have a way of knowing how much it has been used in the past. The motors are generally designed to be used for one year, but you don't know how long the person using it pumped, whether they worked long hours or part time, or if they pumped seven days a week or three. Unfortunately, breastpumps don't come with odometers, so there's not a way to track use.

Is a used pump *ever* OK to use? First of all, technically speaking, you should *never* use a pump used by someone else, except a Lactina, Symphony, Nurture III, or other pump designed for multiple users. That's the ideal, that's me covering my butt. However, this is the reality; there are unused pumps sitting around collecting dust, and there are those of us who can't just throw down $250 on something we're not even sure is going to work out. A lot of us have sisters or friends or cousins or neighbors who have pumped for a little while and then quit pumping, quit their jobs, got new pumps or weaned – and they have that pump just sitting there, ready for us to use. If you have a pretty good idea of how long the pump was used, if this is a person you trust to keep things clean, if there is no noticeable mold or smell or heebie-jeebies on the pump, at this point, me personally – I can't speak for you – I'd say thank you very much and use the pump. In fact, this is exactly what I did when I first went back to work, and it was fine. For 4 months. And then the motor died, the suction conked out on me. But by then I was committed to pumping for a full year, so it wasn't a problem to just buy a new one to finish out the year and use it for my second baby. If you have a used pump and you're not able to pump enough, take it to a lactation consultant who can test the suction and let you know if it's still working properly. And remember, medically, I cannot advise *ever* using an unapproved used pump. You make your own decision, and even though it worked for me, I can't make any promises for you.

Pumping basics
Starting to pump at home

Take at least a full two weeks after your baby is born to not even think about work. This is your time to really master breastfeeding and establish a good supply with your baby. Your body is doing a lot of work to heal after the birth, and it's not a good time to try to learn any other new skills on top of breastfeeding, and you certainly don't want any added stress. Your baby doesn't need any bottles during this time "to learn how" – there's time for that later. Nurse as often as your baby wants to and work through the initial difficulties you may have with breastfeeding. If you're having a hard time with cracked nipples or thrush or just not feeling comfortable, give yourself more time for exclusive breastfeeding. Even if you have to go back to work at 6 weeks, you can start pumping at 4 weeks and still be ready. This time is for you and the baby.

> If you have had a lot of oversupply and engorgement issues, you may have started pumping already to manage your comfort and possible plugged ducts. Save this milk in the freezer if you want to. There's nothing wrong with pumping in the first two weeks if you have to – but you shouldn't put any pressure on yourself to do it if there's no need.

Ideally after about two weeks you and your baby are starting to fall into some comfortable rhythms of being a nursing pair. Sure, sometimes the rhythm your baby chooses is the one that wakes you every half hour through the entire night, and you may not be feeling exactly "rested," but hopefully you're starting to feel more confident and comfortable. Now's a fine time to get out that pump and see if you can figure out how it works.

Your goals for these first few pumping sessions are modest. Figure out how to work your pump, start conditioning your body to respond to the pump, and gradually accumulate a little bit of extra milk for that first day back to work. Contrary to what you may have heard, you don't need gallons and gallons of milk in the freezer to go back to work. Enough for one day is all that is absolutely needed, because after that first day you'll be pumping for missed nursing sessions, and the milk you pump each day will be what you use for the next day. However, having a little buffer in the freezer is nice, and saves you the feeling of always being only just barely ahead. Just be sure you read the section in Chapter 6 on "Proper use of the freezer stash" BEFORE you start back to work!

How often (and when) to pump before going back to work

Once you go back to work, you will pump once for each missed nursing session. You'll find lots more information on scheduling in Chapter 6 - Your first days back at work. Before you go back to work, you'll want to start pumping a little bit, but there's no set answer about how much is best. You want to pump an amount that takes minimal effort and causes minimal stress, while accomplishing your modest goals. There's no need to pump more than once a day, and pumping too much can get you into trouble.

> If you pump too much, you can develop an oversupply. This means that you won't be emptying your breasts at most feedings – which leaves you at higher risk of plugged ducts and mastitis.

I recommend pumping in the morning, since that's when your body's prolactin levels are highest, so milk yield is often highest in the morning. It is best to start at a time when you're likely to have success, so you'll feel encouraged.

> Note: Prolactin is the hormone released from your brain to stimulate milk production. It's levels cycle daily with a peak at about 2 AM and a low point in the evening.

Here's a sample routine: Wake up and take a shower – ha ha, that was a little joke - you just had a baby, you don't have time for showers! OK – for real this time:

Wake up and nurse the baby (this really means the baby wakes you at some ungodly hour and you nurse). Once you have your baby back to sleep or settled in someone else's arms, this is a good time to pump. You can pump right after you nurse, but if you expect there will be a couple hours until the next feeding, try to pump about half way between the time you just nursed and the next expected feeding time. This way you'll have the satisfaction of getting some milk out, while still leaving time for your breasts to make more for the next feeding. If you end up pumping right before your baby wants to eat again, don't worry. A baby is always better at getting milk out than a pump – there will still be milk for your baby. He may want to nurse again sooner, but this too is fine – it will gradually increase your milk supply to accommodate the pumping session you've added. If you're starting at least two weeks before your return to work, pumping once a day should give you plenty of milk in your freezer.

Getting a late start

If you're returning to work soon, you can still pump enough to save the milk you'll need for the first day. Remember, after the first day, you'll just send what you pumped the day before. A freezer stash is nice, but not at all necessary. After the first week, you can pump a bit on the weekends to get a supply of milk stashed away if you need to.

In the days before you start back to work, you can pump after each feeding through the day. If you pump right after a feeding, you won't get much milk, but it will give your body some time to get used to the pump, and over a few days your supply will increase to match the new demand. If you're going to be pumping this often, it's best not to wait too long after a feeding so that your baby still gets plenty to eat at the next feeding session. You may only get a few drops, but keep them all, over several days it will add up to be enough for the first day. You'll only need about 10-12 ounces to start.

Pump one side, nurse the other

If your baby usually nurses on only one side each feeding, you can pump the other side while your baby is nursing. This requires about 12 hands the first time you try it, but with practice, it's not so hard. Try holding your baby in a "football hold" and try this order: turn on the pump (if you have a double, be sure it's set for one-sided use), get your baby's body well-supported with pillows, latch the baby on, let go with one hand and put the pump on the other side. If your baby does want the other side, go ahead and switch sides – the baby can always get more out than the pump.

Pumping How-tos

Here are a few things that you'll need to know when you first start using your pump.

For most women, the pump is a plug and play unit – ready to go out of the box. Follow the instructions and it should work.

To start pumping, first sit in a comfortable position. If you lean slightly forward, it can help keep milk from leaking into the flanges and direct it into the collection bottles a little better. Starting on one side, center your nipple in the tunnel and press the flange against your breast. Turn on the pump at a low suction and speed. (If you're going to use two sides at once, you often won't see much suction on the first side until the second is attached.)

> When you're first pumping, it can be easier to do one side at a time. If you're pumping only one side with a double pump, you'll often need to close off the second piece of tubing somewhere to have suction in the first one.

If you're pumping both sides, once the first side is attached, bring the second side to your other breast. This sometimes dramatically increases the suction, so be careful – this should not hurt! If it does, turn down the suction, and be sure to read on to find out if you have a good fit. If you are not getting suction, check that the valves (usually a white flexible rubber material) are well seated in the pump, and all parts are attached together snugly (just don't overtighten, they'll break).

I need to be an octopus to do this!

How do you adjust the suction when both hands are holding the flanges to your breasts? Do I even get to have a drink of water when I'm on this milking machine?? One way to free up a hand is as follows: When you hook up the first side, do it with your opposite hand (right hand to left breast). Then bring your same-side hand across your body so that your forearm is holding the flange in place (left forearm over left breast). Then that hand (in this case the left hand) is free to hold the other flange in place (left hand to right breast) and one hand (the right) is free to adjust the pump or turn the pages of a magazine. If you act it out as you read, the directions will make more sense. For fully hands-free pumping, be sure to see pages 102-103.

What to pump into

Most pumps are designed so that you can either pump directly into bottles or into milk storage bags. For day-to-day pumping, I preferred to have enough bottles that I could pump directly into bottles during the day, and then send those bottles to daycare the next day.

A typical routine would go like this: Take 4 bottles to work. First pumping into bottles 1 and 2, combine the bottles after pumping into #1. Second pumping, pump into bottles 2 and 3, combine into #2, third pumping, pump into bottles 3 and 4, then even out all 4 bottles, or combine into 3, depending on what I needed for the next day. If you have extra or are building up a stash, then you can pour it into storage bags for the freezer.

My friend Lili recommends the "shingle" method for milk storage when space is tight – when milk is being stored in bags, lay the bags flat in a small box to freeze them into flat rectangular units (this works best for bags with a zip top). Then you can file them upright in the box, with the oldest in front so that your stock is rotated.

Where to store the milk

If it's more than a week before you start back to work, most of the milk should go into the freezer. You're saving up for your first day back at work, and to have a little extra in case milk is spilled, wasted or spoiled along the way. If it's less than a week before you go back to work, keep the first 10-12 ounces you pump in the refrigerator. Expressed milk is good in the fridge for up to 8 days, and milk that has not been frozen is healthier for your baby. Anything beyond the ounces you need for the first day can go into the freezer for backup. The section "Care and storage of expressed breastmilk" later in this chapter has lots more information on milk storage.

Getting a good fit

What do you mean a good fit? I thought pumps were one-size-fits-all! Well, yes and no. Pumps come with a standard size flange that should fit *most* women, but what they neglect to tell you in the enclosed literature is that they make a lot of other flange sizes for a lot of different nipple sizes. If you have large nipples, it's easier to tell that if your flange is the wrong size. Your nipples should be pulled quite a bit into the pump – it looks weird, don't be concerned – but they should not rub against the sides of the flanges. Center your nipples carefully in the tunnel part of the flange, and if they are rubbing, look into purchasing larger flanges. Any pain or discomfort with pumping also means you should have a lactation consultant fit you for the right size flange (or turn the suction down!). Even women with small nipples can need a different size, because if the flanges are too big, the pressure maybe insufficient to extract the milk.

Pumping technique

Different brands of pump have different settings available, but they break down into two general categories: suction strength (which I'll just call suction) and cycling rate (a.k.a. speed). The cycling rate is how often the pump sucks in a minute. Play around with the settings until it feels the most like how your baby sucks.

> Remember this: using a pump is not like using a straw to suck milk out of your breast – the pump uses the cycling to stimulate a let-down, then gradually draws the milk that is being ejected from the glands into the ducts and into the pump. More suction is not necessarily better, and can damage your breast tissue.

A pattern that works well for a lot of women is to start with low suction and a relatively high speed to simulate how a baby sucks when they first latch on. Some of the newer pumps do this automatically with the push of a button (Medela calls this feature "Natural Expression"). Once you feel a letdown or see milk start to flow, increase the suction a little bit and reduce the speed. Your nipples will get drawn into the pump flange, just the way they are drawn into the baby's mouth. This will look freaky – you may not have known your nipple could stretch that far – but it's normal.

If there is a lot of milk accumulating on the inside of the flanges (not in the tunnel, but against your breast), stop pumping and wipe them off. Too much fluid will break the suction and decrease the effectiveness of the pump.

Now here's the kicker – once the milk starts to flow, look away! Focus on something other than pumping, and take deep relaxing breaths. Maybe this was just my personal issue, but I always found that watching the pump made me worry about how much milk I was getting and inhibited my letdowns. Besides, the pump isn't nearly as irresistible to look at as your baby, so this is a good opportunity to stretch your neck.

Neck Stretches: Nursing and holding a baby can make your chest muscles very tight, since your arms and head are generally being brought forward. While you're pumping, take a minute to look at the ceiling and roll your shoulders back to open your chest. You can stretch in a doorway when you're not holding the baby – raise your arms to shoulder height with your elbows bent so your hands point toward the ceiling. Lean forward into a doorway so that your elbows are supporting you. This works wonderfully to open your chest muscles.

Pump for 10 or 15 minutes, store the milk, and put the whole apparatus away until next time. Some women find that if they pump longer, they will have multiple let-downs and can collect more milk. You can try this when you go back to work, but there's no need to pump longer than 15 minutes before you start back to work.

But there's no milk!

Your first time pumping, you may have gotten three or four ounces of milk or you may have gotten a half an ounce. The amount is not important. Remember that while you are home, you're pumping ON TOP of providing all of your baby's food for each day, so don't expect to pump a lot, especially right at first.

The first few times pumping are conditioning your body to 1) respond to the pump and 2) produce a little more milk. If you pump once a day for a week, at about the same time each day, you should start to gradually see more milk in the bottles.

Won't my baby be hungry?

But won't my baby be hungry if I'm pumping out all the milk right before he eats? Well, two things: one, your baby is much better at getting milk out of your breasts than the pump, so even if you've just finished pumping and put the baby to breast, he'll still be able to get a fair amount of milk. Two – yes, there will be a little less milk for your baby, and you may notice that he nurses more frequently after a pumping session. This is fine – in fact, it is wonderful, because by nursing more, he is increasing your supply so that you'll have more to pump. Things will balance out very quickly.

Intentional oversupply or not?

There is some debate about how much to pump before you start back to work. Any regular pumping will cause a bit of oversupply – meaning that your body is producing more milk than your baby is taking in a given day. Some people believe that you should induce an oversupply before you go back to work to provide a "buffer," since some women see a dip in supply when the pump is providing most of the stimulation. In the early postpartum weeks your supply is very high and very responsive to stimulation. Pumping even a little bit at this time trains your body to make just a little more milk.

However, too much of an oversupply can cause real problems. You may find yourself leaking between nursing or pumping sessions, and you'll be more susceptible to plugged ducts and mastitis. Only you can find the balance point that is comfortable for you. Don't feel like you need to spend your entire maternity leave pumping. If it's going to be a long time until you go back to work, you may only want to pump every other day, or just a few times a week.

If you are consistently pumping a decent amount of milk (meaning maybe three, four, five ounces in a session), then I don't think you need to pump any more than once a day. However, if you're having a hard time getting even two ounces, or if your return to work is very soon, a little more pumping is fine. You can add a little pumping time without making yourself crazy by:

    ⁖ Learning to tandem pump, and pump one side while your baby nurses the other side.

    ⁖ Adding in another pumping session later in the day or right before you go to bed. This could be every other day instead of every day.

   ∞ Working on your pump skills to get more milk from one session. This can include doing some deep breathing relaxation (read on in this chapter, and see the biofeedback exercise in the "Troubleshooting supply problems" section in Chapter 8).

   ∞ Pumping slightly longer at each session

Improving your pumping output

Here are some tips if you're having a hard time getting any milk with the pump:

1. RELAX! You're going to be fine! Keep in mind that you are feeding your baby 100% of her food - AND trying to pump. This is a big job. Once you go back to work, you'll be pumping for missed nursing sessions instead of on top of full time nursing. There will be a lot more milk in your breasts, and it will be a LOT easier.

2. Don't watch the bottles. Just look away, think of something else.

3. Take care of yourself. One reason for not being able to pump much is that your body is exhausted. Be sure that you're well hydrated and resting. Your nursing/pumping station should *always* have a full bottle or pitcher of water for you to sip on. You don't need to force fluids or drink gallons of water every day – but you will be thirsty when you're nursing – so be sure you're drinking to thirst and not putting off getting another glass when your mouth feels dry.

4. Breast compressions. When the milk stops flowing during a pumping session, you can often get quite a bit more with some gentle breast compressions. It takes a bit of practice to free up a hand to do this, but using the one-hand method I described above, hold the flange in place with the opposite hand, then use the same-side hand to gently squeeze your breast behind the pump flange. You can massage from your armpit towards the flange, or just grab hold and squeeze (gently!). Be sure you're not compressing too close to the flange edge or you'll break the suction. Compress one side

then switch sides, or if you're pumping hands-free, you can do both sides at the same time.

5. Massage-Shake-Pump technique. Another technique for pumping a little bit more is to remove the pump when the milk flow stops, then lean forward, gently massage your breasts toward the nipple for a minute or two (without expressing milk), then gently shake your breasts (again, still leaning forward). Hook the pump back up, and you'll usually see the milk start flowing again.

6. Be sure your pump is in good shape. If you're using a used pump, the valves should be replaced (see the section "Troubleshoot your pump" in Chapter 8). Be sure the valves are put in correctly, the bottles are securely attached, and the tubing does not have any leaks. Take the tubing off the pump and plug one end with your finger. Blow in the other end – do you feel any air escaping? If so, new tubing is cheap, so order more from a pump supply company.

7. Did I mention relax? It could be that worrying about work is just too much for you at this point. Take a few days off pumping to focus on being a mommy 100%. You'll do fine.

Let-down tricks

A lot of us have a special little trick we use to fool our bodies into letting down for the pump. A lot of women look at pictures of their babies, or bring something the baby has worn recently so that they have the smell of their baby nearby. For me, looking at a picture of my baby made me feel anxious – I was upset at having to be away from him, and worried I wasn't providing him with enough milk, so I had to come up with a different visualization, which, to my great embarrassment, I will now share:

> (cue majestic, soaring musical background). An enormous milk truck is driving down the highway. It is spring, flowers line the road, the entire scene is pastoral in nature. There is no highway noise, as if the truck is floating. Slowly, almost gracefully, in slow motion, the truck jackknifes, and ever so slowly and gently, tips over. The large cover of the milk vat bounces away along the highway, as thousands of gallons of milk slosh and spill out over the road. The milk washes off the road, flowing down the embankment in gurgling rivulets.

Seriously, I let-down to this image. Even now, my breasts are getting a little tingly as I write.

Here are some more conventional ideas:

- Have something warm to drink before pumping.

- Place a warm washcloth on your breasts before pumping, you can microwave a wet washcloth at work, or fill a disposable diaper with warm water and cup it over your breast for 1-2 minutes (you can microwave the diaper too).

- Fill a sock or cloth tube with uncooked rice and sew it shut (add some aromatherapy oil or lavender flowers if you want). Microwave this before pumping and rest it around your neck to help you relax.

- Think of your last pumping session and how productive it was.

- Try a dose of "Rescue Remedy" from Bach Flower Essences (available at health food stores) – a few drops under the tongue can help relaxation.

- Massage your breasts from armpit to nipple a few times before you start pumping.

Whatever you get used to when you are pumping will become a conditioned response. I have a friend who had a Velcro closure on her pump bag. For months after she stopped pumping, she would still let-down to the sound of Velcro opening.

Hands-free pumping

Figuring out hands free pumping is a huge timesaver. If you work at a desk, you can write or email while pumping. If you use a pumping room, you have your hands free to hold a book in a comfortable position or finish the thank-you notes from your baby shower. If you are tandem pumping (pumping one side while nursing the other) using a hands-free setup leaves you both hands free to hold your baby. In general, hands free pumping allows you to relax more while pumping, resulting in less stress on your back and shoulders and a better pumping output.

There are several companies that sell hands free nursing bras, but you can easily make your own with the extravagant purchase of two rubber bands and any old nursing bra. How you make the hands free setup depends on the type of bra you have, but the principles are the same either way (illustrated on the next page). Basically, you place the flanges through the opening of a rubber band that is somehow hooked to the part of your bra above the cups (where the flap attaches). Most nursing bras have a flap over the breast that closes with some kind of hook and eye arrangement to keep it closed. For a bra with the hook on the strap (with the eyes on the flap), put the flanges through the rubber band so the rubber band is at the opening of the tunnel and put the other end of the rubber band over the hook. This mechanism is not enough to hold the pump in place on its own, but once you turn the pump on and suction is established, the flanges will stay in place on their own. If you have a bra with the eyes at the top and the hooks on the flaps, first pass one end of the rubber band through the eye and then feed it back through itself. Then put the open end of the rubber band around the flange and start the pump. If your bra closes with a snap or has no hooks or eyes, just loop the rubber band around the strap and pass it back through itself. Again, you will need to hold the flange in place until suction is established, and then it will hold itself. You can use the one-hand pumping method described in the beginning of this chapter to get things set up.

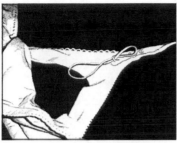

Push one end of the rubber band through the "eye" on the nursing bra's shoulder strap.

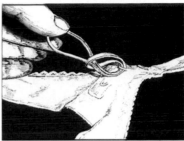

Pass one end of the rubber band through the loop at the other end. Same as for around the strap.

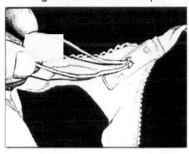

Pull tight. This is called a "girth hitch."

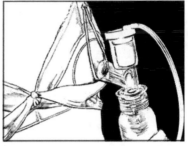

Place flange of one side of pump through rubber band.

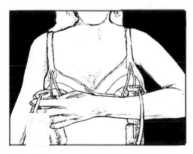

Use forearm to hold first side in place while you put the other side in its rubber band and adjust the suction on the pump.

Let go and relax. Support the bottles on your desk or table if they need to be held up

If you are as lazy as I am, you can just leave the rubber bands in place through washing the bra – they last several washings. If you have very small or very large breasts, the suction might not be enough to hold the bottles in place even with rubber bands – but I found my keyboard tray was just the right height to hold the bottles up at the right level, then the rubber bands and suction did the rest.

A commercial hands free bra works about the same way with built in fabric loops to put the rubber bands through. The Medela hands free bra has an additional loop at the midline of the bra on each side, so you can hook up two rubber bands for each side – giving a little extra stability. There are other hands-free systems that are bands of fabric that you put on over your regular bra with holes to put the flanges through. These systems are nice, but I found the two rubber bands swiped from the office manager worked just fine and were quite a significant cost savings.

Reprinted with permission from
Alison Bechdel, www.alyson.com

Care and storage of expressed breastmilk

Storage guidelines

Knowing about the proper storage, heating and care of expressed breast milk (EBM) allows you to make the most of your precious pumped milk. You will find a ton of conflicting information about how long breastmilk can be left out, how to heat it, how long to store it, etc. The reason for this is that the research that has been done is spotty at best, and conclusions are drawn from a relatively small number of studies. Also, a lot of the information on the long-term viability of EBM has been put out by formula companies. Since they have a financial interest in EBM lasting for a shorter time, I don't consider this information to be entirely reliable.

Here's what we do know about EBM. Fresh EBM contains live cells that actively fight bacterial growth. EBM left at room temperature shows little growth of bacteria after 4 to 8 hours in some studies (Hamosh ct al., 1996) and was bacteria-free for up to 10 hours in other studies (Barger & Bull, 1987). Bacterial growth is much much slower at standard refrigerator temperatures, and almost non-existent in the freezer (Tully, 2000). In fact, breastmilk stored in the refrigerator actually shows a reduction in the bacterial count after a few days due to the activity of the anti-bacterial enzymes in the milk.

Based on these facts, La Leche League has adopted the following guidelines for storage of EBM (also found at http://www.lalecheleague.org/FAQ/milkstorage.html)

- ၰ At room temperature – up to 10 hours

- ၰ In the refrigerator – up to 8 days

- ၰ In a freezer compartment of a fridge (not a separate door, often daycares have this kind of freezer as part of a small refrigerator) – 2 weeks

- ၰ In a separate freezer compartment – 4 to 6 months

- ၰ In a chest freezer – 6 months to one year.

I have found these to be pretty conservative guidelines. When EBM goes bad, you really know it. It's a stink you won't soon forget, so when in doubt, give it the sniff test. The nose knows.

Combining bottles

You can combine milk pumped at different times, as long as you follow a few guidelines. Fresh milk can be combined with refrigerated milk, refrigerated with frozen, but do not mix warm milk in with frozen, as it will cause part of the milk to thaw. I like to only combine milk from a single day; that way when I label it, I can just put on one date. When I pumped at work, I would get a lot more milk in the morning sessions than the ones from the afternoon, so I would just pour the milk between the bottles till they all had about the same amount.

Milk separating

EBM has about the same fat content as whole milk, but amazingly enough, does not come from the breast homogenized, so the fat will separate out as the milk stands. This is fine, it should just be mixed back in when the milk is heated. If you keep your milk in storage bags, be sure to squeeze all the fat from the sides of a bag when you transfer the milk to a bottle. The fatty layer helps your baby feel full after eating and provides valuable fats for brain development, so it's worth it not to lose any! It's interesting to track the fat content of your milk from day to day and see if you can correlate it to your diet or activity levels. Is it fattier early in the day? Later in the week? Every woman makes milk of a slightly different fat content – perfectly matched to your baby's metabolism and body type, so don't feel bad if you have a lot more or less fat then the mom who stores her milk next to yours in the pumping room fridge.

Funny smells

A lot of moms on my message boards ask about funny smelling EBM. It is not unusual for EBM to take on a sort of metallic or soapy smell after a day or two in the fridge. EBM is easily digested by babies because it has enzymes that help break down the fats (call lipases). If these enzymes are very active (it varies from woman to woman), they will start breaking down the lipids while the milk is still in the bottle. This results in the funny smell, but most babies don't mind it at all, and there is nothing wrong with the milk.

If your baby doesn't like the milk once it's sat for a few days, you can stop the enzymes from breaking down the fats by scalding the milk before storing it. Scalding is a cooking term for heating milk until just before it boils. You may boil a batch before finding this point, but scalding can generally be recognized by steam starting to swirl around the top of the hot liquid. This is a gourmet cooking technique, so you'll have practice for when you need to make a mousse or soufflé for a big party someday. Scalding milk also kills a lot of the living immune cells in the milk, so it is better for your baby if they will drink the stinky milk as it is. There is some thought that storing milk in glass bottles slows the lipase activity, so that is another option to try.

My milk is green!

EBM comes in many wonderful colors. If you were only breastfeeding your baby, you would never see the color and wouldn't worry about it – it's only when we're pumping that we see this "problem." However, it usually isn't anything to worry about.

Normal EBM has a faint blue tint to it. If the fat content is high, it will be a bit more yellowish. If you've eaten a lot of spinach the day before, it will be a bit green. I make an Indian spinach dish that contains so much concentrated spinach it turns my milk an intense green for a full 24 hours. Think of all the extra nutrition! You may also see funny colors if you ingest a lot of artificial colors the day before. These aren't harmful, but aren't serving any purpose either, so you can use your milk to let you know when to cut back on the junk.

Blood in milk

It is not uncommon to have a little bit of blood in EBM as well. This can happen for a number of reasons – if you have cracked nipples, some of the blood will get into the EBM and it doesn't hurt your baby at all (but you should try to correct your latch so that you're more comfortable!). Sometimes there is a small amount of bleeding in the breast ducts that results in a pinkish tinge to the milk. Again, this won't hurt your baby, and is not anything you should worry about unless you see blood in your milk for a number of days in a row. A mom I knew was convinced she had a bleeding tumor in her breast because her milk was consistently pink, but it turns out that cutting out cherry soda cleared up the "bleeding" right away, so pink does not always mean blood!

Heating EBM

EBM should be heated by swirling the bottle gently under running warm water, in a dish of warm water, or in a bottle warmer. The milk should be swirled gently to heat evenly and get all of the fat off the sides of the bottle. Don't shake it hard, as this breaks down the living immune cells and proteins.

Easy enough, right – until you find the person who takes wonderful care of your baby but insists on microwaving the milk. In my case, this was my dear husband. He just couldn't see the harm in microwaving, and when the baby was hungry, he didn't feel like he had time to heat a bottle properly. Never mind that maybe he should have been paying attention to earlier hunger cues – he found himself with a screaming baby and a microwave, and that's how he heated it.

So – why not microwave? For one, microwaving heats unevenly. There can be hotspots in the bottle that are scalding even if the outside of the bottle feels cool, so burning the baby's mouth is a risk. In addition, if the milk gets too hot, the living immune cells are killed, so the immune protection of the milk is lessened as well. However, I never could get my husband to heat the milk "the right way." My daycare heated under running warm water, and my husband only gave the kids two to three bottles a week, so I decided to let that battle go. I told him to mix it well and test it for scalding before feeding. I figured 50% of feedings were from me, another 45% from my very careful daycare – so getting 5% of their milk with no immune cells was certainly not the end of the world. Like they say, you have to pick your battles, but its easier if you're well informed.

Reusing an unfinished bottle

What do you do if your baby starts a bottle and doesn't finish it? Do you need to throw the milk away, or can you save it for later and reheat it? Reheating is certainly a good way to reduce waste! There is a small body of evidence demonstrating that for a healthy, full-term infant, it's just fine to reheat a used bottle – the evidence is really just one unpublished thesis, and the experience of the many moms who have done it. If you're not comfortable with this, then don't reheat bottles. However, in my somewhat scientifically based opinion, I think it's OK to do - once. When the bottle goes around for the second time, I would say toss it. And don't reheat milk that was previously frozen. Thawed breastmilk has lost many of the living immune cells that prevent contamination, and should be treated more like formula in terms of preventing bacterial growth.

Your child care provider may be reluctant to reheat a bottle - they've been trained in formula-feeding, and it's absolutely true that formula can very easily become contaminated, as it has nothing to prevent the growth of bacteria. However, breastmilk is very different - in addition to the living immune cells that actively attack bacteria, it also contains numerous anti-bacterial enzymes. In short, it's good stuff.

> Another perk – if it's OK to reuse an unfinished bottle, your care provider may be less likely to pressure your baby to finish a bottle. Your baby's feedings should always end when your baby is ready.

Kellymom.com did a nice write-up of the evidence that re-using bottles is OK – you can find it here (www.kellymom.com/bf/pumping/reusing-expressedmilk.html) if you need something to print out and give to your care provider. There is nothing more frustrating than to find out your care provider is dumping bottles that your baby is not finishing - although if you find out that this is the case, you should probably send smaller bottles. If they insist that they can't reheat bottles, you'll have to just keep sending the milk in small amounts, and let them heat a second bottle if your baby is still hungry after the first.

Frozen EBM

Once EBM has been frozen, most of the immune cells die off, so it no longer has as many natural antibacterial properties and needs to be treated more delicately. Thawed EBM should be used within 24 hours, and should only be heated once (and not reheated).

Thawing EBM. But remember, even if breastmilk loses a lot of its antibacterial properties after it's been frozen, formula has no immune properties at all, so frozen breastmilk is still a better food.

If your EBM is frozen in bottles, you can just send them to your care provider and allow them to thaw in the fridge. However, if the milk is frozen in bags and you need to transfer it to a bottle before leaving it for your baby, this can be done easily without heating the milk up all the way. I find the easiest way is to thaw the milk under running warm water until it starts to break up. You can smoosh it around with your fingers under the water (or just leave it on the counter) until it is about the consistency of a sno-cone. Then you can just squish the slush into a bottle – keeping the milk cold the whole time. This also makes it really easy to get all of the fat out of the bag.

My friend Lili is a little bit, oh, shall we say, compulsive. But she came up with a great way to store EBM in the freezer. Preface this with the fact that she continually struggled with oversupply issues, so she had a LOT of milk to store.

> *The "shingle" method: I only used the milk storage bags with a ziplock top – the ones where you used a twist-tie didn't seem to seal as securely, and they wouldn't lay flat. I always stored the bags on their sides when they were freezing, so they froze thin and flat, like a shingle. Then, once the milk was frozen, I stood the bags up in a kids' shoebox, and that way I could just put the new ones in at the back and pull the milk I needed from the front. They were always in order that way.*

> *Lili says, The Lansinoh bags, they were the best, but they were really expensive and I had to order them online. The Medela bags were good too – they were also expensive, but they had the thickest plastic. I think I remember the Medela bags did have a twist tie, but instead of bunching the top together, I would roll the top to the level of the milk and then fold the ends over, like how you seal a coffee bag. You couldn't fill them all the way up, but then at least they'd lie flat and fit in my shoebox.*

Power failures and thawed milk

For a mom with a big freezer stash, a power outage is the ultimate nightmare – all that milk will thaw! The big trick to a power outage is to keep the freezer door shut. Don't even be tempted to open it; the milk will stay frozen much longer if it's closed. Once the power comes back on, or if you're moving your milk to a new freezer, this is the time to check and see what happened to it. If the milk has thawed to liquid anywhere, let it thaw the rest of the way and use it as soon as you can or — sob — throw it away. If the milk has only thawed to frosty-freeze or slush consistency, it's probably OK to let it freeze again. If your power was out and the freezer came back on when you were out and you really have no idea how thawed it got, you'll just have to take a guess. If the power was out less than a day and your freezer stayed closed, it's probably OK – but give it a good sniff test when you do thaw it, and maybe make a note on the bags that you really don't know.

Rotating the freezer stash

Fresh milk is far preferable to frozen on a day to day basis – both due to its durability and its immune properties. So in general, you should use the fresh milk you've pumped the day or week before to leave with your care provider. However, if you have milk in the freezer, it's also a good idea to rotate it from time to time so it doesn't all go bad at once. It's easy to figure out a system that lets you rotate in the frozen milk a bit at a time while keeping your baby's bottles mostly fresh. Some moms use one bag of frozen milk once or twice a week – just be sure your care provider knows to feed that bottle first, since it's only good for 24 hours. Some moms freeze everything on Friday and use all older frozen milk on Monday – but I think it's a better idea to mix a little fresh and frozen on a given day – that way you won't have to toss out any milk that's not finished. Rotate gradually and your freezer stash will never go bad. And, if you store it like Lili did, it's easy to rotate by just pulling the milk from the front of the box.

What can I do with this milk I have left?

So, you've nursed your baby for a year, you've stopped pumping, you've met your goals, and there's still this milk in the freezer. Given that it passes the sniff test – what are you going to do with it?

Here are some options:

- ℬ Mix it with cow's milk and put it in your little one's sippy cups.

- ℬ Use it for your kids breakfast cereal – either straight, or mixed with cow's milk or soy milk.

- ℬ Use it in recipes – there's a lot of pride in feeding your entire family with milk you made yourself. You may not want to tell your partner or have company over, but a loaf of fresh EBM bread is delicious (scald the milk, cool to a warm temperature and mix with the yeast), or make an EBM spinach soufflé!

- ℬ EBM ice cream – Add enough sugar and heavy cream to anything and it's delicious. Plain, vanilla or get nutty and make chocolate.

- ℬ A note on EBM yogurt – I really wanted to make EBM yogurt with my leftover milk – but after several failed attempts, I learned that once frozen, the milk really doesn't do too well in the whole yogurting process. If you really want to make EBM yogurt, use fresh.

- ℬ Or, you could just do what I did – leave three sad little bags of milk in your freezer for three years. I have no plans to ever use it, but I'm too sentimental to throw it away.

All about bottle-feeding

Introducing the bottle

This section has a big fat case of "do as I say not as I do." I always tell people to wait at a bare minimum two weeks, better three or four, before introducing a bottle. I could have sworn this was what I did. And then the other day I was looking through baby pictures of my son, my first child, and there was my husband giving him his first bottle on something like day 8 of his life. Obviously, he lived, he even breastfed till he was almost three, but still, not the best way to go. But I obviously understand the concern every working mother has about wanting to be sure her child will take a bottle. You want your child to not only be well-fed while you are at work, you want them to enjoy it, to associate the bottle with happiness and good times – just so long as they know that the breast is better. And that's what this section is about – getting your child to take a bottle without preferring it to the real thing.

> Why all the fuss about nipple confusion? If your baby begins to refuse the breast and prefers to feed from a bottle, you may think – well, I can just pump and feed her that way, right? Well, think it through first. Do you really want to have to pump and *then* get a bottle ready for every single feeding? How about at 2 AM? It's so much easier to directly breastfeed, you'll just have to take my word that you don't want your baby to favor the bottle. In addition, remember that "there's more to breastfeeding than breastmilk." There's a wonderful closeness and relaxation that comes from feeding directly at the breast that is well worth preserving. Finally, the pump is not as effective as the baby at stimulating milk production, so you risk supply problems if you exclusively pump. There are many women who choose exclusive pumping right from the beginning, and probably many of them will read this book. My hat is off to you for your valiant efforts – and I realize many women exclusively pump because of medical reasons. But given the choice, I opt to avoid my pump whenever it's not absolutely necessary.

The difference between breast and bottle

When babies get a bottle too early and too often, they can develop what's often called "nipple confusion." The great breastfeeding educator and pediatrician Jack Newman once said that it's not really nipple *confusion*, but flow *preference*. Here are the three main differences in the flow between a breast and a bottle.

Difference #1 - No waiting for let-down: Just about any bottle is going to flow faster than a breast when the baby first latches on. Unless you are profusely leaking, it takes a little bit of time for your baby to initiate the letdown and get the milk flowing. Since a bottle starts to flow right away, your baby may become impatient at the breast, where before bottles were started she was used to waiting a bit, knowing the rewarding milk would be there soon enough.

Difference #2 – No technique needed: Even after you've let-down, your baby has to do some coordinated work to get the milk out when she's at the breast. The latch must be deep, and the tongue has to press on the right spots on the milk ducts. It's much easier with a bottle – your baby just has to move her mouth around some way or other and the milk will flow. She can latch on to the end of the bottle, the top, sideways, whatever, and there will be milk. This leads to an obvious reason not to start a bottle too early – to save your nipples. If your baby learns to latch on to just the end of a bottle nipple, she may do the same on yours, which believe me is no fun.

Difference #3 – Speed of flow: Unless you use very slow-flow nipples, the milk comes out of a bottle much faster than from the breast – resulting in babies who tend to eat more and eat it more quickly. Why is this a problem? Well, they may become impatient at the breast, but more importantly, this can lead to overfeeding at daycare. Why is that a problem? Because you have to pump every precious ounce that is given while you are away, and if your baby is getting too much food, number one, you'll have to pump more, and number two, she won't nurse as much when you're together, further decreasing your milk supply.

And as an aside, eating slowly and stopping when they're full is thought to be one of the reasons that breastfed babies are less likely to be overweight as adults. Breastfeeding takes longer than bottle feeding, giving the stomach time to send the message to the brain that it's getting full. This takes about 10-20 minutes. If a baby is eating too quickly, they will overstuff themselves before they've realized it (like I did last Thanksgiving). I think the composition of the milk also plays a role in formula fed babies being overweight, but if we learn from an early age not to overeat, it certainly can't hurt.

Sorry for the digression – this was supposed to be about introducing the bottle, but I think it's important to understand the differences when you're deciding when, what kind, and how often when you start bottles.

When to start

Some people will tell you that it's absolutely essential that you start bottles at least two weeks before going back to work, or by four weeks of age, or some other set number. But as you may be learning about babies, there are only guidelines, no strict rules. I think some babies will take a bottle no matter when it's introduced, others will struggle even with lots of exposure – there's no way to tell until you try. In spite of my own experience, I strongly encourage that you wait a *minimum* of two weeks, and I hate to even say that – I'd rather see you wait three. Is there some outer limit beyond which babies won't take bottles? Maybe. For some babies. Again, you can't know until you try. This is only opinion, but I think that if you introduce a first bottle by the time your baby is 6 weeks old, you'll have a pretty good idea if they'll take it or if you need to work on it a little bit.

How often to give bottles

Some babies will take milk in any form, at any time. If you have one of these casual eaters and they take their first bottle without any fuss, there's really no need to "keep practicing." You can try every few days if you want to, but you don't need to give a bottle every day. You are blessed with an easy-going child, just enjoy it. If you have a baby who struggles more with a bottle, you may want to start a routine and practice more to get them used to it – but please don't give more than one bottle a day. While you're home on leave, your baby should be at the breast as much as possible. This is important for bonding with your child, important for your rest and relaxation, and is also the best way there is to establish a strong milk supply. Replacing feedings with pumping and bottles can make it hard to keep producing enough milk, in addition to just being way too much work.

Who should give the bottles?

If you have the help, try to always have someone other than mom give the bottles. This is for two reasons – first, many babies will simply refuse a bottle from mom when the real thing is right there. But secondly, I believe that babies should learn that mom is just for the breast. This can help to avoid breast refusal later on, and sets aside a special role that only mom can fill.

If you live with a partner, this person has probably been chomping at the bit to get involved with the feeding end of the baby, and is a good candidate for giving the first bottle. Other good choices are friends, your future child care provider, or your mom or mother-in-law (grandmothers love to feed babies). It may be that your baby won't accept a bottle if you are in the room, or even in the house. Babies can smell that the real thing is in the house. You may need to go out for a little while around a usual feeding time before your baby will accept a bottle from someone else.

How and when to give the bottle

The bottle should be given when your baby shows early feeding cues, preferably before they are crying. If your baby goes from zero-to-starving in 3 seconds, you may want to pump a fresh bottle before you expect him to be hungry and leave it on the counter. That way you don't need to take time heating it once your baby is ready. If the milk is freshly pumped, it's fine to leave it sitting out for several hours. Let your baby explore the nipple with her mouth and only put the nipple in when she opens wide. Never poke a bottle into a baby's mouth when they are not opening for it – if they're not gaping, they're not ready to eat. Once the nipple is in, be sure your baby takes it far back into their mouth so that they don't get in the habit of sucking just on the end – your own nipples will thank you. Most importantly, end the feeding when your baby is ready. Once they release the nipple and turn away or close their mouth, the feeding is over. You can burp the baby and gently offer more (as if you were offering a second side), but if your baby is not gaping for the bottle, that's it, mark down one bottle-feeding complete!

Many babies associate feeding with a certain body position and will take a bottle just fine in the typical cradle hold position. However, some babies strongly associate this position with the breast, they may refuse any substitutes when they're expecting mom. In that case, try different positions – such as sitting the baby on your lap facing out, or a modified football hold. Older babies often enjoy sitting facing out so that they can watch the world go by as they eat.

How about temperature? You can try feeding a room temperature bottle first – if your baby takes it, it will save heating time down the line. Some babies will even drink cold milk right out of the fridge. However, if your baby prefers the bottle warm, you can just run it under warm water from the tap, or set the bottle in a bowl of warm water. Your baby may also like it if you run warm water over the nipple to heat it so it feels more life-like.

What bottles to use

My method for choosing the best bottle system is very scientific. Go through the bottles and nipples you got for shower presents or hand-me-downs and find the one with the slowest flow and start with that one. Even with the slowest flow nipple, your baby won't have to work as hard at the bottle as they do at the breast (part of why breastfeeding leads to healthy jaw development and builds the muscles later used for speaking). You can tell by looking which nipples are the fastest flow – they have 2-3 holes or a slit in the top of the nipple. Set those aside or give them away. Of the nipples with only one hole, test them by putting water in the bottle and holding it upside down. If the water slowly drips out or doesn't come out at all, this is a good nipple to start with. If all you got were high-flow nipples, then go and buy a couple newborn size nipples to fit whatever bottles you have – just don't buy too many until you figure out what your baby will accept. Because the flow rate from your breasts isn't going to change over the first year, you can use newborn flow nipples until your baby weans from the bottle to a cup, so there's no need to get any faster flow nipples.

> If you have a very forceful letdown and an abundant supply, your baby may become overly frustrated with the newborn nipples. In this case try a slightly faster flow, but watch for signs that the baby is getting lazy at the breast and not sucking as efficiently.

Is there a "best" nipple for breastfed babies? The Avent system is often touted as being most suitable for breastfed babies, but I have read enough comments from lactation consultants that the nipple is too long and stiff that I've decided that it really doesn't matter. I used Avent because I had a bunch of them, and then with my daughter I had a bunch of Playtex nipples from a friend, so we used those. A nipple with a wide base encourages your baby to open wide as they would for the breast, but most companies now make nipples like this. I have heard good reviews of the Dr. Brown bottle system because it is supposed to provide *no* milk unless the baby is actively sucking, so if you're starting from scratch and feel like splurging, you can try them – but it's not necessary. Ultimately, the best bottle and nipple system for your breastfed baby is the one that they will use.

I have just heard about a bottle system called Second Nature. This bottle has special holes that only allow milk to flow when the baby is actively sucking. I'm not sure how this is different from the Dr. Brown system, but it seems to be an even slower-flow system. Lactation consultants who I have heard from say that this nipple is not suitable for newborns or babies who need a bottle for sucking difficulties because it requires too much suction to get the milk out. However, for this very reason it may be a good choice for the babies of working mothers. The baby will always have to work for the milk, and may not get used to the easy flow of the bottle with this nipple. As of this writing, I do not have enough information to recommend or not recommend this nipple, but now you have some information to help in your choice.

What about the ages on the nipples – do you need to increase flow as your baby gets older? In a word, no. Formula-fed babies gradually eat more and more each day as they get older. Because of this, it's often convenient to switch to faster flow nipples to make feeding more efficient. However, studies have shown (Kent, Mitoulas et al. 1999, and others cited in this article) that breastfed babies maintain a constant daily intake between one and six months – meaning that they need the same amount of milk in a day at 4 weeks as they do at 4 months. At six months a lot of their increase in calories comes from solid food, so they may take the same amount of milk each day the entire time you are pumping. If your baby starts sleeping through the night, they will obviously need more milk during the day to make up the difference – this is where we see an increase in the amount needed.

Baby won't take a bottle

I'm going to offer a few suggestions here, but then I'll explain why you really don't need to worry about it.

There are a few things to try if your baby won't take a bottle. The first is just to try again later. Your baby may not be hungry, or may need comforting at the breast at that particular moment. If so, let your baby nurse (even if you just pumped for the bottle, there will be enough left for him to breastfeed) and try again later. On the next try, if you didn't leave the building last time, get out.

Have your helper try for an hour or so with you out of range – it may be your baby just needs to realize you're gone before he'll accept this inferior substitute. You can try a few different bottles and nipples if you have them on hand, but don't break the bank buying all different makes of nipple, your baby will figure it out eventually. Try the milk at different temperatures; what feels like body temperature to you may actually be too warm or too cool for your baby. Try different positions, or try the bottle while carrying the baby in a sling and walking gently. Maybe try a nipple with a slightly faster flow, but only as a last resort, and watch carefully for the baby favoring the bottle. The best advice continues to be "wait a week." Babies grow and change so much every single day that in a week you're dealing with a totally different little person who will have only the foggiest memory of this bottle thing. If your baby is rejecting the bottle, don't try it every day – that can cause a real aversion – just give it a little time.

Do not make yourself crazy or make your helper suffer hours of a crying baby if none of these are working. Your baby may not get used to taking a bottle until you are gone on a more routine basis.

If you are taking your baby to a daycare center, you may want to give them a call at this point. Ask them if they're used to dealing with breastfed babies, and if they have experience getting a baby to take a bottle. The answer is probably yes, in which case you can assure them that you've really tried, and then let them take it from there when you start daycare. These people are paid professionals, and it's their job to figure out how to feed your baby. Of course, you would never put it to them like that – one thing you should realize is that breastfed babies are more work for a daycare provider, and you need to suck up to them accordingly. You need your caregiver on your side to make breastfeeding work, so be very apologetic that you haven't mastered the bottle, and then wash your hands of the matter and let them figure it out.

If you are leaving your baby with a family member, this can be a little more challenging, since you need to have this person still like you at the end of each day. But just be honest with them, let them know your baby is having a little trouble with the bottle and may take a few days to get used to it, and again, trust them to work it out. Sometimes it takes a baby up to a week to get the idea that they're supposed to eat while you're away, but it'll happen. The most important thing if your baby is not taking a bottle is to make sure they have free access to the breast whenever you're together. She'll make up for not eating when you're apart by getting more right from the tap. Try to remember that some babies are able to sleep up to 5 or 6 hours by the time they're six weeks old (lucky moms). These babies are going a long time without eating just because they happen to be asleep. This means that your baby has the physical capability to go 5 or 6 hours without eating during the day. If your baby takes only a few ounces during the day and nurses a lot in the evenings and at night, and they look alert and healthy and are meeting their developmental milestones, then they're getting enough to eat. Maybe it's happened, but I have *never* heard of a baby older than six weeks who lost too much weight because of bottle refusal when they had unlimited access to the breast at least half of each day.

If you still have bottle refusal after the first week of daycare, read the sections on "Reverse cycling and Nighttime parenting" in Chapter 8 and the next section on bottle refusal — but for now, just have faith that it'll work out, keep trying the bottle once a week, and other than that, enjoy your baby, enjoy breastfeeding, and savor your time at home.

Solutions for bottle refusal

Once you go back to work, most babies figure out how to eat from a bottle within about a week, so don't diagnose "bottle refusal" until after the end of that first week. If your baby is still refusing after the first week, read on. First of all, try to reassure yourself that if your baby is truly refusing a bottle, this is great for your milk supply, since he'll be nursing a lot when you're together. However, it can be a little grating on your sanity and that of your care provider. The first approach to this problem is to go directly to the sections on "Reverse Cycling" and "Nighttime Parenting" in Chapter 8 – reverse cycling happens when an infant gets most of their nutrition breastfeeding directly at night, when baby and mom are together. Read up on it, compare to your situation, and see if this approach will work for you.

Also – be sure to assess carefully if bottle refusal is really what's happening. It may just be that your baby is not hungry. My friend Jody is a classic example. She struggled for weeks with her son's bottle refusal – trying every bottle nipple on the market, offering milk at every temperature between boiling and freezing, having her husband try feeding in every position known to man. We were so focused on trying to get him to take a bottle that it took weeks before I finally asked how the baby was really doing – this is what we found: Her son was in the 104th percentile for weight and height. He was meeting all developmental milestones on target. He was over 20 pounds by 4 months – the kid was a house. He nursed very frequently during the evening, nighttime and morning – which Jody didn't mind. And finally, he was taking one good feeding during the day, about 4 ounces. So, was this bottle refusal? Probably not. This was a kid who was getting plenty to eat, was holding out for the real thing from mom, took as much from the bottle as he needed to get through the day, then didn't want to be bothered with any more bottles when he wasn't hungry. The clincher was that he was *not* fussy during the day *except* when his dad was trying to give him a bottle that he didn't want. Jody had become concerned because he wasn't taking as much as she was pumping, but by feeding all night and pumping all day, she'd probably convinced her body that she'd had twins, and so she finally cut back on her pumping to match her baby's needs.

If a baby is really hungry but won't take a bottle, you'll know. This child will cry often and act hungry, even as they refuse the bottle, and they won't take the bottle for any feedings at all.

If you decide that you really do have bottle refusal and reverse cycling is not a good strategy for you, or if you would just like to get a *little* more milk in your babe during the day, or if your care provider is at the end of his or her rope from your baby crying, you may want to try some of the following alternate feeding strategies. The previous section, "All about bottle-feeding," has ideas for varying the position and finding a bottle system that your baby likes, which you can also try with your care provider.

The most important thing is work *with* your care provider. You're not the one dealing with this fussy baby, so find out from them what will be the most helpful. You can give them ideas for how to feed your baby, but your caregiver is the person who will have to be OK with the solution. If your care provider wants you to come and nurse during your lunch break, see if you can manage it for a while. However, your care provider might want to work it out on their own, and may be happier to have you stay away. I was just talking to a father who took care of his breastfed baby, and it was infinitely frustrating for him when his wife would come to feed at lunch – he really felt like this undermined his efforts to get the baby to take a bottle. He was trying to work out a solution on his own and felt like she was interfering. She felt like she was sweeping in to the rescue. Like most things in life, communication is key. It's hard to think of your baby going hungry during the day, and the urge to be the rescuing knight in shining Ann Taylor is tempting. But if your care provider would prefer to work it out on their own, try to respect that.

Here are some alternate feeding ideas if your baby keeps refusing the bottle:

Cup feeding

Babies as young as a day old can learn to drink from a cup. I wouldn't recommend starting with a pint glass, but those tiny cups that come with cough syrup work just fine. The way to cup feed a baby is to press the cup against their lower lip so the rim of the cup is at the top of the lower lip. Then gently tilt the cup until a tiny bit of milk runs into her mouth. Once she tastes the milk, she should stick out her tongue to figure out where it's coming from. Her tongue should go into the milk in the cup, and she'll start to lap it up kind of like a cat. It seems inefficient, but small babies can actually drink as rapidly from a cup as from a bottle. You may need to practice in order to demonstrate for your care provider, but many maternity nurses swear by cup feeding as the easiest way to feed a baby who cannot breastfeed.

There are special soft cups you can get for cup feeding if this is what you will be doing on a regular basis. Medela sells one that is pretty widely available.

You can also try a standard toddler sippy cup. With some babies, a bottle nipple is an offensive imitation of mom's breast, but a sippy cup with its hard spout is different enough to be acceptable. Use the sippy cup without the valve, and let the baby drink in a normal drinking position – relatively upright, tipping the cup to the mouth for each drink – not keeping it inverted like you would with a bottle.

Syringe feeding

A syringe can also be used to feed a baby a few ounces of milk at a time. Just use a syringe that comes with a liquid medicine, like children's cough syrup or tylenol, or use a special periodontal syringe from your dentist or medical supply store. Draw the milk up into the syringe, and then squirt it very gently, little by little, into the corner of the baby's mouth. If the baby opens her mouth, you can slowly squirt the milk towards a back corner of her mouth to encourage swallowing, but if she's not opening, you can just put the end of the syringe into the corner of her mouth and slowly squeeze in the milk. Once she has a mouthful, be sure to pause to allow time for swallowing. Only put in a small amount at a time, and feed the baby in a pretty upright position to avoid having the milk pool at the back of her throat. (You want her moving the milk to the back of her mouth with her tongue, not having it flow there due to gravity.)

Finger feeding

If you have a baby who will suck on your finger, you can try finger feeding her. This is done by running a length of very thin tubing from either a feeding syringe or a bottle to the end of your finger. The typical tubing used for this is called a 5 French Feeding tube and can be obtained from a lactation consultant or a medical supply store. The procedure for finger-feeding as used in premature infants is described in detail on the breastfeeding.com website at the URL www.breastfeeding.com/all_about/faq_premature.html. Holding the tubing next to the end of your finger, the baby sucks your finger, and gets milk along with it. In very young babies, finger feeding is used for suck training to direct the tongue while sucking. Cup feeding is generally faster for feeding a baby who's away from mom, but if your care provider is comfortable with finger feeding, it is another option you can offer to them.

Other ideas

We had a little girl named Cara at our daycare who's mother worked upstairs. She would come down and feed Cara whenever she was hungry. However, one day a month, Cara's mom worked out of town. Needless to say, Cara absolutely refused to have anything to do with a bottle, but was used to eating two or three times during the day, so was hungry when her mom was gone. The solution the daycare worked out was to spoon-feed breastmilk to her. They just scooped the milk up with a standard plastic picnic spoon and gently tipped spoon after spoon of milk into Cara's mouth. It took a long time to feed her, but since it was only once a month, everyone was OK with it as a solution. When Cara got old enough to take solid foods, they would mix up rice cereal with breastmilk and feed that to her at all of her feeding times.

Creativity is the key to working this out.

The way *not* to solve bottle-refusal is to start "practicing" with the bottle when you are home with your baby. There are many benefits to your baby getting breastmilk directly from the breast, least of which is that she gets perfect control over how much milk she takes, and so is able to meet her caloric needs for the day by nursing frequently. If it seems your baby is nursing "all the time," and you're convinced you don't have enough milk, keep at it for a few days. Your body should respond to the frequent stimulation by making more milk. Unless there are medical concerns about your child's weight gain or development, if you offer only the breast or breast and solid foods when you and your baby are together, she'll get enough to eat.

References

Barger J, Bull P. 1987. A Comparison of the Bacterial Composition of Breast Milk Stored at Room Temperature and Stored in the Refrigerator. *International Journal of Childbirth Education* 2(3).

Hamosh M, Ellis L, et al. 1996. Breastfeeding and the working mother: effect of time and temperature of short-term storage on proteolysis, lipolysis, and bacterial growth in milk. *Pediatrics* 97(4): 492-498.

Tully MR. 2000. Recommendations for Handling of Mother's Own Milk. *Journal of Human Lactation* 16(2): 149-151.

Kent JC, Mitoulas L, et al. 1999. Breast volume and milk production during extended lactation in women. *Experimental Physiology* 84: 435-447.

Starting daycare

First of all, if it's more than a week till you go back to work, and it's getting you really weepy and stressed to be reading this – put it down. Go back to your baby, lie down with her and take a nap. Maternity leave is NOT for stressing – there's plenty of time for that later. All you need to be doing now is nursing, resting, healing from the birth, and pumping just a little. If you've got those things down, relax! Once you've got about a week to go, come back to this chapter, it'll be here.

Emotional issues

It can be a lot harder to go back to work than you expected. You've fallen in love with a whole new little person who is completely and shockingly dependant on you and your partner for his or her every need. How can you just drop them in the hands of a relative stranger (or even a relative) and just like that be back at work?? Well, it is hard, and it can help to know that you're not alone in this. It honestly stinks to have to return to work when your baby is so small, and if you're really in a lather about it, drop a line to your congressperson asking for better family leave policies and more respect for the importance of the family in society. Then put your indignation aside, and realize that you're going to have to do it, and really, in the end, it's not going to be that bad.

The first few days are the hardest, so see if you can schedule your return to work for a Wednesday or a Thursday (or even a Friday). Having that first week be a short one can make it a lot easier for you and your baby than having 5 days stretched in front of you.

Realize that your baby is going to have a few days of adjustment to go through, and may have a hard time at daycare the first few days. A lot of moms do a "trial" daycare day before going back to work in which the baby is left at daycare for one feeding only. This way, the daycare providers get to know your baby gradually, and you can stand by "on call" for them (preferably someplace relaxing, remember what a coffee shop alone feels like?) and you can come early if he's really having a hard time, or not taking a bottle for them.

But ultimately, as the old saying goes, it's a lot harder for you than it is for your baby. You will miss your child something fierce, even if you are feeling a bit of relief at the same time at re-entering the adult world. Your baby will be in an exciting new environment, meeting other babies his own age, developing new skills, and will be fine. I used to have the occasional horrible drop-off – baby crying inconsolably, me late for work, on the verge of tears myself, and I would always call to check in when I got to work. Lo and behold, I would hear my baby in the background, cooing away, babbling, laughing, having a wonderful time. Call as often as you want these first few days – they're used to it.

Getting your baby ready for daycare

As for ways to get your baby "ready" for daycare, my opinion is to skip it. I was in such a panic sending my son to daycare. He'd been with my wonderful sister-in-law from 2 months till he was 6 months, and had been spoiled rotten. He had never in his life slept in a crib, or slept not being held by someone. He did OK with bottles, sort of, but often Jenn would bring him to me at work if he wasn't taking them, so it wasn't critical. Now here I was, dropping him off in a situation where he had to take bottles, had to sleep in a crib, and wasn't going to be able to be held all day any more. And guess what – he did just fine. I felt so embarrassed telling the daycare providers he'd never slept in a crib – what a lax mother I'd been, doing such a poor job getting my kid ready for daycare. I'd be the one sending him off to kindergarten with no knowledge of the alphabet too, I was certain. Expecting the worst, what a relief when Jane said "oh, don't worry, we get lots of babies like that – he'll be fine." These are professionals – they're used to babies who have never been in daycare before! My infant son and the wonderful Jane worked things out just fine, and are pals to this day. Do your pre-daycare parenting however it feels right to you, and let the daycare folks do what works for them. Your kids will figure out to expect different things in different situations. Kids are smart that way.

Letting go

A strong attachment to you makes attachment to others easier, not harder. This is the foundation of attachment theory – so foster your child's attachment to you, while you also foster strong attachments to others.

Before you go back to work, you are the boss of your baby's life. You and whoever is at home with you are in charge of every feeding, every diaper change, every outfit selected, and the destination for every outing. In short, you are the ultimate micromanager. When you relinquish your baby to childcare, you're still the mom, so you get to be the boss, but you also have to start the painful process of letting go. It can be a very hard adjustment, but you can no longer be in charge of every aspect of your baby's day. The key is to decide what the important issues are.

Let's say you come into daycare and say, "Timmy needs to eat in 45 minutes, he needs to start out with you holding him to the right and switch sides after 17 minutes. Don't give him a pacifier until the afternoon, and only after 3:30. If he has a wet diaper, please use these special wipes, only wipe him from left to right, and if he wets, please put him in the cowboy outfit that buttons up the back not the one-piece." How much do you really think you will be listened to? The care providers will wait politely until you leave, look at each other knowingly, and say in unison, "Control Freak." And then they'll do whatever they need to do to make sure your baby is happy and has a nice day – probably putting him in the one-piece suit because it's not itchy like that silly cowboy outfit, and giving him his pacifier whenever he seems to want it. And yet, there were important things in there – that you like them to switch sides while they're feeding, that he can have a pacifier if he's hungry before you get there. Let's chat a bit about how you can let your care providers have autonomy in their care for your baby while still maintaining control over the important issues.

Everyone cares for a baby differently, which is, by and large, a good thing. Your baby will form attachments to a number of different people, and these people will all teach him different things about what it feels like to be loved and well cared for. Your mother may teach him about singing, your husband about the joy of long walks and hot baths, and your care provider about bouncing up and down on a lap, or bad jokes, or the fun of eating with other babies. Everyone has something to offer (It Takes a Village, right?). While you, the mom, will remain at the center of your child's universe for a long time, these other planets in his solar system make him a more well-rounded adaptable little person. You just need to step back and let them care for him in their own way sometimes.

Workday logistics

Your baby's feeding schedule

These are some ideas that worked well for me when my kids were really little – like up to about 8 months (basically, when breastmilk was A-Number-One for them and solids weren't a big part of the diet yet).

In spite of how rushed you'll feel going back to work, what worked best for me in terms of scheduling was for me to do both daycare drop-off and pick-up. Once my kids got bigger, I happily negotiated with my husband to pick the kids up every day, but when they were tiny babies, it ended up being easier for me to do both because of the feeding schedule.

For many moms, the best schedule works around having as many feedings as possible "from the tap," and minimizing the number of bottle-feedings. Why? First, nursing stimulates your supply better than pumping and you will stay in tune with your baby's changing needs and growth spurts if you are nursing directly for the majority of his feedings. Second, the fewer bottle feedings, the less you have to pump, which you will probably find to be a big relief. Third, it's just nice to sit and nurse your baby at the end of a day apart; it's a nice way to reconnect, to leave the stresses of work in an oxytocin-induced haze, and step back into mommy mode. If your partner feels put off by being excluded from the daycare routine, meet there and do the pick-up together, or tell your dear partner that having dinner on the table for you when you get home is really much more…romantic.

Here is an example of what the daily feeding schedule will look like:

&ufed; Feed your baby whenever he wants to eat in the morning.

&ufed; Feed your baby again when you drop him off. Even if he's sleeping or has just eaten, see if you can wake him and get him to take just a little bit more, so you're leaving him "topped off." This means the first bottle will be given later in the day.

 ℇ During the day be sure that your care providers are feeding your baby on cue only, and never on a schedule. You can help by telling them about your baby's early feeding cues – like mouthing, drooling, grunting – whatever it is your baby does to let you know she's hungry (before it escalates to crying). Make sure your care providers let your baby end the feeding whenever she is finished. Remind your care providers that they should not be encouraging your baby to finish bottles. Once your baby releases the nipple and turns away, the feeding is over. If there is milk going to waste, be sure they tell you so that you can prepare smaller or larger bottles.

 ℇ Your next job is to feed your baby again when you pick him up. This one takes a little planning, because it works best if he is hungry. This is where good communication with your daycare (and having them like you) is essential. Let them know you'll want to nurse right when you get there, and be as accurate as you can about what time that will be. Tell them not to give any bottles after a particular time (I used to write this on the note every single day), probably about an hour and a half before you're going to get there. If your baby is screaming-mad-starving inside this time window, let them know they should give only one or two ounces, just to take the edge off. Then, as soon as you arrive, you can sit down and have a nice relaxing nursing session.

It may be awkward at first finding a place to nurse at daycare, but there's probably a rocking chair or other comfortable chair where they sit to give bottles. Go visit a couple of days before your return to work and let them know your plans – they might be able to set up a little place for you to sit and nurse. This is also a great time to connect with your care provider and talk about your baby's day. The time I spent chatting with our care providers while I was nursing my son really paid off, and I still have a close connection with these people. If you feel uncomfortable nursing in front of them, there may be a separate nap room where you can sit and nurse in a rocking chair, or they may be able to set aside an area for you in a quiet corner. However, I highly recommend working on getting comfortable nursing in front of people. If you spend these nursing sessions chatting with the care providers, you'll feel much more connected to your baby's day.

How much milk to send?

You probably have no idea how many ounces your baby takes in a feeding (and this is as it should be). The best way around this is to send milk for the first day in 1.5 to 2-ounce bottles, up to about 12 ounces of milk. The equation for determining – roughly – how much milk a baby will need in a given day is about 2.5 ounces of milk per pound of baby every 24 hours. So a 10 pound baby will need about 25 ounces per day. Then you divide by the amount of time you are at work vs. at home (usually about 1/3 of your time is at work) to get just over one ounce per hour, so about 8 ounces in an eight hour day for this 10 pound baby. However, this is only a rough estimate, and only accurate for breastfed babies in the first month. Remember, most breastfed babies do not increase their intake at all between 1 month and 6 months of age. In general, count on about 3-5 ounces per feeding with feedings about every 3 hours. If I had to guess, I would say the average amount a breastfed baby takes in a typical daycare day is about 12 ounces, but again, there's a ton of variability. The total amount depends on many factors: your baby's weight and age, how much they nurse at night, and their general metabolism. If you start with only 2 ounces per bottle, you'll get a sense in the first couple days how much your baby wants to eat in a feeding, and then you can adjust the amount in each bottle to match.

> Yes, some babies will take 16, 18, even 20 ounces in a day – which is fine if mom is able to pump this much. The numbers above are just averages – your baby is not weird if they do it differently.

The reason you don't want to send too much in each bottle is because there is a natural tendency when bottle-feeding a baby to encourage them to finish the bottle. You want your baby to eat as much as he feels like and no more.

Try to avoid overfeeding at daycare for a couple of reasons – first, you want your baby to keep feeding according to his own signals of hunger and fullness. Second – and more important in your immediate future – the more your baby eats when you're gone, the more you'll have to pump, and the less your baby will nurse while you're together. The opposite of what you want – so it's important to take steps to avoid overfeeding.

How often to feed

Be sure your care providers know not to feed your baby on a schedule. She should be fed whenever she shows feeding cues, and not any more or less often. When care providers are used to formula-fed babies, they may be surprised to find how often your baby eats. Formula takes longer to digest, so babies do stay full longer. Feeding more breastmilk at a feeding is a good way to increase the amount of spitting up and fussing over a belly that's too full, but is not a very good way to space out feedings. Your baby knows how often and how much she needs to eat, and that should be respected. At the same time, your baby may not need to be fed every time she cries. She may be used to being held a lot at home, and may just want comforting. If your baby cries a lot and then refuses a bottle, or you think she's overeating, you could try taking a sling or front-carrier in for your care provider to use to "wear" your baby so that they have their hands free to care for other children.

Your schedule: pumping

As a rough first approximation, you should plan to pump once for every missed feeding. Think about how often your baby nurses, and plan your pumping on that interval. For most moms, this means pumping three times in an eight-hour day (which is usually more like 9 hours away from your baby, once you add in the commute). Your individual schedule will depend on your line of work, availability of a place to pump, and day-to-day schedule. But as a rough approximation, pumping at 10 AM, lunchtime and 3 PM works for a lot of women. If you have a meeting at your regular pumping time, set aside 15 minutes before the meeting to pump. If you have a private office, plan to eat lunch at your desk so you can pump while you're on your lunch break. Once you figure out how your body responds to pumping (and what your storage capacity is), you can adjust your schedule so that you're pumping the same amount as your baby eats.

If you're not able to pump often enough at work, you can still provide exclusive breastmilk. Many moms pump once before work, either before their baby wakes up, or after the first morning nursing session. You can pump one side while nursing the other in the morning. I liked to leave 15 minutes early for work, and pump as soon as I got there. Many of these scheduling alternatives are discussed in the section on "Troubleshooting supply issues" in Chapter 8, although for a lot of moms, they aren't supply issues at all – just scheduling challenges. Some moms will pump extra on weekends, pump before bed, or wake up at night to pump. There are a lot of solutions available if three sessions at work won't work for you, or aren't enough.

As long as you're pumping about the same amount as your baby drinks over the course of a week, your supply will continue to match your baby's needs, and you can continue to provide exclusive breastmilk. Even if you are not providing exclusive breastmilk, and you're using some formula during the day, pumping when you have the chance keeps your milk supply robust, and pumping at least once during the day will also help keep you a lot more comfortable.

Where to pump

Where to pump is a big issue for a lot of moms. In an ideal world, every business would have a pumping lounge for new moms, and would provide hospital-grade pumps where you just have to provide your own kit. There would be a private fridge for the moms to put their milk in and the pumping room would always be clean and accessible. There are indeed places where this is the reality, but for most of us, it's just a dream.

Second luckiest are moms with their own office, or with an understanding office-mate willing to be elsewhere a few times a day. If you have your own office, it's usually a good idea to let people know you'll be taking a "private" break a few times a day, and it is in their best interest to knock before entering. I had a sign for my door showing a woman milking a cow. Humor is a good way to let people know not to bother you… If you have your own office, you can even use the hands-free pumping trick (see the "Pumping basics" section in Chapter 5 for how to do this) to do some work while you pump, although I would rather see you take a break!

The section "Making plans with your employer" in Chapter 1 has lots more ideas for setting up a place to pump during the day.

Pumping techniques at work

The most important thing about pumping is to relax while you're doing it. See the "Pumping basics" chapter for tips on deep breathing exercises to help with relaxation. Try to release the worries of work, release the worries of pumping enough milk, and let your mind be free of worry for the minutes you are pumping.

The easiest way to release stress while pumping is to take your eyes off the bottles. No Peeking! Counting ounces is guaranteed to stop letdown, at least in my experience. Just look away, close your eyes, let the milk flow, and you'll get plenty – that must be your attitude!

Some things to help you relax: Give yourself a reward for taking time to pump. Surf the web, read your favorite baby and breastfeeding sites. Look at Anne Geddes baby pictures, look at photos of your own baby, think of milk trucks spilling all over the highway – anything relaxing. Take a trashy novel to work, and allow yourself time to read while you pump. Talk on the phone with friends, do your personal email; give yourself a reward for *making* your baby's food *while* you're at work! You are a wonder woman and deserve 15 minutes of pampering three times a day.

And don't tell my boss I said any of this.

Time savers

Taking time to pump can be a real obstacle for a lot of working mothers, so it's important to make it as time efficient as possible. Here are a few tips other working moms have used to make the pumping experience a lot faster:

    ◦ Don't wash the pump parts during the day. In my opinion, this is fine to do. I say this because breastmilk has natural antibacterial properties that keep it from growing bacteria for remarkably long periods of time. One study showed that breastmilk left at room temperature for up to 10 hours had no more bacterial growth than breastmilk stored in the refrigerator for the same period of time (Barger & Bull, 1987). I don't advocate letting the pump parts just sit out – wipe the drops of milk off the flanges and stick the whole works in the fridge or in your cooler pack. You can even hook up the flanges to the next set of bottles so all you have to do for the next session is hook up to the pump. Disclaimer – there has not been a study looking at bacterial content of milk pumped with unwashed flanges that have been refrigerated since the last session. We don't really know if this is OK, yet I have not heard of any bad outcomes from doing this. You have to make your own decision – I'm just telling you what worked for me. If anyone knows a microbiologist who is also a pumping mom, tell her she can get a published paper out of doing this study!

Condensation in tubing: sometimes condensation appears in the tubing of the Medela pumps. This is not a problem on its own, but if you leave it alone it may mildew. To get rid of the condensation, use an eye dropper to drip a little rubbing alcohol in one end of the tubing. Keep hold of the end of the tubing that you put the alcohol into and go outside. Swing the tubing around over your head, and the alcohol will run through, getting rid of the water droplets.

    ◦ Pump directly into bottles. Buy a few extra bottles so you can pump right into the bottles you'll use the next day. This saves transferring milk in the evenings. If you use Avent bottles, you can get adapters for your pump that let you pump right into the bottles. The next morning, you just need to put nipples on them and send them off to daycare. It's worth it to have a few extra bottles, plus if you're transferring milk from those little bags all the time, you tend to lose the healthy fat when it sticks to the sides of the bag.

ᖇᑐ Run your dishwasher every night. If you use a heated setting on your dishwasher or your tap water is hotter than 140 degrees (F), that's all the sterilizing you need to do on a daily basis. Even if it's just the pump parts, I ran the dishwasher to save washing them by hand.

ᖇᑐ Take the weekend to catch up. Every weekend I used to sterilize my pump parts and take the time to organize the milk in the fridge. If there was more then I needed for Monday, I would pour some into bags for freezing, otherwise, just use the milk you pump Friday to send on Monday.

Do it the night before

Anything you can do the night before, do. When I was in college and on the cycling team, the only way I could make it to 6 AM practice on time was by leaving my shorts, shoes, jersey, helmet, etc hanging right on my bike. Needing to look for even one thing was enough to make me late for practice. I found the same applied with getting to work on time. I would pack up empty bottles and as much of the pump kit as wasn't in the dishwasher at night, so in the morning I could just plop in the ice packs and go. My baby's bottles were already made up and in a cooler pack in the fridge. And, if I was really on the ball, that night's dinner would be in the crock-pot insert in the fridge as well, just waiting to be put in the heater – press Start and go.

My baby's diaper bag also had to be packed the night before – clean clothes for the next day, diapers laid out, shoes and socks already chosen. Coffee measured and in the pot with a mug set out – whatever could happen the night before did.

When you get home

Evenings and weekends are for nursing. The best thing for your milk supply and your baby is to allow your baby to feed on demand when you're together, and encourage frequent feedings. In fact, it's the best thing all around for all of you. You need to relax and take time to reconnect with your baby when you're at home, and what better way to do this than sitting and nursing. Run your hands over that soft head, stare into your baby's eyes, just relax. Have you noticed a theme of relaxation yet? It's so hard to find time to relax when you're running around – wake the baby, feed the baby, go to work and be an important grown-up, wash the spit-up off your best suit, rush to pick up your baby, rush home, get dinner together – it's enough to make someone crazy. Especially when your baby is so little, you just have to let it all go sometimes. You'll hear a lot of older moms say things like "the dishes will wait, your baby is only this little once." And guess what - they're right! My daughter is 3, and while she's still nursing, it's only once a day now. I actually have time to clean the kitchen if I want to. I'm still kind of digging out from a few years of neglecting the housework, but I get more organized every day – I have time to write a book! And yet I don't regret a single evening that I spent crashed out on the couch holding a tiny baby. Can you imagine being on your deathbed saying "gosh, I sure wish I hadn't spent so much time just holding my babies"? No – so do it.

And, on a more practical note, if you nurse as much as possible when you're at home, this accomplishes two goals – your baby will need less milk at daycare, so the pressure to pump enough is less, and all of that nursing boosts your supply and keeps your body in tune with your baby's growth spurts.

And finally, if you're nursing, you can't possibly do the dishes, so, honey, could you clean up tonight? Gosh thanks, you're such a dear. Look how happy the baby is to have mommy so well taken care of.

Sample schedules

Everyone's schedule will be different – depending on your milk storage capacity, your work setting, your baby's needs, and your personality. Sometimes it's nice to see what other people are doing so that you can get ideas, or just hear that you're not the only one! Here are some sample schedules, from real working moms (with names changed to protect the innocent). I've included some quotes of how these women describe various parts of their day.

Mandy's schedule

5:30	Baby wakes me, nurse
6:00	Get up, shower, dress, coffee and breakfast
7:20	Leave the house, drop kids at daycare
10:00	First pumping session
Lunch	Second pumping session
Afternoon	One last pumping session

"After work I pick up the baby (usually nurse at daycare), go on to my mom's to pick up my older son, and then head home for dinner (or stay and have dinner with my mom).

At home, I do the laundry, etc while my husband plays with the boys and puts them to bed. I'm in bed by 10PM, and nurse my son at least once by 5AM. I don't mind the night nursing, we co-sleep and all I do is tuck him under my arm when he fusses, he hardly ever cries for night feedings.

I missed my kids terribly when I first returned to work, but work was too far away to visit them at lunch. I enjoy my pumping sessions, it's the time I connect with my baby when I'm at work."

Carolyn's schedule

4:45	Wake up, take a shower and eat by myself for a little quiet time
6:00	Wake baby, nurse her, change her, etc.
6:45	Husband wakes up, hand off baby to him and leave for work
7:10	Work day starts
9:45	First pumping session
12:15	Second pumping session
2:30	Home. Baby nurses every 2 hours and goes down about 10PM.

"Bathing, dressing, feeding and cleaning up after the other kids takes up most of my evening. Every once in a while I can go out for an evening and take the baby with me when my husband stays home with the other kids. It's still easier to take her along than to have to pump another bottle for her."

Jessica's schedule

7:15   Wake up

"We co-sleep, so it's up to the baby whether or not she eats before I get up – it's right there if she wants it."

8:45   Get to work

10:00   First pumping session

11:00   Lunch

2:00   Second pumping session

5:45   Third pumping session (right before I go home).

"It used to be that I would only pump twice, but it seemed like every day when I got to the sitter's, the baby would have just finished a bottle – and then I would be bursting until she was hungry again, so now I just pump before I leave work.

As soon as I get home, I divvy up the pumped milk into bottles for the next day, wash the pump parts and put them on the stovetop to boil. Once they're done, I put them on a rack to dry, and the next morning throw them back in my bag. This is the thing about pumping I like the least." (Author's note – it's not necessary to sterilize your pump parts every day – washing in warm water or running through the dishwasher is fine.)

Maura's schedule

6:00   Baby wakes and nurses in bed

6:30   Get up, change diaper, get baby dressed while husband showers and dresses

"Once my husband is out of the shower, he takes the baby while I shower and get dressed. Then I have breakfast and fill out the daily sheet to bring to daycare. I took a blank one and copied it so I can fill it out at home where I have more time to write a note."

7:30   Leave the house

8:00   Arrive at work

8:30	First pumping session
11:30	Second pumping session
2:00	Third pumping session

"One day a week I have a 6PM meeting, so on those days I pump again at 5."

| 4:30 | Leave work |
| 5:00 | Pick up baby |

"Some days she wants to nurse as soon as we get home, other days she waits till bedtime at 7."

| 9:30 | Go to bed. Usually one nursing session during the night. |

"We use the Avent bottles, so I bought the adapter so I can pump right into the bottles. It's a time-saver since I don't have to transfer milk when I get home, and there's less to wash, but it does mean I need a lot of bottles."

Marianne's schedule

5:30-7   Cluster feeding session.
"We co-sleep, so it is easy to feed her and still get some sleep."

6:30	Get up and shower
7:00	Baby wakes up
7:30	Leave for work
9:30	First pumping session
Noon	Second pumping session
3:00	Pick up baby and feed her on my arrival
3:30	Home

"We go get into bed and I nurse her down for a nap, staying with her for 30 minutes to an hour. This is my favorite time of day!"

4:00	Get up, prep bottles and food for the next day
5:00	Husband comes home, baby wakes up, we make dinner together
6:00	Eat dinner together. Baby nurses after we eat

7:30 – 8   Bath, get baby ready for bed, nurse her to sleep

1:00   Nighttime feeding

"Then she'll sleep till the morning milk rush begins."

Bethany's schedule

5-6:30   Cluster feeding session

6:30   Wake up and change laundry over and fold and put away clothes in the dryer.

"I move one load a day through like this – it's the only way I can keep up with three kids."

7:00   Wake older kids, get them breakfast and off to the school bus

"Then I get ready. Hopefully the baby is still sleeping. If he wakes up, he plays on the restroom floor while I shower and get dressed."

8:10   Leave for in-laws.

"We have breakfast there, and I nurse one more time before I leave."

8:30   Leave for work

11:00   First pumping session

4:30   Second pumping session

"I get about 16-20 ounces a day depending upon when he last ate and my stress level."

5:30   Leave work. Pick up all the kids at in-laws, nurse the baby there, then home for dinner, homework, baths, etc.

9:00   Older kids in bed

10:00   Off to bed.

"The baby still wakes up in the middle of the night to nurse. I don't know how often as we co-sleep."

(Author's note – I never would have recommended this schedule – I always did better pumping early in the day, and it seems like this mom goes a really long time between pumping sessions. But obviously, it works for her!)

The original message board thread where these schedules were posted is publicly available at http://www.breastfeeding.com/cgi-bin/ultimatebb.cgi?ubb+get_topic;f=4;t=001069. What appears here is an adaptation of the original thread, simplifying the schedules, removing identifying information, and paraphrasing some quotes from moms about the particulars of their schedule.

Proper use of the freezer stash

Everyone talks about having a terrific freezer stash ready for when you go back to work, but the freezer stash deserves a bit more discussion than just "more is better." A lot of thought should go into how this frozen milk is used once you return to work. I'll start with my story – when my son was 6 months old, I started to have trouble pumping enough for him at daycare. But I had this great freezer stash, so I figured I was all set, I'd just send in extra milk from the freezer until my supply came back up (see the Chapter 2 "Demand and Supply" for why this assumption was inherently flawed…). I was only adding about 2oz/day to what I was pumping the day before, but I just couldn't get my supply back up. I was still pumping as frequently as I had been before my supply dropped – what the heck was going on? I was proud that my son was still getting 100% breastmilk, and thought I had been doing OK. I was determined not to give my son formula, so I called a lactation consultant to ask what else I could give him – a little rice milk? I even considered goat's milk or some homemade formula concoction. My freezer stash was dwindling rapidly at the rate of 2oz/day, and I couldn't see any way to build it back up! The lactation consultant asked me a bunch of questions about how much I was pumping and how much he was drinking, and after talking with her for about an hour about what I needed to do, I finally figured it out (Thank you Sally – you gave me my start!) So – here's what I learned. Every day that I was sending milk to daycare from the freezer stash I was telling my body that I needed 2oz less to feed my son. However, my son wasn't getting the message that he needed 2oz less to eat – because he was still eating the same amount! So his demand was outstripping my supply by 2oz every day that I went to work and pulled one of those precious bags from the freezer! It's pretty easy to play this out to its natural conclusion if you think about it. Your body isn't getting a signal that it should be making more milk; you keep taking milk from the freezer and not putting any in, and gradually the freezer stash diminishes till it's gone – then what? Unfortunately, most moms recognize the problem when the freezer stash is almost gone, not when they first start using it – which is when the real problem started, the problem of a supply-demand imbalance. So, what's the darn freezer stash for, anyway? I can't use it to send to daycare because my supply will decrease? Why did I do all that pumping??

Well, here are some examples of when you'll be glad you have it:

   ⁎ You leave all your milk sitting out on the counter overnight and have to toss it.

   ⁎ You spill a whole bottle down your best suit while pumping (the dry cleaning is a separate issue!)

   ⁎ Your daycare has just heated and started a bottle as you arrive, and that whole bottle has to be tossed so you can nurse (the far better choice, and a good use for the freezer stash).

   ⁎ You go out and really tie one on at the bars, and want to pump and dump and feed your baby a bottle instead of getting her tipsy.

   ⁎ You miss a pumping session one day, you know you'll pump enough the next day, and you just have to add a little bit to cover. Caution: here starts the slippery slope! Pump extra the next day so this doesn't get to be a habit (see above).

   ⁎ You have to go out of town overnight. You'll be pumping while you're gone, but need milk to get through the hours you'll be away.

   ⁎ If you have to temporarily take a medication that you don't want to pass to your baby and you'll be pumping and dumping while you're taking it.

So – the next time you're ready to reach for milk from the freezer, think about addressing the real issue first – that you're not pumping enough. See the section on "Troubleshooting supply issues" in Chapter 8 for how to fix the real problem and pump more milk. Also read the section on "Overfeeding at daycare" to make sure your baby isn't overeating. And, if you really do need more milk than you can pump, then by all means, use up what's in the freezer, and flip right to the section on "Smart supplementing" also in Chapter 8.

How much is enough?

If you're not going to be using the freezer stash on a regular basis, then how much milk do you need to have in the freezer? In my class for working moms, I tell them it's more of a personality test than a biological absolute. If you're the kind of mom who will be stressed out every time you pump if you don't have a really solid backup, I would say you need about 100 ounces. If you're a fly-by-the-seat-of-your-pants type, then I think 6 ounces should suffice. Only you can decide.

If you're home with your baby before you go back to work and have an abundant supply *and it doesn't stress or tire you to pump*, then you could consider pumping once or twice a day to stock up the freezer. If your work schedule is going to make it hard to pump enough, or if you just know you'll feel better having a backup, then make the time to pump. But if nursing your baby all day long, taking care of other kids, managing a household, and getting to the shower at least once a week are all you can manage, put the pump away. You'll get by somehow, and as I hope I've made clear, a huge freezer stash is not necessarily the key to breastfeeding success. Pumping should never replace time spent enjoying your baby while you're home – it's all about priorities, and we all do the best we can.

Reference:

Barger J, Bull P. 1987. A Comparison of the Bacterial Composition of Breast Milk Stored at Room Temperature and Stored in the Refrigerator. *International Journal of Childbirth Education* 2(3).

Finding a good support group makes working and pumping about a billion times easier, conservatively speaking. Knowing that you're not alone in this endeavor boosts your spirit and gives you a live source for tips and encouragement – but if you're working full time, how can you find this essential support group? There are a few options for finding real life local support, but don't forget the Internet in your searches for support and information. I know, geek city, right? Before I started working and pumping, I thought the only people finding friends online were geeky high school guys playing real-time dungeons and dragons, or creepy pedophiles in chat rooms. Granted, this was in 2000, before the Internet reached its pinnacle of hipness (has that happened yet?), but I was a bit of a snob... And then I found the working and pumping board that changed my life. Really, it did! I learned most of the information that is the basis of this book from the experienced working and pumping women on the old iVillage Working & Pumping message board. I got the support I needed to make it through my 6 month slump and have made lifetime friends. There's something about being united by breastfeeding and working that makes for a special group of women, so I had to give up my D&D preconceptions and dive into the electronic world... But first – there are other options:

Real live groups

La Leche League

La Leche League (LLL) has been around as a breastfeeding support group since my mother was breastfeeding me and has traditionally been where breastfeeding women turn for support and information. LLL was originally opposed to "routine separations" of mother and nursing baby, which pretty much rules out working a full time job, but the official position of the group is gradually changing to be more inclusive of working mothers.

You can find the meeting schedule for your area in a lot of places – Use the "Find a Leader" feature of the LLL website (www.llli.org), look in the Yellow Pages, call the maternity floor of your local hospital, or check with childbirth educators or midwives. Look around for a group in your area that meets in the evening

– that's where you'll usually find the other working moms. If you find a meeting that seems unfriendly to working mothers, see if you can find another one in your area, or try to strike up a friendship with other working moms you run into at the meetings.

As with any support group, if you recognize the benefits you can get from a LLL meeting – such as meeting other breastfeeding moms, learning new information, and seeing how others are raising their babies, you can take what's useful for you, and discard the rest. You may encounter some attitudes at LLL that if you're working, you're not *really* breasfeeding – but rest assured, you are indeed a terrific breastfeeding mom, and therefore meet their criteria for inclusion.

Hospital groups

Many hospitals run groups that encourage breastfeeding moms to get together after the baby is born, often with a lactation consultant or maternity nurse. Again, you need to pick and choose what information is useful to you at these meetings, but they can be a great way to meet other breastfeeding moms, build connections and establish a supportive community before you go back to work. If the group meets regularly, you can keep in touch with other breastfeeding moms as your babies go through similar stages.

Other daycare moms

I met a number of other breastfeeding moms through my daycare. You'll be able to figure out pretty quickly who's breastfeeding and who's not – look for the babies with the Medela bottles in the fridge, or those who don't have their own labeled can of formula. I'm not saying you should be friends with the breastfeeding moms and not the formula feeders – I'm not *that* much of a snob – just that forging connections with other breastfeeding moms can be a great way to get encouragement on rough days. It's nice to have a buddy who you can email through the day for support, or somebody you see every day at daycare who knows what you're going through. I've found that now that I have no time for a social life (between mothering and working), the families we've met through our daycare continue to be our closest friends.

Online resources

There are a few excellent support groups for working and pumping moms. Just started is the message board that I host on my website, www.workandpump.com. The message board can be found at www.workandpump.com/talk. Of course, I have a vested interest in having you come to my site, but if you want to chat with me or one of my hand-picked moderators, this is the place to go.

There are many other places to find working and pumping message boards. A few of my favorites are the pumpmoms group at Yahoo Groups (an email list-serve, not a message board, but it's a similar idea), the iVillage Working & Pumping board (http://messageboards.ivillage.com/iv-ppworkpump/) and the Pumping and Working Outside the Home board at breastfeeding.com (www.breastfeeding.com/cgi-bin/ultimatebb.cgi).

The groups are generally in the format of a message board, on which people can post questions at any time, and others respond when they get around to it. Some message boards begin to have a sense of community, in which members recognize one another, and some even establish private email communication "off the board."

So – why join a message board? A message board for working and pumping women is a group of women who, while in different careers and with wildly different personalities, have a remarkably strong bond of making the commitment to provide breastmilk to their children while they are at work. You'd be surprised how powerful a bond this can be between women! You can post any question you want, if it's too silly, no one will answer it, but there's no loss to you, and if you really want the answer – post it again! You can add your suggestions when women are going through problems you've had yourself, and often, the group works out an answer to something that no one person would have been able to solve alone. Even if you never post anything, you can learn so much just from reading what other working and pumping moms are writing and asking about.

A few message board basics if this technology is new to you:

When a question or comment is posted, the original post along with all of its responses is called a "thread." Message boards have different formats – some show all posts in a given thread when the first message is selected, others show only one post at a time with options to page through the thread (or "discussion") or to skip to the next thread. Some have the option of an "outline" view, in which the first line of each post is seen on the main page. In general, all display the most recent thread headings on a front page, then you select the thread you want to read. You can start a new thread by posting a question, reply to an existing thread, or just read (this is called "lurking," and is perfectly fine and legal).

The message board display is always changing as new threads and responses are posted – some boards keep the threads in chronological order, some bump a post to the top of the board every time there is a new response, so that the most active conversations stay at the top of the board.

Most message boards require you to register to post, but you can read anonymously. Registering is usually free and can be as anonymous as you want it to be. Most users make up a username that is pretty generic so their real identity cannot be randomly guessed, and all personal information that you provide in registering is hidden from the public.

When you first go on a message board, if you're not a veteran of instant messaging and chat rooms, you'll wonder what language they're speaking. The language of the message board is the acronym. For example, "I was LMAO when DH said FIL had been a troll on the W&P board! I always said I didn't know anyone that weird, but now I've BTDT."

Huh?

A brief glossary:

LOL – laugh out loud – can also used to convey sarcasm

LMAO – lauging my a.. off

ROTFLMAO – rolling on the floor laughing my a—off – something has to be really darn funny to warrant this one.

DH – dear, darn, dunce, darling Husband

DS – dear or darling Son

DD – dear or darling Daughter

FIL – father in law

MIL – mother in law (etc with the ILs)

IMO – in my opinion

IMHO – in my humble opinion

BTDT – been there done that

YMMV – your mileage may vary (offered with advice – as in "worked for me, but YMMV")

BTW – by the way

OTOH – on the other hand

OT – off topic, anything not directly related to the board title

PITA – pain in the a—

AF – Aunt Flo – a cutesy name for your period (get it? Flow? LOL)

A lurker – someone who reads and doesn't post

A troll – a creepy weird individual who pretends to be someone they're not to infiltrate an online group. Very rare in the W&P world – I think a few lurk for a while to hear talk about breasts, then leave when they realize how boring it is to talk about pumping output and storage closets and supply boosting foods all day. However, be aware that a troll could always be out there, so hold your personal information close. Only reveal yourself over email with someone who you've been able to verify is a real person (google comes in handy for this).

Working and Breastfeeding and Parenting specific acronyms:

W&P -working and pumping

PIS – Medela Pump in Style breastpump (also PNS)

PY – Ameda Purely Yours pump

BSL – big splashy letdown (a good thing – "wishing you PPV and BSL")

PPV – positive pumping vibes

EBM – expressed breast milk

DC – daycare

DCP – daycare provider

(o)(o) – breasts – see also (.)(.), (O)(O), (*)(*), (^)(^), etc, depending on size, position and temperature

AP – attachment parenting

FB – family bed

CIO – cry it out

MER – milk ejection reflex, also known as "let-down"

WOHM – work outside the home mom

SAHM – stay at home mom

SAHD – stay at home dad

As you get the hang of it, you'll be able to figure out the new ones on your own – and don't be afraid to ask – sometimes people just make them up on the spot, and it's part of the game to figure them out.

And you can be way more touchy-feely online than you are as a real person, so you'll see lots of (((((((hugs))))))) – with each set of parenthesis making the hug that much tighter.

Common Concerns in the First Six Months

Troubleshooting supply issues – what to do if you can't pump enough

The number one problem I hear from working and pumping moms is that they're not able to pump enough. If this is you, don't feel alone, you haven't done anything wrong, lots of us have been there before, and there are plenty of solutions before you run out to the store for some formula.

Take a few minutes to read through this entire section if you are having supply problems. There are a lot of different strategies, and you certainly don't need to use them all. Some combination of the suggestions here will probably work for you, but it's up to you to find the right "fit."

There are plenty of ways to fix supply problems, but most involve a little 'tough love' and a cooperative daycare provider. Here goes the list:

Take a nursing holiday

If it's at all possible, the fastest way to fix a supply shortage is to take a few days off as an intensive Nursing Holiday. Take yourself and your baby to bed and set up a nursing station like you had in your first post-partum days: lots of water, nutritious snacks, a good pillow, the remote… Spend a few days nursing entirely on demand, letting your body rest from the stresses of working, and sleeping when the baby sleeps. Allowing your bodies to get back into a shared rhythm can often restore any supply imbalances. This increases supply, is a great stress-buster, and remember, it's totally justifiable because you're saving money not buying formula!

Nurse more

Nursing more is the number one way to signal your body that more milk needs to be made. If your baby is hungry at the end of the day, this is terrific. Go home, settle in on the couch, and nurse as much as possible. This is easier with a first baby and a cooperative partner at home, but try to boost the amount of nursing you do when you're together no matter what your living situation. Some ideas:

- ❧ nurse right when you pick your baby up from daycare (before you head home).

- ❧ nurse as much as possible in the evening before your baby falls asleep (this is also a great way to get out of doing the dishes).

- ❧ wake your baby up to nurse before you go to bed.

- ❧ be sure you allow for time to nurse in the morning.

- ❧ make every weekend a nursing holiday, and allow your baby to nurse as often as he wants to through the entire time you're together.

- ❧ limit pacifiers and thumb-sucking when you're with your baby – offer the breast instead, even if it is just "comfort sucking" (it will still boost your supply).

- ❧ encourage your baby to nurse more at night. This can result in more sleeping and less feeding during the day (called 'reverse cycling'). It can be tiring, but if the baby's in bed with you (cosleeping), you may find you get used to feeding without totally waking up, and manage to get a very decent rest even with nursing 3-4 times a night.

Don't overfeed at daycare

Hopefully your daycare has the handout from the Appendix on bottle feeding the breastfed baby. You should be using a low-flow nipple on the bottles so that it's not too easy to get the milk out. There's no reason to "upgrade" from a newborn nipple – after all, your breasts don't change as the baby gets older, why should the bottles? The daycare providers should be aware that breastfed babies need to eat more often, but usually eat smaller amounts. After all, this is one of the reasons we breastfeed, so our babies learn to recognize what full feels like, and won't struggle with a lifetime of overeating. Your childcare provider should be using comfort measures other than feeding; after all, breastfed babies are used to being held a lot, and expect a lot of skin-to-skin contact during the day.

However, in the real world, daycare providers are very busy people (as well as frightfully underpaid), and the reality is that it's often a lot easier to give a crying baby a bottle than it is to comfort them by walking or holding them. I think it's vitally important that we acknowledge to our daycare providers that taking care of a breastfed baby can be harder than a formula fed baby. Let them know that we really appreciate their efforts; they are the ones largely responsible for our ability to keep breastfeeding after we go back to work. Be gracious, buy gifts, bake cookies. Talk to them about what you can do to help. And accept that sometimes they may give your baby a bottle even if she's not hungry just to get her to sleep so they can care for another baby. Inconvenient, yes, but not the end of the world.

Send what you pump

If you have a cooperative daycare provider, the best solution to a supply slump is to just send what you pump the previous work day. Your baby may have a few rough days of being hungry at the end of the day, but she will adjust by nursing like crazy when you're home together. If you are going to try this strategy, set aside your evenings for nursing and nursing only. Schedule your partner to make dinner, wash your pump, etc., and before and after you eat your own evening meal (a healthy and nutritious one, of course) just park it on the couch and nurse. If your baby falls asleep early, wake her again before you go to bed and see if you can get her to nurse again. Let her nurse at will through the night (co-sleeping makes this a LOT easier). After a few days of this, your supply will increase to meet the needs of your baby. You will probably be able to pump more at work, and if you can't, your baby may begin to take in more of her nutrition in the hours the two of you are together.

If you are going to start this method, be sure you talk it over with your daycare provider so they're on board with the plan, and they will know that dealing with a cranky hungry baby is only temporary.

A note on shorting bottles

I will add that if you're only short by an ounce or so per day, you could probably just reduce the day's bottles by a little bit each bottle, and your baby may not actually notice the difference between 3.5 ounces and 4 ounces. Or, send the same amount of milk in a larger number of smaller bottles, so that if the daycare is encouraging your baby to finish her bottles at each feeding, she won't be overeating. Be sure to check with the daycare about whether bottles are actually being finished. If they're consistently chucking ½ ounce from the bottom of each bottle, it doesn't seem like much to them, but the 1½ to 2 ounces over the course of the day may just be the make-or-break amount for you.

This won't work for me...

If this method won't work for you, either because your day care provider can't tolerate a hungry baby for a few days, or you don't have the time in the evenings to nurse as much as you need to, then read on – there are a lot of other suggestions in this chapter. Read all the way through, and decide what method is the best fit for you.

Pacifiers can help...

So, what can help this situation of a baby overeating at daycare? Maybe a pacifier (binky, wooby, nuk, plug, paci). I know, all the breastfeeding experts advise against using pacifiers to avoid nipple confusion. But know what? Your baby is already getting bottles, it's a bit of a moot point by now. See if your baby can be interested in a pacifier during daycare hours. Some babies just have a very strong need to suck (I know, I had two of them). They "comfort nurse" for hours when they are very small, and have a very strong attachment to the breast well beyond a year. These babes can be trying for a daycare provider, who will often just keep feeding them because they seem to want to suck all the time. Then, of course, the baby who wasn't hungry in the first place, also spits up a lot. Buy a range of pacifier styles and let the daycare have at it, see if they can find one that your baby will take in lieu of a bottle when she's between feedings.

If your baby shows any inclination towards thumb or finger sucking, this can be a big help at daycare as well. My son was (OK, I'll admit, until he was 4) an avowed binky-boy, but my daughter is a serious thumbsucker. Ask me if my opinion changes after the orthodontic bills are paid, but for now those breast-surrogates have made my life a lot easier. Neither over-ate at daycare, and they can easily comfort themselves in new situations. I'm sure to get a lot of flak for this position, but a working mom has to do some things for survival, and this was one of them for me.

...But not with mom

The key to using a pacifier effectively in a daycare situation is not to rely on it when your baby is with you. To keep your supply up, you should be nursing as much as possible when you're together, even if it is "just comfort nursing." Try to hold out on the pacifier as much as possible when you're together, or if you see the thumb going into the mouth, try offering a breast instead.

Reduce bottle need at the beginning and end of the day

If you can manage to do daycare dropoff, it's a great time to nurse. Nursing at drop-off and again at pick-up effectively shortens the amount of time your baby must be fed by bottle. The result of this is that you need to pump less. Nursing right at drop off and at pick-up can mean as much as one fewer bottle per day. And, if you nurse at drop-off, your baby won't need a bottle for a few hours, more closely corresponding with your first pumping time.

If you can be the one to pick up your baby, plan for her to be hungry when you arrive, so that you can nurse as soon as you get there. Talk to your daycare provider, and explain that nursing your baby right when you pick her up will be a lot easier if she is hungry, but not frantic. The best plan is usually for them to feed your baby about an hour and a half before you are expected to arrive. Then your baby will be ready to feed as soon as you get there. If she's not hungry, extend the time to two hours.

But where will you feed, in the car? No way! This *is* a childcare facility, there should be a rocking chair or comfortable place to sit and feed somewhere. I was very lucky in that there was a rocker in the small, dark naproom of my daycare, so I could take my son in there and nurse as soon as I got there. I used this at first, when I was self-conscious about nursing in front of the care providers, but after a few months, I'd just sit on the floor wherever I happened upon my baby. If there isn't a private space and you're not quite to the point of sitting on the floor, you should still be able to find a spot in a quiet corner to sit and nurse a bit. This is also a great time to chat and connect with your child's caregivers. You'll have more than the usual two seconds to talk as you rush out the door, and it's nice to find out a bit about their lives, in addition to finding out more about what your baby did and accomplished that day.

The schedule doesn't always work out; your baby may be napping an hour and a half before pickup and wake up starved thirty minutes before you arrive. In this case, it's a good idea to keep a small bottle on hand, maybe 1.5 to 2 ounces of milk that they can heat up and give to satisfy your baby until you get there. Usually this works, but if your baby is truly starved for a whole bottle, see if you can get the daycare to call you at work, that way you can pump one more time before you leave.

Hidden supply busters

Before you pull out all the stops to boost your supply, take a look for some of these supply busters. Sometimes you'll need to pump a little extra as you work through a stressful time or illness, but once the cause of the supply dip is taken care of, your supply should bounce right back up.

Stress

Look for other reasons your supply is dipping. Are you under a lot of stress? OK, the stress question is a little redundant, you're a working mom, of course you're stressed. But how are you managing the stress? Do you have enough help? Are you carrying the weight of the world on your shoulders? Learn to say NO and YES. Here's a practice exercise: Question 1, "Is there anything I can do to help you?" The correct answer is:

a) no, I'm fine

b) oh, we'll manage

c) YES YES YES and start with the dishes, OK?

(You know that for a working and pumping mom, c is the correct answer, but it takes a little getting used to – practice saying it!)

And, if the question is "can you…?" as in, "manage this new client?," "stay home while I go fishing with the guys next week?" or "put together mom's birthday party for 800 guests?," this is the time to practice saying NO. Well, maybe not about the new client, but hold the line on the home front!

Supply will bounce back once the stressful situation is resolved – give yourself a little breathing room!

Illness

When you're sick, your supply will usually go down. All the more reason to use those sick days if you have them, and really baby yourself. Become your husband when he's sick – take to your bed, act unable to lift a finger, and hydrate like a camel about to head across the Mojave. You have two people depending on that body – give it a chance to recover. Once you're better, look for supply to return along with your health.

Decongestants

Speaking of illness, what do you take when you have a cold? Most of us reach for the Sudafed (pseudephedrine) for a stuffy nose – but it's been found (Aljazaf et al., 2003) that these decongestants can reduce milk supply by *an average of 24%* with a single dose! Instead of decongestants, try natural congestion remedies like long hot showers (my dad, an ear, nose and throat doctor, recommends three 20 minute hot showers a day for congestion), neti pots, increasing fluids, chicken soup, and here's a novel idea – resting. If you must have a decongestant, use a nasal spray – these do not affect your milk production.

Antihistamines may also decrease supply, but this has not been studied.

Return of menstrual cycles

For a lot of moms, a supply dip is noticeable right before the arrival of "Aunt Flo" each month. This can be particularly vexing the first post-partum cycle, since you're usually not expecting it. This supply slump lasts 3-4 days, and should bounce back as soon as your flow begins. Take the same supply boosting measures, but expect that if this is the reason, recovery will be blissfully rapid. And, it's small consolation as you're dragging out the tampons and pads to know that at least you have plenty of milk again.

Some moms have found that taking calcium and magnesium from about the middle of your cycle until your bleeding starts can help prevent the supply dip – and maybe helps with other pre-menstrual symptoms. The kellymom website suggests 500-1500 mg calcium and 250-750 mg magnesium, or a calcium/magnesium/ zinc combination (http://kellymom.com/herbal/natural-treatments. html#calcium). Generally, the more meat you eat, the higher dose you will need, as the phosphorus in animal protein increases your calcium need.

Birth control pills

In theory, low-dose birth control pills don't have any effect on a mom's milk supply. In theory. There is now quite a lot of anecdotal evidence that while many moms can take these pills without an effect on supply, quite a few do suffer a significant dip in supply when they start on the pill. If you do choose to take hormonal birth control, pay careful attention to your milk supply. Most moms who have trouble with supply after starting on the pill see an effect within a few weeks. If you don't let it go too long, your supply should rebound relatively quickly once you go off the pill, although it may take a bit of extra pumping to get it back up. However, as you'll find out when you read my friend Emily's story in the section "Smart supplementing" in Chapter 8, if you wait too long, it can become a significant struggle to get your supply back up.

I really need to pump more milk

If none of the above solutions solve the supply problem, then you probably will have to pump more milk for your baby. The next sections have many suggestions on how you can do this. It does require effort, this is true. But you're providing the very best for your baby, and it's only for a while that they're depending on you for all of their nutrition.

Pump more often

The simplest way to meet your baby's needs through a supply slump can be just to pump more often. Adding in one pumping session a day can really boost your supply, and make the difference between balanced supply and demand or depleting your freezer stash.

Add a morning session

Prolactin levels are reportedly higher in the morning hours, so many moms find that their pumping output is best if they can add a pumping session first thing in the morning. Oh, but when?? My mornings are packed already, you cry – believe me, I feel your pain. I know a lot of moms who would pump before leaving for work (more on that in a bit), but for me, the easiest way to increase my pumping was to bump my whole morning routine forward by 15 minutes, arrive at work a little earlier, and pump then. I know, I just told you to nurse at drop-off, and hopefully you just did. But for me and lots of other moms I know, you can pump 30 minutes later when you get settled at your desk, and still have a great session. While I think this is in part due to the fluctations of your hormone levels, I'm placing bets that it also has a lot to do with your state of mind. You're still relaxed from your last nursing session (if the commute wasn't too hairy) and you haven't hit the stresses of the workday yet. Try this one for a week – you won't necessarily get much milk the first couple days, but this was often my most productive session of the day once I got used to it.

> When adding any new pumping session, give your body time to adjust to the fact that it's being expected to make milk at a new time. Allow 3 days to a week to determine if a new time is going to work for you. Remember, new pumping and nursing times not only are for getting milk in the moment, but also "place the order" to make more milk in the future.

You can also browse your emails, check the news, and start the day feeling a little more "connected."

Nurse-shower-pump

Another way to fit in an extra morning pumping session is the "nurse-shower-pump" routine. When you first wake up, nurse your baby for as long as he wants to, then either put him back to bed or hand-off to your partner. Next, take a nice relaxing hot shower, and then pump. Again, those high morning hormone levels are on your side, and the relaxing shower makes it possible for lots of moms to have another let-down almost right away. If you get up before your baby, switch to Pump-Shower-Nurse. Even if you've just pumped, your baby is so much more efficient that they can always get more milk.

Tandem pump

Another way to sneak in an extra pumping session is to tandem pump – that is, to nurse your baby on one side and pump the other. Most double electric pumps can be easily set up to pump single-sided, and once you get the coordination down, the letdown stimulated by your baby will give you a nice bottle's worth on the other side. If your baby is still hungry after finishing the first side, go ahead and offer the second side – he'll be able to get out milk the pump couldn't access. If you don't feel like taking your pump back and forth, a manual pump like the Avent Isis can be kept at home for tandem pumping sessions. If you choose to use your electric pump, it's generally easier to get the pump set up first, and then latch the baby. A hands-free set up for your pump makes this easier (see the "Pumping basics" section in Chapter 5).

Pump before bed or during the night

If your baby goes down for the night very early, or sleeps for a very long time at night, you're probably counting your lucky stars for all the sleep you get! Well, if you're willing to interrupt your own sleep but not your baby's, you can pump while your baby is sleeping. Pump right before you go to bed, or set an alarm for the middle of the night to sneak in an extra session. For me, this option was about as appealing as another root canal, but my friends who did this swear it's not that bad. The secret is to have your pump all set up the night before, then leave a cooler right by your bed. That way, you wake with the alarm, pump 10-15 minutes, milk goes in the cooler, save the pump washing for morning, and then right back to sleep with you. Bless you if this works for you – it was more willpower than I could muster!

Power pumping

Power pumping, what I sometimes call dry pumping, is when you pump for an extended time after the milk has stopped flowing. Power pumping should be done with a good distraction present – a movie, a good book, a phone call to a distant friend. You can do this several times a week, up to once a day. Just hook up your pump on a relatively gentle cycle and let it run for about 30 minutes. Stop if you start to feel any soreness – this shouldn't hurt! A power pumping session simulates a baby lolling at the breast for a long time, and should result in a boost in supply within a few days. If done right, it can also be a nice relaxing time for you, and you may get more milk than you expected from it. Go into a power pumping session not expecting to get any milk, but just use it as a tool to increase your supply a few days down the road.

Other ways to increase total pumping time

Pump longer each session

Add 5-10 minutes per pumping session. With good relaxation, a lot of moms can get a second letdown, and several more ounces per session. At a minimum, it "places the order" for more milk in a few days.

Add an early morning session

If you can predict when your baby is going to wake up, you can pump before your baby wakes up. Even if you pump both sides, your baby can extract milk better than any pump. You can nurse when he wakes up, then again at drop-off or immediately before you leave.

Pump on the weekends

If you pump just once a day on the weekend, you send your body the message that more milk needs to be made. You'll also stash away a little extra milk in the fridge if you fall short one day during the week.

A Note on Weekly vs. Daily Supply/Demand Balance:
In an ideal situation, a mother's milk production and her baby's intake are perfectly balanced every single day. However, for the working mom, sometimes this just isn't a reality. A long meeting means a missed session one day, an early pickup means one less bottle given at daycare. Striving to balance each day is an excellent goal, but balance week by week should be the bottom line. If you miss a pumping session one day, be sure to add in extras later in the week. Weekend pumping can be used to make up for mid-week shortfalls.

After nursing all weekend, a lot of moms find their supply highest on Mondays – lowest on Fridays. As long as the amount pumped equals the amount your baby drinks for the whole week, you're on a maintainable schedule. Stockpiling a bit extra on Monday for a shortfall on Friday works fine, and then it all comes back into balance over a long weekend of nursing.

Pumping efficiently

Pumping results can be affected by technique – both physical and psychological. First the physical:

Pump settings

A breastpump does not really work like a straw – sucking milk out by brute force. The secret is in the let-down. A good pump works by simulating the sucking of your baby to stimulate a let-down. Once the milk is ejected from the milk glands into the ducts behind the nipple, the pump can then gently remove the milk with suction. Babies have all different suction rates and intensities, and so do most breastpumps. Play around with the settings until you achieve the fastest let-down, the milk flow will follow. If you have been using your pump at the highest setting, experiment with slowing the rate or decreasing the suction and see if this more closely mimics the sucking action of your baby. It may be that a more gentle suction at a faster rate changes your response, or a you may need a stronger and slower suction.

Troubleshoot your pump

An often overlooked cause of a drop in pumping output is a problem with the pump. If you got a used pump from someone, be sure that you replace the valves before starting to use it. Valves should be replaced periodically (maybe every six months or so) in new pumps as well.

> The valves in the Ameda pumps are the white cone-like things with a slit in the end. In the Medela pumps, they are the white flippy membranes about the size of a dime. In an Isis, the valve is the white dime-sized rubber piece with a star on one side.

Also, check the tubing for leaks by plugging one end with your finger and blowing in the other end; no air should escape. Check around the flanges for cracks in the plastic, and replace as necessary. There are plenty of companies on the Internet selling replacement parts, and any time I've ordered, I've gotten the parts in 2-3 days. Finally, if you have a used pump that's been in use for more than a year, the motor may have tanked on you. Many lactation consultants have machines that can test the suction on your pump.

To see if the problem is your pump, you may just want to rent a hospital-grade pump for a month (it runs about $50) and see if you have a jump in supply. The boxes are ugly and heavy, but often the increased, or just different, suction can work wonders to boost your output.

Try a different pump

This is related to the above – I found with my first pump (a Medela Pump In Style) that my output gradually decreased over time. The pump was the same, the motor was fine, valves were good, but output was decreasing. I was sure it was a problem with my pump's motor, so I rented a Lactina for a month (commonly known as a 'hospital-grade pump'). I was so pleased when my pumping output went up almost immediately. So, convinced that my pump was defective, I ordered a new one (an Ameda Purely Yours). However, it had not arrived by the time the Lactina rental was up, so I was stuck with my old pump for a few days. Amazingly, switching to the old pump, I had another boost in supply. Then when the new one arrived, another jump. What was going on?

I concluded that sometimes a different pump can cause an increase in output just because it's *different*. I guess our bodies get used to a certain stimulation and stop responding to it as well, and sometimes mixing it up a bit can help. There isn't really a practical way to implement this suggestion on a regular basis, and I'm not recommending trading pumps with your friends every month, but maybe renting a hospital-grade pump for one month when you're in a slump is worth a try.

Pumping psychology

This is perhaps the most important piece – the psychological component of effective pumping. Stress and worrying about how much you're pumping really can inhibit a let-down – here are a few ways around it.

Relaxation

Mostly pumping efficiently means learning to RELAX while you're pumping. It's so hard when you're worried about pumping enough, but relaxation is the number one way to increase your pumping output. Sometimes herbs can help this – the Bach flower essences Rescue Remedy is a well known let-down enhancer for pumping. But my number one tip for this is – **Don't Look at the Bottles!** Read an article online, stare out the window, look at the wall – but for some reason, watching the bottles and counting ounces is the number one way for me to abruptly halt a letdown. Close your eyes if you have to. Picture waterfalls, milk trucks spilling on the highway, whatever it takes.

There are also relaxation exercises you can do to condition yourself to relax when you're pumping. A nice website called The Working Cow has a good relaxation routine, which I have paraphrased here. This is based on principles of biofeedback, and was written up for the website by Diane O'Brien Juve.

1. Start by taking slow, deep abdominal breaths, maybe 15 to 20. Count to 4 slowly with each inhalation and exhalation. Breathing should be done slowly and deliberately through this whole relaxation exercise. You're training your body to relax in association with this breathing pattern, so the breathing is the core of the practice.

2. Next, single out one part of your body, for example, your fists, your toes, your legs, etc. Create as much tension as you can in this part of your body and hold for 5 seconds (for example, by clenching your fists, or curling your toes). Keep the rest of your body completely relaxed. Then completely relax for 5 seconds. Tense and relax individual body parts on and off at 5-10 second intervals while concentrating on deep relaxed breathing. You can tense and relax as many different muscle groups in your body as you want, even working head to toe or toe to head. Just stay focused on the relaxed breathing. (This is paraphrased from Jacobsen's Progressive Relaxation exercises.)

3. As you relax, you will feel increased heat in your fingers and toes – this is because your sympathetic nervous system, the one that controls the "fight or flight" stress response, is being inhibited by the relaxation.

4. These exercises take time, so don't rush. The key is that once you get used to doing these relaxation exercises, beginning the focused breathing alone will increase your state of relaxation, and along with it, your letdown of milk

into the bottle. It may take a week or so of training yourself to relax "on command," but you can get quite good at it in a short time with these exercises.

A note on biology: There are two branches of your autonomic nervous system, the sympathetic and parasympathetic. These control all of the "involuntary" functions of your body, including milk let-down. The sympathetic nervous system responds to stress by increasing your heart rate and breathing, shunting blood to your muscles and away from your digestive system, and making you more alert – remember "fight or flight" from high school biology? The parasympathetic nervous system causes your body to relax, decreasing heart rate and breathing, etc, and also – increasing milk let-down. The sympathetic and parasympathetic nervous systems work in opposition to each other. However, the sympathetic nervous system tends to be dominant, and has a pesky habit of responding to any and all stresses as if you were being chased by a tiger – including inhibiting milk let-down. So, long story short, if you're worried about pumping enough (=stress), your milk let-down is actually inhibited by your brain. Sucks, doesn't it? But that's why it's important to learn to relax.

Feed your mama-body

There are three primary ingredients in breastmilk – water, protein and fat. Be sure your body has enough of these to make milk. For some reason, the fat is pretty efficiently moved from your butt, belly and thighs into the milk even if you don't have much in your diet (hooray for biology!), but protein and water are different. You need a high daily intake of protein and water to keep milk production up. Try keeping peanuts in your desk, or bringing hard-boiled eggs with your lunch. And be sure you have a big water cup or bottle that sits on your desk at the ready all day. Dehydration is Lactation Enemy Number One! If you don't like drinking a lot of water, try juice, flavored seltzer, or decaf iced tea. Try to avoid lots of sodas, even diet sodas, or caffeinated beverages, since they dehydrate you even more.

For the sake of completeness, I will point out that numerous scientific studies have shown that there is virtually zero correspondence between a mother's diet and her milk output – when a baby and mother are together. However, throwing separation and a pump into the mix seems to change things, and a lot of pumping moms report that their pumping output goes up with drinking more water or eating more protein. Strictly anecdotal evidence, but it can't hurt, can it?

Galactogogues and herbs

A galactogogue is any substance that causes an increase in milk production and supply. These can be dietary changes, herbal remedies, or pharmaceuticals.

Dietary milk boosters

The number one dietary galactogogue is supposedly oatmeal. Perhaps this is an old wives tale, but I know dozens of women who swear by it. There are many ways to add oatmeal to your diet: Oatmeal for breakfast, Oatmeal granola bars, Oatmeal cookies, Oatmeal breading on your chicken (OK, I made that last one up). And, like many old wives tales – it may work, it may not, but oatmeal is a hearty, high-fiber nutritious food, so what could be the harm in eating more?

B vitamins are also thought to boost supply, as are vitamin-B-rich hops – but I'm thinking the experts here mean more than just in beer. Brewers yeast is rich in B vitamins, and should not be confused with the yeast that gives us yeast infections and thrush, which is called candida. Brewers yeast can be added to all kinds of foods – sprinkled on popcorn is my personal favorite, or just mixed by the spoonful into whatever you're cooking to increase your vitamin B intake.

Herbal milk boosters

There are many herbs and herbal concoctions used to increase milk supply. Fenugreek is probably the most well known, either taken alone or as part of an herbal blend. Listed here are several herbal remedies and their recommended usages. It should be noted that herbal milk supply boosters seem to work incredibly well for some women, and not at all for others. If one works particularly well for you, it may not work for someone else, but they may thrive on something that was worthless for you. They are not free of side effects, and Things to Watch Out For are noted for some of the remedies. Many people are more comfortable with natural herbal remedies than pharmaceuticals, and they have the advantage of being available without a prescription.

Fenugreek

Fenugreek is an herb used in middle-eastern cooking, and has also been used as the "natural flavoring" in artificial maple syrup. Fenugreek is available in capsule form at many health food stores, or can be ordered by them. The typical dosage is three capsules three times a day, modified until your sweat and urine smell slightly of maple. It can also be taken in combination with an equal dose of Blessed Thistle, the combination recommended by Dr. Jack Newman for low milk supply.

Things to Watch Out For: Fenugreek is known to increase the anticoagulant effect of warfarin, exacerbate asthma, and have a hypoglycemic effect. It should not be taken by anyone with diabetes, asthma or any bleeding disorders (including both mother and baby). Fenugreek should also be avoided in pregnancy. The maple scent to your urine should not be confused with Maple Syrup Urine disease, a severe metabolic disorder. It is just a normal byproduct of taking in a lot of fenugreek.

Alfalfa

"If you want to make a lot of milk, eat like a cow" is the old-time reasoning behind adding alfalfa as a galactogogue, but it does seem to work. Alfalfa can cause allergic reactions in some people, but it is a pretty incredible food. Alfalfa is high in B vitamins as well as Vitamin K (an essential clotting factor – so it should not be taken by those with clotting disorders). In addition, if you're still taking pre-natal vitamins and have "issues" (i.e. constipation) with taking such high doses of iron, alfalfa is a wonderful natural laxative. Alfalfa tablets or capsules are more readily available than fenugreek. The dose on the bottle says three tablets three times a day – I found the laxative effects a bit too aggressive at that dose, and felt like two capsules twice a day helped maintain my supply and my fiber intake.

Other plants

Other herbs in this category include blessed thistle (not milk thistle), anise, fennel, goat's rue, etc. I am not as familiar with the effects of these herbs taken alone, but they are often included in herbal blends. History shows that many of these herbs were used for breast augmentation purposes, so it kind of makes sense that they might also increase milk-producing tissue.

Herbs to avoid

Sage is known to deplete milk supply. It is difficult to get a high enough amount of sage in your diet to decrease your supply, but it has been known to happen. If you're having supply problems, cut out sage from your cooking for a while. I've also heard that peppermint and wintergreen can decrease supply, but don't know the source or validity of this information. I just know I gave up my beloved peppermint tea as soon as I heard this information.

Herbal Blends: More Milk Tincture

More Milk Tincture was the herbal galactogogue that really worked for me. It's available from a company called Motherlove Herbals (at some health food stores, or readily available on the Internet). This is a liquid extract of several herbs (also available in capsule form). The dosage is one dropperful per waking hour until milk supply is seen to increase, then gradually decrease the dose until the desired supply is maintained. This blend contains fenugreek, so it should be avoided if you are pregnant, but they conveniently sell a fenugreek-free formulation called More Milk Two for nursing and pregnant mothers. This stuff is pretty nasty – but you just put the dropperful into a shot glass of water and down-the-hatch. It helps if you had practice with drinks like Cement Mixers in college.

Mothers Milk Tea

This tea is from the Traditional Medicinals tea company (who also make a terrific herbal Throat Coat tea for sore throats that is amazingly comforting). Again, this is a blend of herbs, but in tea form. It also contains fenugreek and many of the other herbs listed above. The recommended dose is three cups per day. Some moms find this tea absolutely unpalatable, but I find that enough honey makes any tea drinkable, and I was weird enough to actually like it.

Medications

Your last resort should be pharmaceuticals. As of this writing, the pharmaceutical situation in the United States is complicated. Reglan used to be the drug of choice for milk supply issues, but once Domperidone became available on the U.S. market, it became much more widely used than Reglan. Domperidone has few side effects and is considered very safe for nursing mothers, however the FDA has recently issued a warning that domperidone should not be considered safe as a galactogogue. There is some investigation into where this recommendation is coming from. The studies on which the warning is based found some cases of heart trouble in people taking intravenous domperidone at doses hundreds of times higher than the oral dose used for milk supply issues. This is true of many drugs deemed safe for nursing mothers, so it's a bit of a puzzle why domperidone has been singled out at this time. In addition, domperidone is used in other countries to treat reflux in babies, so passage of the drug in the milk is not a problem, as the dose used to treat reflux is considered safe for infants, and is much much higher than the amount that passes in the milk.

For both domperidone and Reglan, you should know that using them to increase milk supply is considered "off-label" use. This means that the FDA has approved the drugs for other uses, but not for increasing milk supply. It is legal and safe to prescribe drugs for off-label use, but your doctor may not be able to find information in the standard references. The decision to use an off-label drug is one that is considered to be in the realm of "the practice of medicine," and thus is between the doctor and patient. For more information on these drugs, please refer to Dr. Jack Newman's handouts on Domperidone (www.breastfeedingonline.com/domperidone.shtml and Reglan http://www.breastfeedingonline.com/reglan.shtml) or his book *The Ultimate Breastfeeding Book of Answers*.

The Breastfeeding After Reduction website (www.bfar. org/domperidone.shtml) maintains current information about the Domperidone issue, which includes statements from several prominent breastfeeding researchers. The International Academy of Compounding Pharmacists even posted a statement to their own membership stating that the FDA overstepped its bounds, and stating that they should still provide Domperidone when it is prescribed. Unfortunately, this statement was removed from their website. You can view this statement on my website at www. workandpump.com/domperidone.htm.

So, all caveats aside, there are many moms who, when separated from their babies, just cannot respond to the pump the way they do to a baby, and when all other methods fail, these drugs can be a real blessing. They increase supply effectively and rapidly, and in the case of domperidone, without significant side effects. Reglan should not be taken by anyone with a history of depression or migraine, as depression and headaches are among the potential side effects.

Supply problems in older babies

Once your baby is taking solids well, supply issues can be dealt with differently, and are not nearly as complicated. Just because you need to supplement your baby's intake of breastmilk during the day, it doesn't mean that the supplement needs to be formula. Once your baby can take a variety of nutritious foods (well, at least two or three), you can use solid food as a supplement to the breastmilk that you are able to pump. I say this assuming that you are nursing as much as possible when you are together, so that your baby only needs to be supplemented about 1/3 of the time (the 8 hours you are at work each day).

If this is the case, see if your daycare can encourage your baby to eat more solids during the day to reduce the need for as many bottles. The easiest way to do this is to just let them do ALL of the solid food feeding. Nurse before drop-off, then let them feed breakfast or cereal or baby food. Have them space lunch between morning and afternoon bottles, then let them feed him "dinner" about an hour before you get there. Then when you are together, only offer the breast. This way he is getting as much breastmilk as possible "from the tap," while learning to eat a variety of other foods during the day. Daytime is for food, evening and night is time for mommy's milk. This can get you through a lot of slumps, and for me it worked till my kids were about 9 or 10 months old (at which time they wanted food at home as well...)

> Important: Don't forget to feed your kid on the weekend! You'll be in the habit of only offering the breast, when they're in the habit of sitting at the table for some spoon action. Offer the breast first, but don't forget to throw in a meal or two as well on the weekend! It can be slightly less food than they usually get at daycare, since she'll be getting more milk from you than you can pump. I can remember leaving to be out for the day with my son after he'd started solids, and totally forgetting to pack food for him. Then I wondered why he was nursing all day long...

Even if your baby is getting some solid foods at home during the week, be sure you're offering the breast first so that the maximum amount of their diet is perfect, nutritious breastmilk.

If your baby is almost a year old, ask your doctor about adding in alternate milks during the day instead of formula. Even if you're not ready to introduce cow's milk, many babies enjoy having a few ounces of rice milk or soy milk. In addition, yogurt and cheese can be used to supplement during the day as well. The key is variety – once your baby is taking less breastmilk, she will need sources of protein and iron, as well as vitamins and fiber. As long as your baby can eat a variety of foods, I don't think that formula needs to be one of them.

Overfeeding at daycare

A woman I had just met, Hannah, emailed me to ask about how she could pump more. She had taken my class on working and breastfeeding, and said "I remember you said something about overfeeding at daycare, I wonder if that's why I can't keep up?" I asked her a bit about her situation – her baby was only 14 weeks old, she was pumping between 16 and 18 ounces a day, and her daycare was giving her baby 23 ounces a day! In 9 hours!! Just so we're clear, that is a LOT of milk for a 14 week old baby. I asked Hannah if her baby was nursing much at night, and she said "No, not really at all. A little before bed and maybe once in the morning." No wonder she was having to pump so much.

Sadly, this is woefully common.

Babies will almost always take more than they need from a bottle as long as it's just flowing into their mouths. One post on a message board told of trying a bottle with a 5 week old baby, and then being amazed that the baby gulped down 3 ounces in a few minutes, and still "fussed for more." So they gave the baby a second 3-ounce bottle, which she also finished. The baby was still fussing, so they put her to breast, where she immediately fell asleep. The poster's interpretation of this event was that her baby was going to need more than 6 ounces for each feeding. My interpretation was that it was a fast-flow nipple, and the baby just kept swallowing as milk poured into her mouth. She was probably fussing because her belly was alarmingly full. Once she got to the comfort of the breast, she was able to relax and fall asleep. I'd bet that if the baby had been held and rocked after the first bottle, she would have been content, or maybe would have had a huge burp, but didn't actually need more food.

My friend Jen tells a funny story about overfeeding:

Aidan normally took about 10-12 ounces a day. The teachers were usually good about holding him off until I got there so we could nurse at the end of the day. When I was pumping at work, I generally had just enough, so this help was really great. But we had one teacher who wouldn't hold him off at all – one day she fed him 24 ounces! She told me "oh, he's just been hungry all day!" I got there and it was obvious that he had not slept at all – he was just exhausted. Luckily she wasn't there for too long. Usually our daycare was really good about this.

As my friend Beth put it, there is a "bottle-feeding culture" at a lot of daycares, and they are just so used to giving a bottle whenever a baby is crying, or at certain scheduled times of day. This is how your baby might be getting more than they need, or it may be that they're urging your baby to finish bottles once they're started, or feeding instead of trying other comfort measures.

How to avoid overfeeding

- Find out how your care provider is soothing your baby. Some babies like to be held a lot, and will cry when they are put down. Sometimes this crying is mistaken for hunger, resulting in feeds when they are not necessary. See if your care provider will try carrying your baby in a sling or front-carrier until they are a little older.

- Use the slowest flow nipples your baby will take. We never graduated from the newborn flow nipples, which my kids were still using at a year.

- Make sure your care provider knows never to encourage your baby to finish a bottle once she has stopped sucking or turned away. Babies know when they've had enough.

- Let your care provider know it's OK to re-use a bottle your baby has already started. This can prevent pressure to finish bottles.

- Send slightly smaller amounts in bottles. Just because a baby can finish a 6-ounce bottle doesn't mean that they won't be satisfied after 5 ounces. Just like when I have a second piece of pie put in front of me, I'll eat it, when really, I would have been quite satisfied without any dessert at all. The five helpings of mashed potatoes were really sufficient.

- Let your daycare feed all solid foods that your baby is taking. By offering only the breast at home, you can make sure your baby gets as much breastmilk as possible, while still having plenty of choices available for feeding times at daycare.

    ဆ Think about offering a pacifier if your baby needs a lot of non-nutritive sucking for comfort. Try to leave the pacifier at daycare if you can, so that your baby does all her sucking at the breast when you are home.

Pacifiers

Wow, a whole section on pacifiers, what's the big deal? Pacifiers can be used for a lot of good reasons, and misused for just as many. Here's the dirt on pacifiers – scientific fact mixed with a healthy dose of my opinion, as usual.

Pacifiers and sleep safety

Unfortunately, pacifiers are at the heart of a very confusing debate right now (the early spring of 2006). The American Academy of Pediatrics (AAP) has just released a statement that recommends pacifiers for all babies to help prevent SIDS, also known as Sudden Infant Death Syndrome, where babies die for no apparent reason, usually in their sleep (AAP Task Force on SIDS, 2005). What we're learning about SIDS shows that it seems to happen mostly when babies sleep too deeply, so keep this in mind when you get frustrated with your baby waking up every two hours – this is normal and healthy for babies up to about six months of age – when the incidence of SIDS drops dramatically. It is true that sucking during sleep keeps babies in a lighter sleep state, which seems to be protective against SIDS, but why recommend a pacifier over sucking at the breast? Studies have shown that pacifiers were protective against SIDS, especially in premature infants, but these studies don't take into account whether the babies were breastfed or not, whether the breastfeeding was exclusive or supplemented, and whether the babies had access to the breast during the night (these studies are cited in the AAP statement). Many sleep researchers believe that if a baby is breastfed and sleeps close to her mother, enough natural sucking takes place that a pacifier is not needed. Additionally, sleeping close to mom helps regulate a baby's breathing and sleep cycles so they don't fall too deeply asleep. If your baby sleeps near you (in the same room or in your bed), nurses some at night, and doesn't seem to need a pacifier,

I myself would not push it just for the sake of SIDS protection. Again, just my opinion, not medical advice, but I have looked at the literature and don't see a reason to push a pacifier in a breastfed baby. For the record, the AAP recommendations were met with quite a bit of controversy. The US Breastfeeding Committee wrote a response to the AAP statement (www.usbreastfeeding.org/News-and-Events/USBC-SIDS-PR-10-17-2005.pdf), as did La Leche League (www.lalecheleague.org/Release/sids.html), both refuting the basis for a blanket pacifier recommendation.

While I don't believe that pacifiers are needed to insure safe sleep for breastfed babies, they do have their place, particularly for a working mom. Read on.

Pacifiers and comfort sucking

Many well-meaning advice givers warn against letting your baby "use you as a human pacifier." However, there is no reason on earth to limit your baby's time at the breast if you don't feel like it. I think many of us don't realize the extent of a baby's need for sucking – sucking gets them their food, helps them feel calm and content, lets them know that mom is near. Sucking satisfies more needs than just hunger. If you are uncomfortable with a lot of sucking, first make sure your baby has a good latch. If the latch is not quite right, "comfort sucking" can be excruciating. But if your baby is latched correctly, you shouldn't feel any pain, and non-nutritive sucking can be very relaxing for both of you. It can be very hard to just let yourself sit with your baby, but I think there is value to this exercise! Teach yourself to sit down and enjoy this quiet time with your baby – time to just sit is so lacking in our busy world, isn't it?

So – if that zen-like mantra doesn't work for you, and you just need to *get up out of this chair already,* you can try wearing your baby as you walk around. Sometimes movement is as relaxing as sucking. You can let your baby suck your finger. And, if a couple of months have gone by, if you have no breastfeeding problems at all, and you're just going crazy with all the sucking and your baby hasn't found her thumb or fingers yet, then fine, get the pacifier.

Pacifier vs. thumb-sucking

You may wonder what my experience was – I had two kids with very high sucking needs. My mother-in-law started my son on a pacifier when he was two months old (you can see the section in Chapter 2 on childcare for the full story – I was in no position to object) and he never looked back. He'd been nursing a lot and working the fingernails off my hand one by one sucking on my fingers before the pacifier started, so we happily embraced it. Then less happily as he passed one, then two, then three... let it be known that I have no willpower at all when it comes to getting rid of a pacifier, and we have a slight jaw alignment issue to show for it. So, if you start a pacifier, I recommend "losing" it as close to a year as you can – it does indeed get harder to get rid of. I'm a little embarrassed as a breastfeeding advocate to look back at all the baby pictures with the binky in them, but hey, you do the best you can, right? One thing I will say for the pacifier is that it made it really easy to keep mittens on in the winter – he never tried to take them off to suck on his hand like my daughter did.

My daughter bypassed the pacifier for her thumb, which she found at about 8 weeks and has yet to lose. As a mom of an infant, I was so pleased to have a thumb-sucker. She was a calm baby anyway, but the thumb gave her a phenomenal ability to soothe herself. And guess what? You can't lose it, it never falls out of the bed, and you don't have to get up in the night to find it. A hungry baby will never choose the thumb over the breast. A toddler has to take their thumb out of their mouth to talk or carry things, so you don't get that annoying "talking around the binky." Full disclosure – my daughter is only 3 now, and yes, she still sucks her thumb. She's not "allowed" to suck it at daycare anymore except for naptime, so she's able to limit it. Yes, her baby teeth came in a little funny around it, and I may completely change my tune when I get the first orthodontist bill, but at this point, I have no complaints (except for the aforementioned mitten issue). She still gets great comfort from sucking her thumb when she's tired, and it's oral satisfaction that's non-fattening, nicotine-free, doesn't use any resources and doesn't hurt anyone. If she wants to suck her thumb in college, I really don't care. And I think peer pressure takes care of most of the public sucking.

Pacifier cautions

If your baby is using a pacifier, make sure they're still eating enough. Don't plug in the binky with every cry – always check first to see if your baby is hungry. A baby who is "hungry all the time" may just be going through a growth spurt or may not have taken much from bottles that day, and overusing a pacifier can lead to not eating enough (although most babies will ultimately spit out the pacifier if they're hungry enough). Pacifiers can cause jaw alignment problems and can increase tooth decay, so try to get rid of it before your baby is old enough to be as addicted as my son got! As for how to get rid of the pacifier – I'm not the one to ask, I'm no good at it. My friend Kim trimmed the tip off of her son Wyatt's pacifier so that it sucked flat and then he didn't like it anymore. You have to watch for sharp edges, but it worked for her, right at 12 months. Other ideas are to limit where your baby can use the pacifier – like just in the car or just in bed, but my friend Becka's son Dylan will go get in his bed in the middle of the day just to suck the bink. At least he understands the limits!

Pacifiers to avoid overfeeding at daycare

Many breastfeeding advocates are strictly anti-pacifier. But I think there is a real place for the pacifier for a baby who consistently needs more and more from bottles during the day and mom is having trouble pumping enough. It could be that this baby just has a high need to suck. And, it could be that your care provider is giving a bottle every time this baby is fussy, which is satisfying, since the baby does need to suck – but ends up being way more food than your baby needs.

If the amount your baby is taking during the day is always more than you can pump, how do you tell if your baby is being overfed, or if you're not keeping up with his needs?

It's pretty easy to tell if your baby is being overfed at daycare. He won't be hungry when you pick him up and won't nurse much in the evening or at night. He'll be growing on or ahead of his growth curve, and may refuse to eat when you offer. This baby is a prime candidate for a pacifier at daycare. If your baby is eating too much when all he really needs is to suck, a pacifier can really save the day. If at all possible, leave it at daycare and only provide sucking at the breast when you are at home. A pacifier is addictive, for babies *and* for parents. It's so easy to just "plug in" your baby when they cry – but if you avoid the pacifier when you are with your baby, you can learn a lot more about other ways to soothe them.

If your baby is nursing a lot at night, is hungry when you pick him up and you're not able to pump enough to meet his needs, then you'll want to turn to the "Troubleshooting supply issues " section at the beginning of this chapter and skip the pacifier. Keep an eye on your baby's growth curve (remember to use the one for breastfed babies – see the section "Do I need to supplement?" for more information about normal growth in breastfed babies) and watch for signs of dehydration, like crying without tears, sunken eyes, and excessive sleepiness.

Help! I forgot my ....!

Note – you may want to photocopy this section and keep a copy of it at work…

First of all, you are not alone!! Every single pumping mom I've ever known has forgotten some key piece of equipment one day. If you're lucky, you live close to home or have somebody who can run something over to you. If not, you can improvise just about anything.

Forgotten bottles

If you have forgotten your collection bottles, this is inconvenient, but not the end of the world. In most pumps, the valve in the flange unit creates the suction above the level of the bottle, so the bottles do not need to fit tightly to have suction. Using a substitution bottle, you can rest the pump flanges over it, and use it for collecting. This is a lot easier if you have a hands-free setup (as described in Chapter 5 "Starting Pumping and Bottles"), so that you can hook the flanges to your bra, and then use both hands to hold the bottles in place. So – where do you get a substitute collection bottle? Luckily, most of us work near a drug store or convenience store, and have access to a microwave. If this is the case, buy a glass bottle (must be glass) or your favorite beverage and drink it all. Next, rinse out the bottle (you don't need to wash with soap). Finally, put about 1 inch of water in the bottom of the bottle and cover it with something microwave safe – plastic wrap, a piece of a plastic bag, the plastic cap it came with (not a metal cap!). Microwave for one minute on high – the water will boil and steam-sterilize the inside of the bottle. If the bottle came with a metal lid, just wash it well in hot water with soap.

And, this will be the reminder you needed to always keep a few spare collection bags in your desk. If you have collection bags, you can use a rubber band to attach them to the bottom opening of the flanges without the bag holder.

Forgotten ice packs

If you forget your ice packs, there are a few options. One is to store the milk in the fridge at your workplace (well labeled, of course) and then just hurry home at the end of the day. An hour or so at room temperature won't harm the milk, just refrigerate or freeze it as soon as you get home. If you don't have access to a fridge, your nearby drug store will come in handy again. In the section of the store where the pain relievers are you can generally find some sports-use instant cold packs. With these, you squeeze to break open a bag inside the pack, mix by shaking, and get instant cold that should last for several hours. If you don't have an insulated container to keep them in, some drug stores or grocery stores sell small Styrofoam containers for a dollar or two, or you can ask at the butcher or fish department of a grocery store for one of the insulated boxes in which their food is shipped.

Forgotten pump

OK, this one is the biggest challenge, but you can manage! Many things effectively count as a forgotten pump – including forgetting the power supply (unless your pump will also run on batteries), forgetting the valves or membranes (keep an extra set in your desk) or the forgetting the tubing. All of these effectively render your pump useless, but fear not, even this is manageable.

First, remember that you've followed my every word of advice and have already learned the fine art of hand expression. (And if you didn't, you will now, right?) So – now you can get the milk out, what do you do with it? Sterilize a collection bottle as described above, and do your best to direct all of the various ducts into the bottle. You'll probably want to spread some paper towels or your jacket in your lap before taking this on, but it can be done. You can also express into a clean coffee cup or bowl and then transfer the milk to a bottle.

Or – if you're close to a baby supply store of some sort and don't already own my favorite back-up pump of all time, the Avent Isis, now may be the time to run out and buy one! It's a purchase you won't regret (and I really have no financial stock in the company, honest) and it will make your forgotten pump day fly by in style.

Forgotten presentation for the boss

Sorry, can't help you with this one. Good luck! Maybe the daycare will call with a sick kid and you can put it off till tomorrow…

Nighttime parenting

Parenting at night can be particularly exhausting for a working parent. You don't have the luxury of lying down for a few minutes when your baby is napping during the day, or of scheduling a less taxing day after a particularly trying night.

There are a million books on the market to help you train your baby to sleep longer, so I'm not going to venture into that realm at all. Besides, I don't know that it's always the best idea. Babies need to eat at night, and if you go away to work, they miss you. Nighttime can be a time to spend some special time with your baby, to enjoy breastfeeding without the mechanics of the pump involved, and to just appreciate this tiny little person who really (really) will only be this small for a short time.

I know, the little old ladies who say "enjoy it while it lasts" haven't been up at 2 AM with a screaming baby any time since the Nixon administration, but they do have a point – it is only for a short time, and when they're annoying teenagers, you'll always have the memory of that sweet milk-drunk face staring up at you in the moonlight.

If you're a person who absolutely needs uninterrupted sleep, then I recommend *The No-Cry Sleep Solution: Gentle ways to help your baby sleep through the night* by Elizabeth Pantley to help teach your baby to sleep longer on their own. I also like Harvey Karp's book *The Happiest Baby on the Block: The New Way to Calm Crying and Help Your Newborn Baby Sleep Longer*. However, many of us can adapt to occasional wakings if they're not too disruptive. This is where shared sleep comes in – and in my opinion, it's the secret to making "breastfeeding" and "a good night's rest" fit in the same sentence. Try bringing your baby to bed with you.

What?? – you cry – if she's in bed with me, she'll nurse all night long – how is *that* supposed to get me more sleep?? Well, I'll tell you a secret if you promise not to tell my husband. If your baby is sleeping with you, you can feed her *without waking all the way up*. I can remember mornings when my husband would get up and say "boy, you had a really rough night. Kai was up so many times to feed – you must be so tired. Here, let me take him, I'll go get your breakfast." I would agree with him, that indeed, the night had been rough, wondering what on earth he was talking about, but certainly enjoying the service. I could remember one, maybe two feedings at most, and only in the haziest way. After the first few nights with my son in bed with us, I got used to just rolling over, getting him latched on, and both of us drifting back to sleep. If you tend to leak a lot, you may want a towel under your chest and your baby's head, but that was the only adjustment we made. If your baby needs to burp after feeding, you can sit up and do it without leaving your bed (and your partner can do diaper changes, Thanks Hon!), but for the most part, you'll feel like you're getting a mostly uninterrupted night of sleep.

Another reason that shared sleep provides improved rest is that your baby will fall back asleep faster. If she were down the hall, she would have to wake all the way up to get your attention, crying to let you know she was hungry. Since your baby is right there with you, you can respond to her earlier feeding cues, like little coos and grunts, and you can start to feed before she gets all worked up. After eating, she'll tend to settle back down faster as well. Try it for a week, you'll be hooked.

The safety of shared sleep

But isn't co-sleeping dangerous? There was a study released in 1998 by the US Consumer Product Safety Commission showing that babies were at an increased risk of death when sleeping in bed with an adult. This study got a lot of press attention at the time, but has since been exposed as having many flaws. First, the study did not take into account the presence of alcohol or drugs in the parents. Obviously, you should not co-sleep if you are under the influence of anything that makes you less alert – even a strong nighttime cold medicine.

In addition, the study did not consider if the mother was breastfeeding. Breastfed babies are at an infinitesimally low risk of harm when sleeping next to their mothers. Nobody quite understands why, but co-sleeping is actually protective against SIDS in breastfed babies. They are thought to get in tune with their mother's breathing rhythm, which helps them "remember" to breath through the night. The only people who should not co-sleep are smokers, as smoking somehow interferes with infant sleep making co-sleeping more dangerous. In addition, there is some thought that very obese women should not co-sleep because of loss of peripheral nerve sensitivity, but I don't think this is very well supported by the research.

Finally, studies showing increased risk with bed-sharing often do not take into account the sleep surface of the adult bed. Is it free of heavy blankets? Is there any way for an infant to become trapped? It is possible to make an adult bed safe for a baby, but it does take a little bit of work.

The AAP released a statement in 2005 that recommended against bed-sharing with infants, but this is because co-sleeping is a very complicated public health message. There is a long list of qualifiers: you should not sleep with your baby if you smoke, if you take any drugs or have been drinking, if your bed is too soft, if you have heavy comforters and pillows, if the baby could fall off or get trapped against the wall, if there are other children in the bed, if you are not breastfeeding, or if you have a waterbed. Do you see how this is a very hard message to portray in a sound bite like "back to sleep" or "babies should be in a carseat"? It can be confusing, and there are questions like "how firm is a firm mattress" that are hard to answer in black and white.

In short, here are the guidelines:

- ∞ Babies should sleep only on a firm sleep surface. Crib mattresses are a good indicator of how firm is firm enough. Deep pillowtop mattresses aren't a good idea. Sheets should fit tightly and obviously not have any holes in them.

- ∞ Keep pillows and blankets away from your baby's head and face. This doesn't mean you can't use them. If the baby's head is by your breast, your pillow should be out of the way. I started sleeping in a warm shirt, and keeping the blankets at waist level when my babies were tiny.

- ∞ The baby should only be covered by a light blanket, or better yet, should just sleep in temperature-appropriate sleepware.

- ∞ Don't overdress your baby. Your body temperature will keep them warmer than if they were sleeping alone.

- ∞ If you have a gap between your bed and a wall, fill it with rolled towels so that the baby cannot get trapped there.

- ∞ Never let older children sleep next to a baby. If you have a family bed, there should be an adult between older children and the baby.

- ∞ Parents who are biologically related to the baby are more likely to be aware of where the baby is during the night.

- ∞ If your partner doesn't feel safe sleeping next to the baby, put the baby on your side of the bed. Just make sure they can't roll off or get trapped.

- ∞ Never sleep with a baby on a couch or chair – it's much more dangerous than a bed.

- ∞ Don't let your baby sleep alone in an adult bed. The presence of the parent is protective.

∞ Your baby should still sleep on their back. After breastfeeding, it is natural for babies to roll over to their back when falling asleep.

∞ No co-sleeping with drugs on board – alcohol, illegal drugs, pain killers, cold medicine all mean put the baby in a crib for the night.

Only you can decide whether co-sleeping feels right to you, but here are a few facts: In cultures where co-sleeping is common, like Japan, rates of sudden infant death syndrome (SIDS) and "overlying" (rolling over on a baby) are *extremely* low. When people from those cultures come to the United States and adopt more "Western" practices like bottle-feeding and separate rooms for babies, the SIDS rates rise to match our own.

Follow safe co-sleeping guidelines, bring your baby into your bed, and you will all have a better night's sleep.

Dr. Jay Gordon's book *Good Nights* has a lot more information about getting good rest when you are sharing sleep with a small baby – a great reference on the subject, and written in a way that's very reassuring to parents.

Co-sleeping is not for everyone, as my friend Sara is kind enough to remind me. She is a light sleeper, needs a lot of rest, and has trouble sleeping if even her husband gets too close during the night. She tried cosleeping for a while, and felt exhausted every day at work, so it was not the best solution for them. They kept each of their babies in a bassinet next to their bed for 3 or 4 months, and after that, everyone slept better with the baby in her own room. For me, having to get out of bed during the night to feed, even once, was more tiring than feeding three or four times in bed. We're all different. If you are not comfortable with the idea of having your baby in your bed, or know that you won't get good rest worrying about the baby, consider a co-sleeper (a side car bed that hooks to your bed) or having your baby's crib right next to your bed, at least for the first few months. That way you will hear your baby sooner, neither of you have to wake up as much, and you will be able to get her without getting all the way out of bed.

Whatever sleeping arrangement you choose, the evidence is very strong that babies younger than about six months should not sleep in a separate room at night, because sleeping close to parents is very protective against SIDS, which can be a tragic consequence of babies sleeping in isolation.

For more information about safe co-sleeping, be sure to check out the websites of James McKenna, a researcher and wonderfully engaging speaker who studies mother-infant sleep patterns (www.naturalchild.com/james_mckenna/ and http://www.nd.edu/%7Ejmckenn1/lab/faq.html). You can also find links to more research and information from Attachment Parenting International's website (http://www.attachmentparenting.org/cosleepindex.shtml).

Reverse cycling

Reverse cycling is when your baby does most of her nursing when you are together, and takes very little milk during her day away from you. Some people worry that co-sleeping will cause reverse cycling. Ultimately, I don't know that we really have that much control over our baby's eating preferences – but I do know that co-sleeping and reverse cycling are great bedfellows (so to speak).

Reverse cycling may seem like a drag – to be up all night nursing seems like it will be exhausting, but there are a lot of advantages. In the first place, you can rest assured that your baby is getting plenty to eat. Her constant nursing at night is your assurance that she has a healthy appetite and will not let herself starve. You get the benefit of a lot of close contact time with your baby, helping you to feel close to her as she grows. You get a wonderful supply boost from all the time your baby spends at the breast, and you probably have to pump less during the day – thus reducing your stress. Well, you say, this sounds great on paper, but when, *exactly*, am I going to be sleeping?? In general, as a strategy, co-sleeping is essential for the reverse cycling mom. If your baby decides that they want most of their milk "from the tap" and nurses all night, cosleeping will let you nurse with as few disruptions as possible.

If your baby is a particularly vigorous nurser, or if you have trouble falling back asleep, reverse cycling can indeed be tiring. You'll need to ask yourself just how tiring when deciding if you want to try to change it. If you're not pumping much during the day, are you willing to pump more if your baby wakes less at night? Is that trade-off worth it? If you decide you want your baby to sleep more at night, you can encourage your care provider to try to feed her more during the day, and you can cluster nursing sessions in the hours before bed. If you've pumped extra milk during the day, you can even try giving a bottle of milk right before your baby goes to bed (but only if you've got extra from that day – don't throw off your demand and supply balance!) In the end, I'm not sure how much these things help for a baby who just loves to wake up and be with you at night, and may just result in an uncomfortable baby with a distended stomach – but it's worth a try. Again, I'll defer to *The No-Cry Sleep Solution* for more ideas on how to get your baby sleeping longer.

Some moms actually try to encourage reverse cycling – and it's a great solution for moms who can't pump enough during the day. However, just as it's hard to get a reverse cycling baby to stop, it can also be hard to get a dedicated night-time sleeper to start waking up to eat. You can try limiting feedings during the day – just by ½ ounce per feeding, not enough that your baby will be crabby all day, just enough so that they'll be a bit hungrier at night. Bringing your baby to your bed to sleep with you encourages reverse cycling as well – and should certainly be a first strategy for the mom who struggles to pump enough.

Moms who can't pump at all should also be encouraged to co-sleep, so that the baby gets as much breastmilk as possible when baby and mom are together.

Undoing co-sleeping

When my son was born, my doctor was very supportive of co-sleeping. However, when he got to be about 6 months old, she suddenly switched course and told me that if I didn't move him to his crib soon, we'd be co-sleeping "forever." I know a lot of people share that concern about co-sleeping – it's fine when your baby is tiny, but not something you want to be doing with a 3 or 4 year old.

I can only share my own story and those of my friends, but I don't know anyone who got stuck co-sleeping against her will because she didn't move the baby to her own bed by the magic date of 6 months. We did a very gradual transition from full time co-sleeping to independent sleep that happened between 8 months and about 16 months, and really, it went just fine. Here's what we did – once my son could scooch and crawl, we didn't feel safe putting him to bed in our bed by himself, because we were afraid we wouldn't hear him wake up and he'd roll out. So we started putting him to bed in his own crib, and around this time, also gradually stopped nursing him to sleep. It is true that in order for a baby to be able to self-soothe at night, they need to be able to reproduce the conditions in which they fall asleep – so if you want your baby to sleep longer stretches at night (not before 6 months, but sometime after that), it's very convenient if they learn to fall asleep without being rocked, or nursed, or being held. (I'm happy to admit that not everyone feels this way, and many parents think it's best for babies to be soothed to sleep for as long as they need it.)

Anyway, we started a new bedtime routine in which I would nurse Kai till he was sleepy, then give him to my husband to put down in his crib. At first, he was pretty resistant to the crib; understandably, he'd never slept alone before! I had the idea that he should know that the crib is not jail, and that he could get out whenever he wanted, so there was a lot of up-and-down those first few nights, but my husband managed to get him to sleep through a combination of rocking and walking and singing and reassuring and patting of the back. Our initial routine was that the first time he woke up after we'd gone to bed, I'd just bring him into bed for the rest of the night. This worked well till he was about 9 months old, then we started to feel like maybe he could sleep longer on his own, and that we were actually waking him up moving around at night. So I started getting up and nursing him the first time he woke up, and then putting him back in his crib. Then the second time he woke up, he'd come in bed with us for the rest of the night. Doing this, we eventually had our first nights when he stayed in his own bed (aside from one feeding) all night. From there, it was just a gradual back and forth till he slept most of the night through most of the time, which was good enough for us. With my daughter, we were more used to waking up at night and having a crowded bed, so she stayed full-time in bed with us a lot longer, and by the time we moved her to her own bed, she was old enough to think it was neat to be in a room with her big brother. They still wake up and come into our bed sometimes during the night, but at this writing, they are three and five years old, and I'm pretty confident they won't want to sleep with us when they're teenagers. I'm not in such a rush for them to grow up, and when we say "go back to bed please," they do.

My friend Beth just told me that her son Marty just moved to his "big-boy bed" – and he'll be 5 in a couple of months. They chose to do the full-on family bed, and the move to the new bed was as much motivated by Marty as it was by the parents. Marty started complaining that "Daddy's hogging all the covers," and would complain when the baby woke up to nurse in the night, so he just decided it was time to move. Beth had asked him on his 4th birthday if he was ready yet, and he very much was not. But six months changed a lot, and now he sleeps all night long in his own bed. Choosing a family bed is not a life sentence, and families are amazingly adaptable to the changing needs of their members.

Sleeping through the night

Normal sleep

Sleeping through the night is like the holy grail of parenting. You're such a "good" parent if your kids sleep through, somehow a failure if they don't. But really, neither is true, and there's not that much you can do about it. Before a baby is 6 months old, they have a biological need to eat during the night, and they also have a very strong psychological need to be near their parents. Babies are not built to be alone for 10 hours at a stretch until they're much older – it's just the way they are.

And then, guess what – they sleep alone for a few years, then start the process of searching out someone else to share their bed with. Maybe human beings just aren't meant to sleep alone…

Sleep disruptions

Babies also change their sleep patterns based on what they're doing when they're awake. Sometimes a baby who always slept through the night from a very young age can start waking up a lot at night. This is far more distressing than the baby who's always been up, because you've had the luxury of some uninterrupted sleep, you can remember what you're missing. However, this too is perfectly normal – when babies are learning a new skill, it is very common for them to start waking more at night. It's like their little brains just short out and can't manage the skills of learning *and* sleeping all in the same day. (Babies also tend to eat less when they're learning something new, or regress in other skills.).Watch for signs you're about to hit a developmental milestone – rolling over, sitting up, crawling – when sleep gets rocky for a few nights, and chances are his sleep will go back to normal once the new skill has been mastered.

Another reason a baby who usually sleeps well will start waking is a growth spurt. You may have heard that formula digests more slowly, leaving baby feeling full longer, so you may be tempted to try a bottle at night. But a few nights of extra nursing at night has the effect of boosting your milk supply to meet the new needs of your bigger baby, so in the long run, the easiest thing to do is just wake up and nurse for a few nights. Be sure that you're eating particularly well around a growth spurt – extra water, extra protein – and take a couple nights to go to bed when your baby does so that you can get the rest you need. Or, if you stay up later than your baby, try waking her to nurse right before you go to bed so she'll be "topped off" for as long as possible. But you are a working mom and have to function all day, so if the extra night nursing is really wearing you out, consider co-sleeping! Honest, you really will get more sleep, and you'll wonder where all this milk is coming from during the day. Extra sleep, supply boost, what more could you want??

I really need a drink! Can I still breastfeed if I...?

What was your favorite vice that you gave up for pregnancy? Coffee? A beer after work? Wine with dinner? You may be ready to put some of these vices back into your life, but you're not sure if they're compatible with breastfeeding. I can't give you an absolute yes or no, but what I can give you is some perspective.

Alcohol and breastfeeding

The jury is surely still out on breastfeeding and alcohol. You'd be hard-pressed to find anyone who will flat-out recommend it, yet the breastfeeding advocates assure us that the "occasional" drink is safe – indeed, it is far better to have an occasional drink than to wean from breastfeeding. But what exactly does "occasional" mean, and what are the effects on the baby?

I keep this in perspective with a concept called "relative infant dose." That means that for every drug or food that you take into your body, a certain amount is passed in your milk to your baby. For some drugs, the relative infant dose is zero, meaning that none of the drug will appear in your milk. Some drugs concentrate in milk, which means that the amount in your milk will be higher than the level in your bloodstream. But in general, the amount of any drug will be somehow related to the amount of that drug in your bloodstream – the more in your blood, the more will be in your milk.

So – in terms of alcohol, let's look at percentages. Hard liquor is about 40% alcohol (that's what 80 proof means). Wine is about 15%, beer is about 6%, give or take. But what ends up in your blood? You can get some idea from your state's laws regarding drinking and driving. In Vermont, "over the limit" means 0.8%, which means that your blood as a beverage is 1.6 proof. Not a terribly strong drink, some "non-alcoholic" beers are almost that much. Alcohol does concentrate slightly in your milk, so it may be a tad higher – but remember, that's if your pretty well zooted – too drunk to legally drive.

Now you get to decide – do you give your baby a small amount of a low-alcohol drink? The younger your baby, the less mature their liver, so they don't metabolize alcohol as well as grownups, but if you have one or two glasses of wine, we're talking about a pretty small amount being passed. And if you've abstained since conception, don't worry, one or two glasses of wine will be *plenty*!

I never worried about drinking small amounts – one or two drinks in an evening (OK, once or twice there were three). I think (my opinion here) that the bigger concern if you're drinking a lot is your ability to take care of your baby – much more of a concern than the small amount of alcohol being passed in your milk.

What about pumping and dumping?

A lot of moms talk about "pump and dump" after they've had too much to drink, so the baby doesn't get the alcoholic milk. This is fine to do, but is only necessary to protect your milk supply or keep you comfortable. Alcohol clears from your milk at the same rate as it clears from your blood, so once you're sober, your milk is mostly clear of alcohol as well. However, if you're going to miss a feeding during your bender (and assuming that you have someone sober and responsible to give the baby a bottle during that time), you may need to pump for comfort or to maintain your supply. If you do pump, yes, toss the milk, it's got some ethanol on board (or keep it to sniff later if you're curious). If you don't pump, then just nurse your baby at the next feeding. The only issue is that you may be uncomfortably full.

How about coffee?

Whether or not you can drink coffee is up to your baby, not you. As you reintroduce caffeine, watch your baby, they'll let you know. Are naps shorter? Is your baby irritable? Up more at night? Loose stools and diaper rash are also a sign of too much coffee (though not a factor with tea).

It's different with every kid. With my son (who tends to be more sensitive in general), I couldn't drink any coffee at all – not even decaf. He would get terrible diarrhea and diaper rash, and would be cranky to boot. I could tolerate one or two cups of caffeinated tea, and beyond that, I'd see effects in him. When I was nursing my daughter (who, of course, has a thicker skin), she didn't care what I ate or drank. She was even-tempered, a great sleeper, and regular in her schedule in spite of my gradually increasing coffee intake. I was happy to have the lattes back in my life, and the only ill effect was that I wasn't sleeping well. I only drank 2-3 cups a day, maybe 4 before a deadline, so I'm not talking pots and pots, which would probably make any baby miserable. Just see what your baby tolerates, and if nobody's getting good rest, it might be time to cut back on the cappuccinos.

What about medications?

Most medications can be taken while breastfeeding. I talk about this more in the section called "If your doctor recommends weaning" in Chapter 10. You can use Dr. Tom Hale's excellent book *Medications and Mothers' Milk 2006* (available from www. ibreastfeeding.com, and yes, we share a publisher) to look up the safe doses of most drugs for breastfeeding mothers.

As for over-the-counter drugs, the only one to really watch out for is Sudafed. Read labels carefully, because the active ingredient (pseudephedrine) is hidden in almost every "cold remedy" you can buy. Sudafed is on the caution list because it can decrease your milk supply, not because of any effects on the baby (although it can cause some jitteriness). Some mothers report an anecdotal decrease in milk supply with antihistamines as well (like Benadryl), but this has not been studied as much.

Breast refusal

Sometimes after you've been working for a few weeks, your baby will begin to be fussy at the breast, or even refuse to nurse. This can be heartbreaking for a working mom, who counts on that nursing time to reconnect with her baby at the end of each day. This situation can also trigger all those guilt feelings about being away from your baby too much – you may feel like your baby is rejecting you, and it's a really hard situation. However, like almost all breastfeeding problems, it can be solved with good technique and a little perseverance.

I find it reassuring for working moms to know that breast refusal happens in a lot of babies around 3-4 months of age. This is not just because you are giving bottles, it seems to be a phase that a lot of babies go through whether they are with their mothers all day or not, and nobody really understands why. The good news is that it generally resolves within a few days – so while those days can be very stressful, just know that you'll get through it, and it generally only happens at two times in the first year of life – around 3-4 months, and around 7-9 months.

So – how to treat this? Your baby is rejecting your milk! What can you do? While you may be tempted to pump and give a bottle just to get something in your baby's belly, this is the one thing you should NOT do. This will just add to any favoritism the baby has for the bottle, and reduce the chance for the breast refusal to pass naturally.

The way to get through breast refusal is to frequently offer to nurse in a gentle non-pressuring way. Some moms find they have the best luck if they offer the breast when the baby is very sleepy. Your baby will begin to suck out of habit as he is falling asleep, or just as he is waking. Keep your baby with you as much as possible, and whenever you can, have your breast exposed and available and hold your baby skin-to-skin with you. Try to be as relaxed as possible, since tension can cause your milk let-down to take longer. You can try nursing with your baby in a sling while gently walking, nursing in a dark room with no distractions, or nursing in a warm bath. Never pressure your baby to take the breast by forcing his mouth to your nipple – he will feed when he's ready, and you just need to have faith that this will pass. Skin-to-skin contact helps your baby relax and helps the hormones that will get him interested in nursing again. Holding him against your skin can also be a relaxing time for you, when you can just enjoy your baby without worrying about feeding him. Most of us don't spend enough time just holding our babies against our skin – it's one of the great opportunities of parenthood, in my opinion.

If you think your baby is impatient waiting for your milk to let-down (and your let-down is delayed because you're so stressed about whether your baby will eat), it can help to hand express or pump until the milk starts to flow and then put your baby to the breast.

If your baby is frustrated when he feeds, try putting him to the breast when he is not very hungry. He may have more patience, or may explore sucking out of curiosity when his needs are not as pressing.

It can be very reassuring to start tracking wet and poopy diapers again like you did when he was first born. He won't be pooping once a day like he did as a newborn, and in fact, may go a week without pooping, but as long as the diapers are consistently wet, you can be assured that he's getting enough to eat. It may seem like your baby is "never" eating, but even if he just latches on and feeds for a couple minutes, he is getting some food that will keep him going as he works out how to get back to the breast.

> Note: Watch your baby carefully during the time he is refusing the breast. Keep an eye out for signs of dehydration such as crying without tears, sunken eyes, and excessive sleepiness. Most babies get plenty of nutrition nursing just a few times a day when they are sleepy or relaxed, but if you start to have any concerns take your baby in to his doctor to be checked. Rule Number One is "Feed the baby." Finding the balance is hard – you want to be confident that your baby will return to the breast without giving any bottles, yet also be mindful of your baby's health. If you do need to feed your baby when you are together, try using a cup, syringe, or spoon so as not to further confuse him with artificial nipples.

You'll need some help at home during this time, so that you can focus on being in constant contact with your baby whenever you're home. This is a good time to enlist your partner to do more cooking, or splurge on a little take-out for a week. The typical experience is that the baby goes along for several days on seemingly nothing, but is actually getting enough during the feeds when he's sleepy or takes a bottle at daycare. Then one day, he just decides that his early experiment in making autonomous decisions went pretty poorly, and he'll latch on and feed beautifully, never looking back.

One important thing you can do to end a nursing strike is to keep your milk supply ample so that when he does decide to nurse, he'll be greeted with a rewarding mouthful. If your baby is refusing to nurse, you can pump after each feeding attempt to keep your supply bountiful. This is a great time to boost your freezer stash – but don't use it to send more to daycare so they can "fill him up" during the day – this only makes the situation harder. Keep sending the same amount of milk to daycare, steel yourself to deal with a few days of a fussy baby, try to keep yourself as relaxed as possible, and chant with me: This Too Shall Pass.

If breast refusal lasts more than three days or so, call your local La Leche League leader or a lactation consultant for more ideas. It could be that your baby has a medical problem that is making feeding uncomfortable, so while it is fine to treat this on your own for a few days, it is important to get more help if it is not getting better.

The six month slump

It is very common for women to start to have trouble pumping enough right around the time their baby is six months old. This doesn't mean that it happens to everyone, but it's common enough that it's got a name and is worth discussing.

There are a number of factors that tend to converge around that six month landmark that make it hard to pump enough to keep up with your baby. These are a few of the things that can contribute to a supply slump:

    ဢ Your baby's 6 month growth spurt – Normal growth spurts happen, *generally*, around 3 weeks, 6 weeks, 3 months and 6 months. When your baby is 6 months old, he's probably not taking much (if anything) in the way of solid foods, but is a very large, very active little person with pretty major caloric needs.

    ဢ Return of menstrual cycles – Yup, around this time, good old Aunt Flo often comes around to visit, and in response to the hormonal changes there can be a definite dip in supply right before your flow begins.

    ဢ Baby is learning to move – Your baby might be learning to scoot or sit at this point, increasing her caloric needs.

    ဢ Your schedule – You can get away with a lighter schedule at work for a while after you have a baby, but when your baby is about 6 months old, you're usually starting to ramp back up to full speed at work. You may be taking on additional responsibilities, and putting yourself under more stress around this time.

    ဢ Taking care of yourself – You were probably really careful about what you ate when you first started breastfeeding, but maybe by now you've gotten a little lax about it, and aren't concentrating on protein intake and good hydration the way you were at first.

⅚ The superwoman syndrome – A messy house is OK for a month or two, but this may well be the time when it just starts to get to you. You're staying up later tidying up, you're taking on more stuff in your non-work time, you've finally decided to get all the newborn pictures in the album – you know what I'm talking about – it just gets to you seeing it sit there not finished, right?

⅚ Dieting – This is about the time the last of that baby weight and having no normal clothes that fit gets really annoying, and a lot of moms decide it's time to diet – without leaving enough calories for making milk. It's hard to produce calories without enough coming in.

⅚ Supplementing from the freezer stash – Maybe you've been sending a bottle here and there from your freezer stash, not even so much as you'd really notice. But if you're in this habit when a big growth spurt or AF hits, you may very quickly find yourself running out of milk, and wondering how you got in this mess in the first place.

Wow – unbeatable odds, right? How could your milk supply not go down? While this may seem like an insurmountable bundle of obstacles, and any normal person would let this breastfeeding thing go, this supply dip is not irreversible. You actually can get through it pretty quickly with just a little bit of extra work. It may be hard to see out of this hole you're in, but you just have to trust me – it gets easier. As in, a *lot* easier. Once your baby starts taking solids you probably won't have to pump as much, and you'll know that there are nutritious alternatives on days you don't pump enough milk. Your baby will also start sleeping longer *very soon*, so you won't be nursing at night as much. And if you can keep nursing for just a little bit longer, you'll be able to keep breastfeeding once you wean from the pump. Then you'll have the option of nursing for as long as you want to.

Getting through the six month slump:

⅚ Try not to supplement more. If you're supplementing some from the freezer, try to gradually decrease the amount you're taking out, or at a minimum, hold it steady as you boost your supply. Remember, supplementing from the freezer stash tells your body that it doesn't need to make more milk, so if you can avoid using that frozen milk, please do.

ಬ Take care of yourself. Give the house-cleaning a rest for a few more weeks. Start going to bed earlier. Stay hydrated, eat lots of protein, and put off that diet (or at least, add back a few healthy calories). If you've just started working out, step back on the intensity a little bit to give your body time to rest. Set a date to start the diet and exercise again so you don't let it slide forever, but give yourself a rest for now.

ಬ Reduce stress. If you've taken on too much at work, see if you can scale back a bit. If you can't, try to reduce stress at home as much as possible. This is a good time to call in those promised dinners from friends and family, or declare Wednesday "take-out night" for a mid-week break. Or declare every night take-out night!

ಬ Reduce stress. Try not to worry about how much milk you're getting when you're pumping. Don't look at the bottles, practice your relaxation exercises when pumping, and tell yourself that any amount of breastmilk you can pump is good for your baby.

ಬ Start solids. If your baby is close to six months old, you can reduce the amount of milk you need to pump by starting solids – but have your daycare give all of them. You should be nursing full time when you're home to build up your supply, so even though it's fun to have strained peas all over the place, if your supply is low, have daycare do all the solids. You don't have to mix cereal with breastmilk every time, either. My kids really liked rice milk mixed with rice cereal when there wasn't enough EBM for it (it has a sweet taste that is very much like EBM, and is very non-allergenic). It says on the box "Not to be used as infant formula" because it's not supposed to be a primary food in your baby's diet – this doesn't mean they should never eat it. Just be aware that rice milk is pretty nutritionally empty, so don't rely on it for healthy calories.

ಬ Add a pumping session. Around 6 months, I started pumping when I got to work. Pumping in the beginning of the day usually has a higher yield because your prolactin levels are highest in the morning, but I could never bring myself to wake up before my baby to pump. I solved this by leaving for work 15 minutes earlier. I would nurse Kai right when I dropped him off, then drive 20 minutes to work, then pump as I read my emails. It was before the hurry and stress of the day had begun, and was usually a very productive session, even if I had just nursed. Any time you add a pumping session, give your body about a week to get used to the new schedule and start producing for that session.

∾ Nurse as much as possible evenings and nights. Take a few days to wear your baby close to you in the evenings and co-sleep. Let your baby have free access to the breast so that he makes up for whatever he's not getting in bottles during the day.

All of these strategies should have you through a supply slump in no-time-flat – and then you'll be well on your way to smooth sailing through the next 6 months. Really, it does get easier.

Do I need to supplement?

Is my baby getting enough to eat?

Many working moms wonder if their baby is getting enough to eat during the day. Usually a mom will start to think about supplementing with formula if her baby always takes more breastmilk during the day (or during her work shift) than she's able to pump, or if her care provider starts telling her she needs to send more. Some moms truly aren't able to pump enough, either because they have trouble responding to the pump or because of their schedule, but in many cases, the problem can be fixed without supplementing.

The root of the pumping/eating mismatch is either because you're not pumping enough or your baby is eating too much. Or, you've gotten worried about your baby's health because they're not sticking to their "normal" growth curve. I'll address both of these issues here. Yes, there are cases in which a baby truly is not getting enough to eat – but trust me, it's rare. More likely than not, you can provide plenty of milk for your baby by just adjusting your schedule a little bit or having a heart-to-heart with your care provider.

The baby who always needs more at daycare

You may be hearing from your childcare provider that your baby is always hungry during the day and you need to send more milk. Before you add in bottles of formula, take a few minutes to look at how your baby is doing. It could be that your baby is being overfed at daycare, so here are a few ways to tell.

The easiest way to tell if your baby is taking too much from bottles is to look at how hungry she is at home. Is she ready to nurse as soon as you pick her up? A baby older than seven or eight months may be more interested in playing when you pick her up, but a baby six months or younger should be very interested in nursing when you arrive. If she's not, how long is it until she's hungry? Write down how long it is until your baby is hungry for a few days and see if there's a pattern. If you track it for a few days, you'll have pretty good evidence that you're baby doesn't need that last bottle that's being used, or maybe you can substitute a smaller bottle at the last feeding time. Maybe your care provider says that she can't hold off on bottles or your baby just cries and cries. Ask her what else typically calms your baby during the day. If your care provider says, "only the bottle satisfies her," that would raise a red flag for me. There should be other ways to soothe a baby – holding, carrying, a pacifier, songs, books, playing with other babies – the list goes on and on. It's hard to have a conversation in which you're basically saying, "you're not trying hard enough to soothe my baby," so as you talk, keep in mind the value of a smooth relationship with your care provider. But it could also be time to start asking around about other care providers if they're not willing to work with you.

How much is too much?

How much does your baby really need during the day? One equation that a lot of moms use is to take your baby's weight, multiply by 2.5, and that's the number of ounces the baby needs in a given day. So, if you have a 10 pound baby, that means she will take about 25 ounces in 24 hours. It's a nice equation for starting out, but a study by Kent has shown that breastfed babies do not increase their intake the way formula fed babies do, and can have the same daily intake from 2 months through 6 months while having perfectly normal weight gain (Kent et, al 1999). It can help to start with 25 ounces as a really rough first approximation of how much your baby needs in 24 hours. If you're at work 8 hours, then that's 1/3 of your day, so your baby could only need 8 or 9 ounces during that time. Some babies need more, some less – there is a *ton* of variation. But based on that rough estimate, you can start to make some guesses about whether your baby is being overfed or not. For example, a mom emailed me last week about not being able to pump enough. I'd spoken to her before about overfeeding at daycare, so she knew about it and wondered if her baby was getting too much during the day. I asked her how much he was eating, and she told me 20 ounces between 9 and 5:30. What's your guess? My guess is that kid was overfed. 20 ounces is a lot – the baby is only 14 weeks old, and about 12 pounds. That leaves only 5 of her 25 ounces that she needs to get from mom – not all that productive a situation for maintaining a milk supply. This mom is now trying to cut back on the amount in the bottles, encourage more daytime non-food comforting, and waking the baby for more nighttime nursing – we'll see how it goes!

What if your baby is hungry when you get to her, but is also eating everything you've been pumping and is still fussy for more? It might be time for you to turn to the "Troubleshooting supply issues" section at the beginning of this chapter and see if you can increase your pumping output a little bit. For me the easiest thing to do was to add in a pumping session when I first got to work – it was not at all disruptive and gave me three more ounces each day!

Finally, if you've been through the whole "Troubleshooting supply issues" section, tried a lot of different things, and still can't satisfy that hungry baby, go ahead and add a bottle of formula when you need to. Your baby needs to eat, and at some point (what we call the point of diminishing returns) the added stress of pumping all the time and the added worry is just not worth it.

There are certainly other options to consider – work an hour less each day, see if you can go to your baby to nurse during the day, stay home with your baby one day a week until she's older, increase nighttime nursing – but these options are not realistic for everyone, so take the time to figure out what works best for your situation.

The baby who falls off her growth curve

Here's the typical scenario (raise your hand if this is you). You baby is about 4 to 5 months old, and you've been back to work for two or three months. Your baby always finishes all of the bottles that you send, but still nurses well in the evening and seems happy enough in childcare. You go in for your well-baby check and your doctor points out that your baby is falling off her growth curve. He asks you about how you're feeding your baby, and that seed of doubt is planted about whether your baby is getting enough. Your doctor may even tell you that you need to either pump more for your baby or supplement with formula.

At this point, it's time for you to start asking questions. First, what growth curve is your doctor using? Most doctors have not updated their growth charts since the early 1970s, and these are based almost exclusively on the growth patterns of formula fed babies. We now know that formula-fed babies gain more weight than breastfed babies, especially between 4 and 6 months of age. Is it coincidence that formula-fed babies are also more likely to be obese as adults? The WHO (World Health Organization) and the CDC (Centers for Disease Control) have both put out new growth charts. The ones from the CDC include breastfed babies in the proportion that they are found in our population, so the average weight is still higher than for an exclusively breastfed baby, but they're closer. You can view and print out these charts at the CDC website (www.cdc.gov/growthcharts/). WHO has just completed all-new charts for exclusively breastfed babies. It is very important that all pediatric care providers are given these new growth charts for assessment of normal growth in breastfed babies – so feel free to print out a copy to take with you to your next appointment. You can print out the charts from the WHO website (http://www.who.

int/childgrowth/standards/en/).

The differences in the growth curves between breastfed and formula-fed babies are striking. Breastfed babies gain weight faster in the first two months, but level off to very little weight gain between four and six months. Sound familiar? It's normal. It's the formula-fed babies who are gaining "too fast" if you consider the breastfed baby to be the normal one.

The other important thing to understand is what a growth curve means. Parents should realize that just because a baby is in the 10th percentile, doesn't mean there's something wrong with them. Growth charts plot the growth of normal, healthy babies. They're all normal, even the 99th percentile and the 1st percentile. Somebody's got to be there! If all babies were in at least the 50th percentile, the old 50th percentile would become the new 1st percentile for a vastly upward-shifted chart of an obesity epidemic. 1st percentile just means the smallest normal person – but still normal. Hey, some people are just small, and others are big. So it goes.

So, enough science – let's look at your baby. Is she meeting her developmental milestones? Does she look healthy? Are her eyes shiny and alert? Does she spend her awake time looking around and exploring her world? Does she nurse vigorously when she's feeding at the breast? If the answer to all of these questions is yes, and if you allow your baby to nurse whenever she wants to when you're together, then try to buy some time on the supplementing. Your baby is healthy and growing just fine. It's hard not to worry when your doctor mentions that awful growth curve, but have faith in your mommy-instincts. You can ask your doctor to thoroughly assess your baby's development and general health (without regard to weight gain). If her health is otherwise good, then please, keep doing what you're doing and try not to worry. There is more discussion of this topic in the section "When your doctor recommends weaning or supplementing" in Chapter 10.

The baby who really needs more milk

If your baby does not look healthy and alert, isn't producing lots of wet diapers every single day, if she's lost that full chubbiness in her face, arms and legs, and is either hungry all the time when you're together or seems overly sleepy, then you might want to worry. The first step is to see if you can pump more, and there is more than enough information in the "Troubleshooting supply issues" section to help you do this. If your schedule is just so crazy that you can't pump anymore, or if you're just not able to get any more milk out with the pump, and your baby seems to be suffering for it, then giving some formula is clearly the best choice. First, feed the baby. Before you start supplementing with formula, pay a visit to your doctor. There are rare neurological and muscular disorders that can first show up as a loss of interest in eating or unusual weight loss, so you'll at least want your baby looked at. Besides, it's a good idea to chat with your doctor about what kind of formula you should use and any special concerns you may have about introducing your baby to new foods (and yes, formula is a new food for your baby).

All or nothing?

It can be heartbreaking to need to supplement – but does it mean that you need to quit breastfeeding? Absolutely not. Many moms tell me they gave up breastfeeding when they weren't able to pump enough, but there's no reason to do that. You can continue to nurse when you're home and on weekends, and you may find that just pumping once a day is enough to keep your supply strong for the times you are together with your baby. It doesn't have to be all or nothing, so don't beat yourself up. Adding formula after your baby is six months old isn't that different from adding other solid foods, and it happens to be pretty nutritious for the older baby. The next section, "Smart supplementing," has tips for combining breastfeeding and formula. It can be done while allowing you to keep breastfeeding. My friend Emily started adding in some formula at about six months with both of her kids, and is still happily nursing her two-year-old, who has replaced all formula in his diet with things like hot dogs and milk and macaroni and cheese, but he loves his "nursies." Personally, I chose to avoid formula, but that doesn't mean that's the choice that's going to work for everyone. Many moms have successfully combined breastfeeding, pumping and the occasional bottle of formula.

Smart supplementing

If you've decided to supplement with some formula, now it's time to learn about how to do it smartly. What does that mean? Well, it means supplementing in a way that does not compromise your breastfeeding relationship, in a way that will let you keep breastfeeding for as long as you want to, and in a way that works for you. Even if you're supplementing as a path to weaning sooner than later, give this a read so you understand the process.

In this chapter I say a lot of disparaging things about the formula industry, because I think their marketing practices are really appalling. This doesn't mean it's not good for your baby, or that you're a bad person for using it! Formula can be a very healthy supplemental food. You're doing your best for your baby, and sometimes this means making sure they're getting enough to eat no matter what. It's just that I wish the formula companies didn't try so hard to get us to "need" their products or entirely replace breastfeeding with formula from day one for so many babies.

Choosing a formula

Your doctor may have an opinion about what formula is best. You can ask them what they base this recommendation on, but it probably has to do with which formula rep they have the best relationship with. Not to be jaded (who am I kidding, I'm totally jaded), but the formula companies spend millions of dollars on things like gifts to physicians, free samples, professional dinners and the like so that your doctor will recommend their brand to you. So if your doctor recommends the brand that also happens to supply all of their pens, notepads, waiting room books and free samples, you may wonder if this is just coincidence.

Cynicism aside, you should still ask your doctor for a recommendation if you're going to start with formula, but my opinion is that it doesn't really matter that much. All formulas are very similar. If your baby is still getting the majority of their nutrition from the breast, you can save money by skipping the DHA/AHA additive formula – your baby is getting these essential fats from your milk. Most formulas have iron, which can be a convenient way to add iron to your baby's diet, though extra iron is not needed until six months in babies who are exclusively breastfed (it's needed earlier in babies who get formula because of changes in the way minerals are absorbed when babies get formula). A lot of moms I know swear that Carnation BestStart is the most like breastmilk in taste and breaks down the most easily. This may or may not be true. Just like in choosing a bottle system, the most important thing when you first buy formula is not to buy too much until you know what your baby will take. Before you run to Costco and stock up on the million-gallon size tub, be sure your baby will drink the stuff, and give it a week or so to make sure their digestive system tolerates it. Some babies will react to the milk proteins, but you can try a more hydrolyzed formula (this means the milk proteins are broken up already) before going to soy. Personally, I would think long and hard about giving soy formula, since soy is a natural source of plant estrogens, which babies probably can do without, whether they're boys or girls.

How much to supplement?

How much should you give your baby in supplements? The short answer is only as much as is absolutely necessary! If you've been supplementing from your freezer stash and have run out, you'll have a pretty good idea of how many ounces you need each day. You can leave a tub of powdered formula for your daycare to mix as needed, or you can prepare the bottles at home if you feel like this gives you more control.

Cutting back on pumping

If you cut back on pumping once you start supplementing, remember to do it gradually. If you decide your baby will be getting formula for the entire time you will be at work, you will still need to pump some during the day to avoid engorgement and the risk of mastitis. You can gradually ease your pumping sessions to later in the day to let your body slowly adjust. The section on "Weaning from the pump" in Chapter 12 has a lot more information on making these changes.

To mix or not to mix

There is no consensus at all about whether supplemental formula should be mixed with breastmilk before feeding. Here are a few considerations: Your baby may only take the formula when it's mixed with breastmilk if they don't like the taste. If you mix, your baby gets some breastmilk at each feeding. If breastmilk is mixed with formula, you can't reuse an unfinished bottle – once the bottle has been started, it should be finished or tossed out – resulting in possible waste of breastmilk. If you mix and the supplemental amount is not needed, then your baby has had formula when it wasn't needed.

Given these considerations, I guess I would try the formula alone to see if my baby would tolerate it. Then I would have my care provider give all the breastmilk first, and only use formula as needed at the end of the day. While I like the idea of having some breastmilk at every feeding, I hate to see breastmilk wasted, so I come down slightly in favor of not mixing – but there's no evidence either way, so do what works for you. Your baby makes the final choice, and if they refuse the formula on its own, then you'll need to mix.

Avoiding the slippery slope

A lot of moms who start supplementing early in their breastfeeding relationship find it to be a *very* slippery slope. One bottle a day becomes two, then three, then before you know it, your milk supply is shot and you have a bottle-fed baby. Once your baby is older, it's easier to avoid this, but it is something to be aware of.

Even if you've decided to supplement, you can preserve your milk supply by continuing to pump. If part of the reason you started supplementing is so that you could cut back on pumping, that's a great reason to do it – but see if you can pump just a little bit. If pumping three times a day is making you crazy, how about pumping twice, or one time? If adding in extra pumping sessions isn't getting you enough milk, you can keep the sessions you already are doing to keep your baby getting as much nutritious breastmilk as possible.

Try to keep exclusively breastfeeding at home. Your baby may get used to the stupefyingly full feeling they get from a bottle of formula (which sits in the stomach more heavily than breastmilk and digests more slowly) so he may seem restless after feeding. But as I've said before, babies are smart, and if you just let your baby know that mom is for breast only, they'll get used to the differences. Your baby may nurse frequently – but try to remember, you only have an infant once, and if you let your baby nurse frequently, they usually get enough.

A note about weekends – if you've been supplementing several ounces of formula during the work day, your milk supply is not quite as much as your baby needs. You can try exclusive breastfeeding on the weekend – some women can rapidly adapt and have plenty to feed a baby directly, but others need to add in a little extra food on days they're home. If you have someone else to give the bottles, then you can still keep the "mom for breast only" rule which really helps keep your baby breastfeeding for as long as possible.

Weaning from supplements

If you've started supplementing, it doesn't mean you need to keep supplementing forever. Some moms decide to gradually reduce supplements if their baby doesn't tolerate the formula well, others start supplementing with the intention of it being only temporary, others have a change in work situation that makes exclusive breastfeeding more possible.

My friend Laura had a really rough start with breastfeeding her first, and was so pleased to be having a better experience with her second, even after she went back to working full time. However, when Tara was about 7 months old, Laura decided she was ready to stop pumping at work. She cut back on her pumping sessions, and left bottles of EBM from her freezer stash until it was gone. The she started introducing formula - which was an awful experience for them. It turned out that Tara was horribly allergic to milk, vomited up all the formula they gave her, and developed hives wherever any spilled formula or spit-up touched her skin. Laura decided to start pumping again right away, but since she hadn't been pumping at all in a while, it did take some time to build her supply back up. Luckily, she was able to pump as often as she wanted to at work, and between pumping every two hours as well as some on the weekends, she had enough milk to send exclusive EBM bottles again within a week or so. But the moral of the story is this: if you're going to stop pumping, it's better to do it gradually at the same time as you try a bit of formula - just to be sure your baby will tolerate the switch.

How easily you can stop supplementing depends on how much formula you've been using and for how long. If it's just been a couple ounces a day for a week or two, you can usually stop the supplements very quickly by just pumping and/or nursing more and following the suggestions in the "Troubleshooting supply issues" section. As you work on increasing your supply, gradually decrease the amount of formula you send to daycare as the amount you pump increases, or as you increase the amount of milk your baby gets from the breast when you are together. A lot of communication with your care provider will be necessary, and they can let you know if your baby needs more than you are sending.

Focus on breastfeeding as much as possible. For some moms, a week's vacation from work with 100% exclusive breastfeeding is enough to restore your supply so that supplements can be stopped. For other moms, more intensive supply boosting is needed.

When newborns are supplemented, the standard protocol for weaning from the supplements involves having the mom pump after each feeding, collect the milk, and gradually replace the supplemental formula with EBM. Once all of the supplement is coming from mom, the next step is to get the baby exclusively on the breast. You can follow a similar protocol – by pumping after each feeding for several days, you will gradually increase your supply *and* collect more milk to send to daycare. This is tiring, so if you are committed to getting rid of the supplements, eliminate as many of your other responsibilities as possible for a few weeks. Pay careful attention to your nutrition, but most importantly, rest and let your body do the work of making more milk.

Emily and Caroline

One of the first sections of this book written way back in 2001 was my dear friend Emily's supplementing story. I'll include the story here for you – it's such a great example of a mom who struggled to pump enough, finally ended up supplementing, but managed to provide breastmilk for her daughter for as long as she wanted to. I'll let Emily tell the story in her own words:

Breastfeeding was going just great, milk galore. At my 6 week ob/gyn appointment, I asked for and received a prescription for the low dose birth control pill. (Background: I went off the pill and started my period 12/25 – was pregnant by 1/09 – in the interest of not having two babies in the same calendar year, I went back on the pill). My ob/gyn said, "This may affect your supply," but I didn't worry. At the time I could nurse Caroline to satisfaction and then still pump (for my freezer stash) more than an ounce from each breast. I was swimming in milk.

Everything continued well, and I went back to work at 13 weeks postpartum. I pumped 3 times daily and before bed, and gave Caroline the milk the next day that I pumped the day before. The bottles were pretty small (3 3-4 ounce ones). My mom kept her for my first week back, and called me to come over every afternoon because Caroline would be hungry.

At about that time, Caroline got her first ear infection. We took her to the pediatrician on a Saturday because she woke with her eye swollen shut. They weighed her. At her 2 month appointment, she had weighed in at 9 lbs 14 oz (after being 7 lbs 8 oz at birth). She was in the 50% at two months. At this appointment, almost 4 months old, she weighed 10 lbs 6 oz – an 8 ounce gain in more than 6 weeks. I panicked.

I called everyone I knew to see how big their babies had been at her age. I was so concerned about her. We were still nursing every 3 or so hours, and she wasn't gaining. My pumping output had not improved. I immediately quit taking the pill. I nursed her every chance I could get. I investigated ways to increase my supply. I took a course of Reglan. I took fenugreek and blessed thistle. I ate oatmeal every morning. I pumped extra sessions. The Reglan gave me temporary supply boosts, but the effect went away when I was not taking it.

I wasn't sure what the problem was.   We ended more nursing sessions with her crying, but she was a happy baby between sessions and was developing nicely. At her 4 month appointment, she was in the 10% on weight. Her doctor said we would wait until 6 months to make any decisions regarding her weight if she continued to fail to gain.

One night when Caroline was crying and I couldn't seem to nurse her enough, I gave her one of the newborn bottles of formula they had sent home from the hospital. She ate it all right up, and was able to sleep.

Then Caroline went on a nursing strike. One night she and I were up literally all night. She was screaming, hysterical, refusing to nurse. I kept trying to make her nurse, which wasn't helping anything. I was crying. We had an awful night.

The next day at work I cried. I called the LC from the hospital; her only advice was to continue trying. I called a LLL leader. She was wonderful. She gave me some advice, she sympathized with me, but the best thing she said to me was, "You are doing a wonderful thing for your baby." I cried on the phone with her. She had at least restored my confidence that I could confront and overcome this problem, and had given me the resolve to find a solution.

"That night, when Caroline refused to nurse, I gave her to John along with a bottle of formula, and I went and pumped in the middle of the night. I couldn't make her nurse, but I could at least pump and make milk for her to eat later.

The next day she broke her strike and nursed really nicely for me. I was so thankful.

But I still couldn't nurse enough or pump enough to satisfy her. They kept asking for more milk at daycare. I finally broke into the formula cans that I had brought home from the hospital. I sent her to daycare with my bottles of breastmilk and a bottle of formula.

And so it continued. I nursed Caroline every morning before work, sometimes twice, pumped two to three times daily at the office (getting no more than 6 ounces from a day's pumping) and nursed her after work, before bed, and during the night.

As her appetite grew, I began to add formula supplements after a nursing if she still seemed hungry. And so we started supplementing on a full time basis.

At her 6 month appointment, she was in the 25% in weight. She was gaining nicely, and was developing right on schedule.

Caroline was happy because she was getting enough to eat. I was happy because I was able to continue our nursing relationship, but still able to assure that she was getting what she needed, even if it didn't all come from me.

At eight months, she now has 6 ounces of breastmilk and 10 ounces of formula at daycare. She has a nursing and formula in the evening, and then nurses at night and in the morning. We have a good balance that is working well for us. I continue to pump so that I can continue to nurse my little girl. Nursing still calms her down and puts her to sleep the way nothing else will.

I have never been able to regain my original supply, despite every trick in the book. I have been able to nurse and work and pump for my 8 month old, and to find a solution that works for us.

Update, 2006: Despite our troubles, Caroline and I nursed until she self-weaned at 13.5 months. I had made it past the magical one year mark and was pleased.

Thankfully, I was able to learn from this experience and handled things differently with my second child. Caroline used a pacifier from birth, and I wonder if that didn't interfere with our nursing relationship from the beginning, since she had an outlet other than me to satisfy her sucking urges in the early days. With Charlie, I nursed in recovery (I'd been unable to do so with Caroline because of a trip to NICU). I didn't use a pacifier with him at all, and spent those first weeks attached to him. We co-slept. I had learned to sit and enjoy nursing and not try to push myself in the early days to get back to being my version of normal, which is 100 miles per hour. I took advantage of the early milky days to build a freezer stash so that if I had to supplement, I could do it with my own milk.

Most importantly for me, I avoided hormonal birth control. When I returned to work 13 weeks post-partum this time, I was able to pump enough milk. I was still barely keeping up, but it was enough. We did supplement as we neared the one-year mark, but I was able to do so with my own milk.

And now as Charlie has turned three, we are still nursing. I've been a one-side nurser for about 18 months now, and yet we continue. I never would have imagined myself nursing a preschooler. But now I can't really imagine not nursing him.

(Author's note: I wonder also about what growth charts were used to weigh and measure Caroline. The fact that her growth slowed around four months is typical for breastfed babies, but is not reflected on the older growth charts – it could be that her drop in percentiles caused needless worry for Emily).

References

Aljazaf, K, Hale T, et al. 2003. Pseudoephedrine: effects on milk production in women and estimation of infant exposure via breastmilk. *British Journal of Clinical Pharmacology* **56**(1): 18-24.

AAP Task Force on SIDS. 2005. Policy Statement: The Changing Concept of Sudden Infant Death Syndrome: Diagnostic Coding Shifts, Controversies Regarding the Sleeping Environment, and New Variables to Consider in Reducing Risk. *Pediatrics* **116**(5).

Kent JC, Mitoulas L, Cox DB, Owens RA, Hartmann PE. 1999. Breast volume and milk production during extended lactation in women. *Exp Physiol.* Mar;**84**(2):435-47.

Pumping for teachers

I know that teachers have a lot of special challenges fitting pumping into a work day – more specifically, they have zero privacy as they go through their day, and hardly any breaks. However, with a little creative thinking (and maybe some helpful co-workers) you can put together a schedule that works for you to provide breastmilk for your baby while you are at work.

If you can, start planning before you start your maternity leave. Scope out the places where you might be able to pump during the day, and see what kind of adjustments you might have to make in your schedule. Most moms need to pump three times during an eight hour workday – but the times don't necessarily need to be spaced evenly through the day. Most women have a more abundant milk supply in the first part of the day – so even if you can't think of three times during the school day when you can pump, you could make up the difference by pumping before the day starts, or before you leave the house in the morning.

What about fitting in times during the school day? If you have a planning period, you have an obvious time to pump, and by using your planning period, lunch, and either before or after school, you can fit in three pumping sessions. I know that scheduling can be harder for elementary school teachers who are with their students all day, but maybe you could pump while your students are at art, music, gym or lunch. My friend Susan, a school counselor, offers a few ideas:

> The elementary teachers have "specials" – when the kids go to PE, music, art – and they are supposed to be duty free, or it's a planning time. This is a time when they can take 15 minutes to pump – the big question is where. There is often a speech pathologist or psychologist who has a space where they work or test kids, but mostly they don't use it every day. You can ask if they can could give up their space for 15 minutes twice a day (take a break, go to the teacher's lounge) to help a mom out. I guess you would have to be at the school for a while to feel comfortable with that. On days they are not there, the pumper could use the space. And, there's always the car.

My son's kindergarten teacher often has an aid in the room, and she has a large storage closet with room for a chair. With these resources, her plan is to pump for 10 minutes in the closet when the aid is in the room if she doesn't have a time when the kids will be gone – although I highly recommend she get a good set of headphones so she's not distracted by the classroom noise.

A lot of teachers can pump in their classroom when students are gone by closing the door and finding a space away from the window. If not, or if you share a classroom, it can be harder. A teacher on the Working and Pumping message board posted, "When I was pumping for our first child, I had to use the restroom. That was OHH so pleasant. (Hear the sarcasm.) It was tiny, only 2 stalls. My co-workers would walk in, hear the pump, and usually have some not so funny comment." This is less than ideal, to be sure – but you'll note, she did it. She provided her baby with breastmilk every single day, even though it was hard. Kudos to her for sticking with it, and with her second baby, she had a much more supportive administration and was able to pump twice during the day in her own classroom.

However – there are usually better options than the . Take a good look at who has a private space and how much they are using it. Karen, a guidance counselor I know, lets teachers use her office for pumping when she doesn't have appointments scheduled. She suggests that teachers ask the counselors, speech therapist, or school nurses if there are times that they could borrow their office for a few minutes during the day. Bring a creative eye to your building when making your plans. Is there a large storage area that sees little traffic and has a door you could close? Is there a music or art room that's unused for part of the day? If your school has an auditorium, are there dressing rooms? Think outside the box.

Susan also points out that if you are good at what you do, your principal really doesn't want to lose you, and many are willing to make a lot of accommodations to help a good teacher return to work – and stay back at work. When a teacher has a baby, it's no big secret that if she finds her return to work too difficult, she may well choose to stay home instead. Keep this in mind as you are negotiating your return to work – you do have a bit of the upper hand. Sue talked about her school situation – which sounds like it's great – but uses this example to encourage teachers to ask for what they need.

If my principal thinks you are good at your job, she will do anything to keep you. It all depends on the school system and the people. We had a French teacher who wanted to breastfeed and was worried about what it would be like. She asked if she could have the first period of every day as her planning time so she could pump – or come to work late if needed. We granted her that wish (and I was one of the ones fighting for her). It's a very desirable thing (to be off first block) and she got it for one year.

This is why I highly recommend talking with your principal before you go on your leave. I've certainly heard stories of principals totally unwilling to accommodate a pumping mom's schedule, or maybe their hands are tied about the scheduling – but it can't hurt to ask.

After my first baby was born, I needed to return to work pretty quickly because we were so broke, but I didn't let my boss know that. He asked me how long I was going to be out, and I said "A lot shorter if I can take breaks to pump during the day." Using the length of my leave as a bargaining chip won me total freedom over my schedule and an office with a door! A longer maternity leave is always the best thing for you and your baby, but if you have some flexibility around your return date, don't be above using your return date to bargain for pumping accommodations! Be sure to see the section on "Making plans with your employer" in Chapter 1 so you can have the numbers handy on absenteeism and employee loyalty when you present your case. Parents of formula fed babies miss three times as much work as mothers of breastfed babies because their babies are sick more often – a useful statistic to throw around if you're not getting the support you need.

You may be hesitant to make a fuss if you're not even sure that you'll keep breastfeeding after you go back to work. Why rock the boat? But by arranging your schedule before you go on leave (or as soon as you get this book), you at least leave all your options open, right?

A real-life example

It can help to write out your schedule to see when pumping will fit in most logically. A teacher wrote to me for help with her schedule – she had been feeding formula once a day, but wanted to try to get her baby back on exclusive breastmilk since she felt like he wasn't tolerating the formula well. She couldn't fit any more pumping time into her school day, and wondered what to do.

Here's the schedule she sent me:

5:00-5:30   Mommy Feeding

9:00-10:00   EBM Bottle @ Daycare

(Sometimes he sleeps through time for his bottle)

11:00   Pump Session

1:00-2:00   Formula Bottle @ Daycare

4:00-5:00   Mommy Feeding

8:00-9:00   Mommy Feeding

So how can this mom get rid of the formula bottle? She could only pump during her lunch, which was from 10:50-11:10 (they were the first group in a school of 900!). Just looking at this schedule, I can see a few options. First – what's happening between 5:30 and 9 AM? No pumping, no feeding – that's a long time with no milk removed – signaling her body to slow production. This long break is in the morning, when her milk supply was probably highest. Would she be able to leave the house 15 minutes earlier and nurse right at drop-off? Or – leave the house 15 minutes earlier and pump in her classroom before the students come in? Most teachers are required to be in the building at least 15 minutes before the students are let in – so she's probably there anyway. If she pumped hands-free, then that could be a time to look over her plans for the day or check emails. And what's happening between 11 and 4? I know, she's got students until 2:30 or 3, and then is probably rushing like crazy to finish up and get out of there. Her first mommy feeding is early enough (4 PM) that it could be that she's leaving the minute she's done with her students. But if she was staying at school for a while after the students were gone, would it be possible for her to shut her door right after the last bell, pump for 10 minutes, then open the door and go on with her after-school activities? I know, it can be hard to kick out those lingering students, but maybe if you tell them to come back in 10 minutes, you could add in one more session.

Some other scheduling options

ॐ Pump one side while the baby feeds on the other in the morning. This takes a little getting used to, but since the baby triggers the let-down, you can usually get a lot of milk this way. Don't do this if your baby always nurses both sides, but if your baby typically feeds on one side at each feeding, this is a great way to get more milk.

ॐ Pump after the baby goes to bed at night. If your baby goes to sleep hours before you go to bed, you can pump right before you turn in for the night. Milk supply tends to be lower at night, but once your body gets used to the added session, it will gradually produce more milk at that time.

ॐ Pump one side while the baby feeds in the evening.

ॐ Pump one or two times each weekend day to store up a little more milk for the week to come.

> Any time you add in a new pumping session, expect to get very little milk (or none) the first few times. Remember, the stimulation of the pump is placing the order – telling your body to make more, to speed up production. Expect to see more milk for a new pumping session in about 3 or 4 days.

ॐ Encourage more nursing at night by co-sleeping or waking your baby so that your baby will need less during the day.

ॐ Shorten the time when your baby will need bottles by always nursing right before you leave your baby and as soon as you are together again. This can push the first bottle of the day later, and make the last one earlier – resulting in fewer bottles needed.

When work includes travel

If you have to travel for work, you may think that pumping and breastfeeding won't work out for you – but let me be the one to tell you, it has been done, and with great success.

I didn't have to travel much for work, and never had to pump too intensively on the road, so I'll rely on the stories from my friends Jen and Lili for inspiration.

Can your baby come?

If you're heading out on a trip for work, I think the first consideration should be to think about if there's any way you could take your baby along with you. No, of course not, this is a business trip – what would I do with my baby? Well, who could go with you? When my daughter was 9 months old, I had to go to a course in California for a week. At that point, I was not at all ready to be away from her for a week, so I asked my mom if she could go. My mom (who, yes, does have a job of her own) was delighted to come! We stayed with my college roommate, my mom took my daughter out sightseeing in San Diego and visited some of her old friends, and it worked out great. I was gone long days, usually from 7AM until after dinner, but at least I could nurse my daughter each morning before I left, and again when I got home and at night. It was nice to get back from class and put the pump away.

I did have to pump during the class, but I was able to arrange with the front desk of the hotel where the course was held to get a key to an empty room whenever I needed to pump. Which brings me to:

Making plans with your hosts

And by host, I mean the hotel or conference center or business place where you will be working. If you're staying in the hotel where a conference is being held, then it's easy to go back to your room to pump. The only arrangement you'll need to make is to call ahead to see if there are refrigerators in the guest rooms – if there aren't, you can request one. If there's a charge for it, you can often get the fridge for free if you say that it's for storage of breastmilk, or explain that it's a medical necessity.

Where to pump?

If you're working away from your hotel, try to call ahead to the worksite and see what kind of accommodations they have for pumping. Some conference centers now have what they call "infant nursing lounges," which mostly means it's for the pumping moms, (unless the La Leche League conference is there, in which case they all just nurse their babies wherever they are anyway). If there isn't a special place, sometimes there is a medical unit set up – so try to contact the organizers of medical support to see if there might be an area curtained off where you could pump. Or, there's always the restroom. If you usually pump with an electric pump, you may need to get a battery attachment for it, so plan ahead if you'll need to order this. Yes, the restroom is very much less than ideal, but for a few days, it's not so terrible. I don't worry about the safety of pumping in a restroom, I think the enzymes in the milk take care of any germs – it's just a little disrespectful of moms to make them pump in the restroom. But – when push comes to shove, you make do with what you have, not what you wish you had.

Here's Jen's take:

> I never called ahead for a room to pump in, but a lot of times I found it was just as easy to use a restroom. I know it's not the greatest thing, but I sometimes had to pump in a restroom at work, so I was used to it. And you always know there's going to be a restroom. Sometimes you get really good support since the other people in the restroom know what you're doing. It's not all bad. To me it was just one of those things, if you're going to do it, you just do it to the best of your ability; you make do with what you have. If I were traveling every week, I would probably try to prepare better, but it worked fine for what I was doing.

If you will be working onsite at another business on your trip, instead of contacting your work partners directly, it sometimes goes more smoothly to make a call to their HR department. If it is a large company, they may have a lactation room established, and if not, they may be able to steer you to a comfortable location. If HR is not helpful, try to talk directly to the people you will be working with. Explain your needs clearly – that you need to express milk during the day for your baby, and you will need a couple of breaks and a private space. People can be very generous. One time when

I went to a one-day academic meeting, I pumped in the office of the Chairman of Engineering at the university. A little awkward, opening my shirt in his office, but after all, I had work to do. If you present your case as simply one of the accommodations that you will need in order to work there, you can generally get what you need.

Then there are the times when you just have to improvise. If you have a car, you can always pump there. Buy one of those folding window shades for the front windshield, and take along a towel or baby blanket to hang in the front window, and that will get you at least some minimal privacy. This is a time when some kind of drape to put over the whole pumping apparatus can be nice as well. If you set up to pump hands-free and then read a magazine while you pump, people won't wonder why you're just sitting there in the parking lot.

When my friend Nicole was working on a construction job site, she would pump in the mobile trailers that are set up as temporary offices – she just had to coordinate with the other people using the offices. But they were very accommodating (most likely happy for the excuse to go get a coffee).

Lili offers the tip of always keeping extra paper towels in your pump bag in case you have to pump someplace without a sink. Lili was glad she had packed these when she found herself pumping in a taxi on the way to a job interview. Her flight had been late, and while she had made arrangements to pump when she arrived at the interview, she had already missed her pumping time and could feel her milk starting to let-down. "I had on a new suit for the interview, and didn't want to leak all over it, so I just pumped in the cab!" (There was a divider between her and the driver.)

Planning time to pump

Jen told me the story of her first trip away – and what she learned about asking for the time you need:

I was going to Washington DC from Denver for a kick-off meeting for a project. It was an all-day meeting with the project team. The meeting was very long, and the team decided not to take any breaks. I only pumped one time, at lunch; that was hard. The thing I learned was to be more assertive about saying – preferably ahead of time – that I need these breaks. At that time, I was so new to being back to work, it was with a group of people I'd never met before – I was not as assertive as I should have been.

The hardest part (and I found this to be pretty typical) was that while other moms are very accommodating, and men are generally very accommodating, women without children are not. A woman with no kids was the team leader on this project. Her career was her life. She had no comprehension of life outside of work. I think that with her, even if I had asked for breaks, I don't think she would have been very accommodating anyway. But now I'm much more comfortable with just asking for what I need. I'm more comfortable as a mom, and more confident professionally. I feel more comfortable setting my own rules.

Does it matter where you stay?

If you are going to a conference in a hotel, it is convenient to stay right on site. However, if you are able to make your own travel plans, Jen recommends booking a room in a suite hotel if you can (like Embassy Suites, Homewood Suites, that kind of thing). She says:

I was able to book a hotel on my own, and managed to book a hotel with a kitchen area. That worked really well, as far as being able to wash pump parts out in the restroom. Having a refrigerator in the room makes things so much easier. Having a freezer is really nice too, you can do the freezer packs for your pump bag during the day or overnight. There was one time I didn't have a fridge, and it worked out OK - I just kept filling the ice buckets, but it is more convenient to have the fridge and freezer right there.

Whether your baby comes with you or stays home, these suites are nice. If your baby and another family member are traveling with you, it's great to have a suite so that you can put the baby to bed and then sit up and chat or read a bit. In a single hotel room, once the baby is asleep, you have to turn off the lights and just sit there in the dark – certainly something I didn't think of the first time I stayed in a hotel with my kids.

The magic of Ziploc

When you travel, every mom I've talked to suggests packing a bunch of Ziploc bags in your luggage. Why?

- ଛ If you don't have a freezer, you can fill Ziploc bags with ice to put in your pump bag during the day.

- ଛ Put pumped bags of milk into double layered Ziploc bags so you don't have to worry about leaking in your luggage.

- ଛ Ziploc bags of ice keep your milk cold during travel.

- ଛ Ziploc bags of ice can be used to keep milk cold during the day if you don't have a fridge in your room.

What about the milk?

There are a lot of things to do with your milk on a business trip. If you have a huge stash at home and are only pumping to maintain your supply, you can certainly toss the milk before you come home, but I've never met anyone who had an easy time doing that. If you plan to bring the milk home with you, you'll need to decide if you want to carry it refrigerated or frozen. If you transport the milk frozen and it thaws out on the way home, you'll need to use it as soon as possible when you get home, so be sure that you can find a way to keep it appropriately cold en route. If you bring the milk home refrigerated, you can then freeze it when you get home and save it for a longer period of time, but it can be a concern keeping it cold enough.

Here's Lili's solution:

I carried the milk with ice packs in a Styrofoam box. I used the zip locking milk storage bags – then I'd put 4 of those bags in a larger Ziploc, so they could go in the baggage compartment where it's not pressurized without having to worry about the bags exploding. I was gone for four days, so I froze the first two days worth of milk – I just used the little freezer compartment of the fridge in my room. I also froze all my ice packs. When I packed the Styrofoam box, I interleafed the frozen milk with ice packs – I stood them up sideways, layered with more ice packs on top and bottom. Once I'd packed ice packs around the milk that was frozen, I just put the refrigerated milk on top of the ice packs. I didn't pack the box until right before I had to leave (I always ask for a late check-out). When I got to the airport, I checked the box because it was cold outside, so I figured it would stay colder outside the passenger compartment.

This was actually pretty funny, all the checked bags had to go through the huge x-ray thing before they would put it on the plane, so all the carry-on bags had to go through too. First I gave the guy my black bag, and of course he wanted to know what it was. I said "It's a breastpump", and the guy got all embarrassed, but dutifully opened it up and turned it on to make sure it wasn't some kind of breast-pump-looking-explosive-device. Then he looked at the Styrofoam box and said "what's in there?", and I gave him my best "duh" look, and said (as if it should have been totally obvious) "it's breastmilk." He turned bright red and didn't even open the box. Taking the Medela through airport security was always good for a few laughs. The person in the front of the scanner never wanted to hear what it was – "just put it on the belt, it'll be fine." Then they'd have to back up the belt to look at it again, and then they have to call over some other people to see it. Then they ask me what it is. "It's a breastpump, OK?" and of course then they get all embarrassed and hand it back to me. Or they'd want to see the controls, so I'd have to open it up and show them how it worked.

To check or not to check?

Checking your pump is always risky – not because it'll get damaged, but because if it doesn't show up, you're in trouble. But if you carry it on, that doesn't leave you much space to carry anything else. I liked to have my manual Isis pump with me right there on the plane, and that takes up space, too. But it worked, thanks to the magic of tote bags. For carry-on, you're allowed one bag and one personal item, such as a purse or briefcase. The electric pump becomes your "bag." The rest goes in the tote bag (your "personal item"). If you take only a small purse, and then put it in a larger tote bag along with your manual pump (mine fit in a small lunch-bag, that then fit in the tote bag) and a book to read – there you have your "personal item." It just looks like a really big purse. I rarely had to actually pump in an airport or on the plane, but if your flight gets delayed and you don't have a pump with you, it's really a drag! I have pumped in an airplane once – I did it with my small manual pump (love that Isis), but I was stressed the whole time thinking there was probably a line to use the toilet. However, it was better than leaking on my foolishly chosen white blouse.

Travel pumping schedule

To a large degree, your pumping schedule when you're traveling depends a lot on what you'll be doing. You don't always have the control over your schedule to pump at your usual times. But remember, you're not asking for something unreasonable, so just be clear in asking for breaks when you need them. It may mean excusing yourself from a meeting for a few minutes, but as long as you've told people ahead of time that you will need this, it shouldn't be a problem.

Will you need to pump at night? This depends a lot on your baby's normal schedule. If you have a baby who nurses a lot at night, you may find that you're not able to sleep through the night even if you want to. Your full breasts may rudely awaken you.

Lili again:

Before I went to the conference where I had to pump for Isaac, I had already started not nursing him as much at night, so he was only up once at night. On the trip, I didn't wake up to pump, but I did pump about five times a day. I woke up and pumped at 6am, went to the conference, then took breaks to pump at 10 and 2. Then I pumped as soon as it ended at 6, and then before I went to bed at 10 – about every 4 hours, except in the middle of night. I came back with more milk than he drank when I was gone.

Jen adds:

I usually didn't get up to pump at night. I needed my sleep! I'd pump right before bed, and first thing in the morning. I think getting a full night's sleep (which didn't happen at home) was more important. I didn't make a point to wake up, although if I'd woken up and been uncomfortable, I would have pumped.

When I traveled, I would pump for a long time as I watched

trashy TV before going to bed, then another long session first thing in the morning. That seemed to take care of missing the nighttime feedings. However, if you need to bring home a lot of milk, or have very little time to pump during the day, then waking up once at night is always an option.

What happens at home?

You may need to stock up a bunch of milk before you go – if you don't have a huge freezer stash, this can be a challenge, but see if you can gradually increase your pumping in the weeks before your trip, and try to pump at least once on days you're home. It can be hard to think about your baby facing his first night separated from you. But for the most part, babies adapt to the new situation. You may also find that your baby doesn't take as much as you expect when you're gone.

Here's Lili:

When Isaac was six months old, I had to be gone at a conference for three days. I left a ton of milk for him to drink while I was gone, but I came home with so much more than he'd drunk while I was away. He basically just used the bottle for subsistence. He never took much from a bottle during the day anyway, so I guess it wasn't that much of a surprise. He did fine at night with my husband, but would only sip from the bottle, and never really drank that much.

Jen's experience was similar:

Generally I'd have to build up a little stash before leaving so she'd have enough milk while I was gone. If she needed a bottle of formula while I was gone, then so be it, but she never did. There was always extra milk when I got back – I didn't need all that I'd pumped while I was gone, so it helped me have a bigger stash when I got back.

Remember the basics of bottle-feeding when you're gone – use a slow flow nipple, don't pressure him to finish bottles, don't give a bottle every time your baby cries – sometimes he may just need comforting and carrying, especially if he's not used to being away from mom, or if he's in an unfamiliar place overnight. If your baby takes more than you pump while you're away, just pay special attention to letting your baby nurse on demand when you're back, or do a little extra pumping to rebuild your supply. Or, maybe she just drank a lot because it was coming from bottles and she was sucking for comfort. Ultimately, not that big a deal. If you don't pump enough on a trip of more than a day or two, your supply may drop a bit, but you should be able to boost it back up by spending a couple of days home with your baby nursing on demand.

Being away from an older baby

I started to travel regularly when my son was 16 months old. I had already stopped pumping during the day, so I really only had to worry about doing it at night, since my son usually nursed after daycare, before bed, and in the morning. Honestly, it was kind of nice. I would put on the TV (we don't have TV at home, this was a real treat), pour myself a cup of coffee or glass of wine (depending on which end of the day it was), hook up the pump and channel surf for half an hour or so.

I live in Vermont, but grew up in Cleveland, Ohio. One of my first trips away was to Detroit, where I had a ton of fun watching urban TV. I caught the gospel hour, I watched Sanford and Son reruns, I saw one of the first Fresh Prince of Bel Aire episodes! And, because I was so relaxed, pumped about five ounces each session. Not too bad a deal. I didn't bring the milk home with me, and it was kind of heartbreaking to watch it go down the drain. I suppose you could always drink it, or put it in your coffee.

I still go away from my kids overnight sometimes, but now that I'm nursing a three-year-old, it's a totally different picture. I like to keep my supply up just because I don't want a trip away to be the reason that she weans, so I take a long hot shower morning and night and hand express as much as I can while I'm under the running water. That does the trick, and there's no pump to carry or wash.

Will travel mean weaning?

I was always afraid my babies would wean while I was away. I don't have a problem being a working mother and being away from my kids during the day, but it would trigger all of my maternal guilt feelings to hear myself saying: "My baby weaned while I was on a business trip." The sad truth is that some babies will wean after only a few days of separation, but they were probably getting close to ready anyway. I was lucky, mine didn't wean when I traveled. I did a few things that may have helped – although I could be deluding myself, and just got lucky – but it can't hurt to try:

- ❧ Nurse as soon as you get home. If it's nighttime, you can wake your baby to nurse as soon as you get home, or just be sure you're right there to nurse when they wake up.

- ❧ Nurse in familiar places when you get home. Sitting down in your favorite nursing chair when you get back can remind your baby what they're supposed to be doing.

- ❧ Take a couple days off work. Most companies give their traveling employees a day off after a long trip – take advantage of this. Spending an intensive day with your baby after you've been away is a wonderful way to reconnect.

- ❧ Don't offer a bottle. If your baby won't nurse when you get home, don't offer a bottle. Someone else can feed a bottle, or you can offer some other foods or drinks or a sippy cup. Giving her a bottle sends a message that they won't be getting anything from the breast. If your baby refuses the breast, spend some time skin-to-skin – in bed or in the bathtub – and offer the breast when your baby is sleepy and relaxed. You can find more suggestions in the section on "Breast refusal" in Chapter 8 if your baby starts a nursing strike while you are away.

Working and not pumping

While this book emphasizes the importance of pumping to keep up your milk supply and provide your baby with breastmilk during the day, there are a number of moms who keep breastfeeding without any pumping at all. There are a couple of different approaches to this – one involves still giving exclusive breastmilk, but with pumping outside of work or visits to the baby during the day. Other moms wean to formula for the part of the day when they are routinely separated, while continuing to breastfeed during the parts of the day they are together.

Moms make these choices for a number of reasons. Maria chose not to pump at work simply because she didn't have to. Maria started pumping when she was working from home starting when her son Samuelito was six weeks old. She would pump one side while he nursed the other, and saved all that milk in her freezer for her return to work. After she went back to work full time, she was able to pump enough for her baby's mid-morning feeding from one side as her baby nursed on the other before work. She pumped about 3-4 ounces from one side as her son nursed on the other side. She would then come home to nurse at lunchtime, when she would again feed from one side and pump the other. If another bottle was needed, she would pump more that evening to make up the difference. She kept her baby on exclusive breastmilk with this somewhat "fly by the seat of her pants" approach, which was quite comfortable for her and her family. Maria adds "we co-slept since birth, so I always fed Samuelito at night as needed. We've had no supplementation with formula, and I still have gobs of milk in the freezer." It's interesting to me that she did a lot of pumping before returning to work so that she'd have enough milk, but didn't really end up needing it, as she kept up with Samuelito each day. She recently updated me, and had enough milk in the freezer that she stopped pumping before Samuelito was 11 months old, while still providing him with exclusive breastmilk until he was a year old. At a year, she still goes home at lunch to nurse, but no longer gives any bottles during the day.

Another mother I know chose not to pump at work because she simply didn't like the pumping facility available to her. It was a cramped room with awful lighting, and she just couldn't imagine being there three times a day. She weaned her baby to formula during the day, and really loved the closeness of breastfeeding right after work, in the morning, and before bedtime. She returned to work when her baby was six months old, so her milk supply was strongly established, and her baby was getting formula as well as some solid foods during the day.

Don't feel like pumping three times a day in a storage closet is your only option. For moms who can not or choose not to pump at work, you can still have a long and meaningful breastfeeding relationship with your child. It's important to know that not every woman has the ability to go long stretches between pumping sessions without significantly reducing her milk supply. As discussed in Chapter 2 "Demand and Supply," it has a lot to do with your storage capacity. If you are not pumping during the day and see a drop in your supply when you are home with your baby, pumping even one time during the day (even if you can't keep the milk) will do a lot to keep your baby satisfied at the breast when you are together.

Alternate work situations

I'm not going to tell you to quit your job and stay home, don't worry. But sometimes, once we've gone back to work, we suddenly realize that the dream of 40 hour work-weeks combined with parenting is a bit harder than we thought. I know, you need to work – you have to stay on track with your career, you need to pay the bills. Believe me, I know. But – there are ways you can make it easier on yourself with just a little creative thinking. This section will describe ways women I know have changed their schedules to make life a little easier, while still making a living.

My story – working eighty percent

When I was pregnant with my first baby, I didn't believe the people who told me I had to line up daycare the day I got the positive pregnancy test. C'mon, I live in Vermont, that kind of competition is only for the big cities, right? Wrong. By the time I got around to applying for daycare spots, the soonest anyone could take my son was when he was six months old. The only problem with that was I'd committed to return to my job when he was three months old. So I had to scramble. I was able to get my sister-in-law to watch my son some days, a friend had a nanny she was willing to share when her older son was at kindergarten, and my husband could come home early some days. But the best I could do was 4 days a week. So, I went to my boss (this being a new job I hadn't even started yet) and said "I need to work 4 days a week the first three months" – non negotiable, that was what I had to offer. Luckily he said yes. And, since I'd be working 32 hours a week, I was still technically "full-time," so still qualified for benefits – which we desperately needed.

What I learned from that experience was that four days a week is infinitely easier than five. It was a 20% pay cut, but an 80% improvement in quality of life. I had one day a week to play stay-home mom while my husband was at work – we went to play groups, story hour at the library, and I even went to the gym with my best friend. We'd leave our three kids at the gym childcare for an hour and a half and do an aerobics class – which we both desperately needed – then take the kids out for bagels together. Fridays were my favorite day of the week, just so relaxed. When my son was six months old, I negotiated to keep the four-day arrangement with my boss, called daycare and moved our reservation to four days, and kept up the four day work week until my second child was a year old.

The interesting thing was that I was so conscientious about getting my work done, lest my boss take away my Fridays off, that I think I did just as much work in four days as I did in five, once I was back to full time. I didn't see much improvement in productivity, but I did see a big increase in my stress levels and my need to lie down and rest on the weekends.

The other advantage to having a day home is the amount of "little stuff" that gets done. I find that if I'm home, even if I'm not thinking about it, I'll carry a load of laundry downstairs, or clean up the kitchen a little bit. On a good day, I'd get a lot of housework done, but even on a bad day, I'd end up ahead of where I'd started. That took a lot of stress off the work-day evenings and weekends.

Forty hours in fewer days

Sometimes working less than 40 hours isn't an option, but altered workdays are. My friend Eileen, a lawyer, was able to negotiate four 10-hour days a week, with Wednesdays at home. It was hard to have to pump for an 11 hour separation, but she only had to do it two days in a row, then would have a full day home with her baby to boost her supply back up by nursing all day. She really felt like the long days were worth it to get an extra day at home. Eileen ran a lot of errands on her day home, and usually got the week's grocery shopping done with the baby. She's kind of hard-core, so sometimes she'd even make a few soups and casseroles to eat the next week – anything to make the work-days easier. When all of your workday breaks are devoted to pumping, you wouldn't believe how nice it is just to have a few hours free to run errands.

My friend Katie is a nurse, and is going back to work with three 12-hour days. These will be very long days for her, but she'll be home more days than she's working, so feels like the trade-off is worth it. And pumping will be easier for her, since she'll have 4 days home each week to boost her supply by nursing, and maybe sneak in a pumping session mid-day to store up a little milk for the days when she's working (when it's notoriously hard for her to take enough pumping breaks – she's lucky if she gets three breaks in 12 hours).

Working from home

But enough about these other moms, let's talk about me again. When my daughter was born, I had no paid maternity leave, mortgages to pay, and needed to get back to work, at least part-time, as soon as possible. But at the same time, jumping right back into pumping didn't exactly call to me, and I desperately wanted more time home with my baby! So, it was time to get creative.

I had collected just over three weeks of vacation and comp time that I used to get paid at half my regular salary for six weeks of maternity leave. Once that money ran out, I started working two days a week – but I was in the middle of a big writing project at work (a new software manual, if you're curious), and was able to do that work from home. It was summer, so I had a high school student from down the street come over and watch my daughter for eight hours a day two days a week. My son went to his regular daycare, so I didn't have to deal with the needs and noise of a two-year-old while I was trying to work. The sitter would come to my house and take care of my impossibly young baby, and I would shut myself away and work in a tiny little bedroom upstairs. I never pumped during this time, the sitter would just bring my daughter to me when she was hungry, which gave me some nice breaks. Once we got used to her schedule, the sitter could take her out for walks or to the park between meals, so I'd have the house to myself. It takes discipline to work when your baby's in the house, but I was so freaked out about getting my work done and not jeopardizing the luxury of working from home that I really was able to get a lot done.

We could only afford this for six more weeks, and my boss was wanting me to have some "face time" around the office, so when my daughter was 12 weeks old, I started working two days a week in the office with my daughter at the daycare center, and another two half-days from home with the sitter (during which time I was significantly ripped off, since I did way more than eight hours of work from home, but it bought me a lot of good will around the office).

Finally, when my daughter was six months old, she started full time in daycare, and I went back to the office full time (still four days, which was great!).

Once my daughter was a year old and I was finished pumping, I foolishly accepted a teaching position on top of my other job, got involved in volunteer work promoting breastfeeding, and started writing this book in my "free" time. Now I probably work 60 hours a week and I'm completely insane – which is just to say that taking a reduction in the amount you work for a year or two doesn't mean you're stepping off the fast track forever.

Going truly part-time

If your partner carries your family's health benefits, you have a lot more freedom about your scheduling. After my husband started getting benefits as a public school teacher (he'd been at a private school for years with no benefits), I was presented with an opportunity to start doing some contract work for our health department, but in order to do it, I would need to reduce my hours at the software company. I was able to negotiate a reduction in hours with an increase in hourly pay from my boss by going off the company health insurance policy, which was costing him an arm and a leg.

Cutting hours doesn't have to mean as much of a pay cut as you might think, if you have the flexibility to do your job in fewer hours. And don't assume your employer won't go for it – by eliminating your benefits package, they save a huge amount of money, so they might be willing to let you reduce hours in exchange for that savings.

Job-sharing

I know of women who have worked out really satisfying job-sharing positions when their babies were small. Again, this is a beneficial deal for an employer, at least financially, because two part-time workers without benefits are a lot cheaper than one full-time person with health insurance, retirement, etc. It can provide a much easier life for the employees, and the only downside is the loss of continuity in the position.

If you are job-sharing, it's critically important to work out a good communication machine between you and your job-share partner – and being available by phone on the days that you are home is also very helpful. A once-a-week lunch between the partners facilitates communication of the little details that might get overlooked in the formal hand-off of responsibilities, and besides, it's a lot easier if you're friends with the person you share responsibilities with.

If a company is expanding, job-sharing can be a great way to get two people on board for the price of one, with the possibility of offering them both more hours as the need arises (and the babies get older).

What are you, the chamber of commerce?

I bring up a lot of these business points because you shouldn't go into asking for less hours assuming you're at a disadvantage. Remember that you're offering your employer your expertise and experience (which would be very expensive for them to replace) at a reduced cost – this can be a big plus. And, many bosses, when a mother comes to them asking for reduced hours, realize that if they say no, she may just flat-out quit. Think "employee retention" – this is a big buzz-word around business circles. It's expensive to train a new employee, so just the fact that you've been there for a while is worth several thousand dollars.

When your doctor recommends weaning or supplementing

It is possible that your doctor or your child's pediatrician will give you advice that contradicts what you've learned about breastfeeding. How can that be? Did you get the wrong information? Well, you could have gotten incorrect information about breastfeeding (not from me, of course), but also remember – your doctor may not know what they're talking about. Not to be too hard on doctors – but during their training they are generally not required to take any classes specifically about breastfeeding to graduate from medical school. And, as likely as not, there was not specific breastfeeding information offered in their pediatric or OB residency either. Your doctor was influenced by the people he or she trained with, and if they weren't particularly supportive of breastfeeding, your doctor has not been given the tools to help you maintain a healthy breastfeeding relationship. Pediatrician Dr. Jack Newman has said that doctors don't pressure women to breastfeed because they don't want them to feel guilty if they aren't able to continue breastfeeding – but it's really the doctors who don't want to feel guilty if they are not able to help a woman when she has breastfeeding difficulties.

Conscientious doctors will do extra work to educate themselves about breastfeeding, but there is still not a standard for breastfeeding education in the medical community. As I'm sure you've found out by now, sources of breastfeeding information don't always agree, and breastfeeding information is being updated all the time. Doctors don't always have the time to stay up to date on the latest information in addition to all of the other pediatric research. A lactation professional (an IBCLC), however, has been trained according to an international standard, and is required to stay up to date on the latest research.

When to listen?

To a certain extent, you have to trust your instincts. The "mommy gut" is usually right. If your doctor gives you advice that just doesn't feel right to you, or they recommend weaning or supplementing for any reason, you can always call an IBCLC for a second opinion or ask for a referral to a lactation specialist.

Common issues

Poor weight gain

Poor weight gain in a baby seems to be the number one reason women are told to supplement with formula. From reading the Chapter 2, "Demand and Supply," which of course you have, you know that supplementing with a bottle to replace nursing sessions decreases milk production, and this is the opposite of what you need if your baby is not gaining enough.

There are 2 categories of "poor weight gain" that deserve to be discussed separately; failure to gain in the first days after birth (excessive weight loss after the birth or failure to return to birth weight) and falling off the growth curves later on.

Poor gain after birth

A baby can be expected to lose 7-10% of his birth weight in the first few days after birth. Even with an abundant milk supply, this weight loss makes perfect sense. The section "Getting breastfeeding off to a good start" in Chapter 2 discusses this initial weight loss in greater length, but if breastfeeding is going well, this loss should stabilize within a few days, and babies should start regaining by the end of their first week of life.

When to worry

According to sound lactation practices and Jack Newman's *The Ultimate Breastfeeding Book of Answers*, if weight loss is more than 7-10%, a breastfeeding *evaluation* should take place. Some babies do lose too much if they are not feeding well, and as they continue to lose they get more and more sleepy and become even less likely to nurse effectively. So, an evaluation is in order – but this is not the same as supplementing right away!

Evaluation

Check the diapers – if a baby is not gaining well, but is having consistent wet and poopy diapers, and is alert and bright eyed, the proper course is to wait another day or two. Often the weight loss will reverse itself rapidly once the mother's mature milk comes in.

Check the latch – someone needs to watch the baby actually feeding. Trained lactation professionals can watch the baby latch on, watch for the suck-swallow-pause rhythm of breastfeeding, check the nipple shape after a nursing session and tell if the baby is latched well and emptying the breast effectively. Tongue-tie or neurological effects from drugs used during delivery can cause poor latch. The baby may need to be trained with finger feeding to place his tongue correctly, or the tongue-tie can be surgically corrected.

Check the milk transfer – if the latch and diapers look good and the baby is still not gaining, a high precision scale can be used before and after a feeding to measure the amount of milk being transferred. This is the only way to check this.

How *not* to check breastfeeding amounts – ask the mom to pump into a bottle and see how much the baby will eat. It is very rare to be able to pump as much as the baby can get out, and putting the mom on the spot to "see how much milk she can pump" is a sure recipe for a low output.

If early supplementation is necessary, it can be done without interfering with breastfeeding. Jack Newman's *The Ultimate Book of Breastfeeding Answers* is a great resource for more in-depth evaluation of breastfeeding issues and has step-by-step instructions for handling all of the common bumps in the road. La Leche League's *Breastfeeding Answer Book* and William and Martha Sears' *The Breastfeeding Book* are other great resources –and there are many more good sources out there. When in doubt, find an IBCLC, midwife, or a physician who specializes in breastfeeding medicine.

Later weight loss – falling off the growth curve

I think working moms are particularly plagued with concerns about their babies not gaining enough weight. After you go back to work, you spend so much time and energy working to pump enough, if you hear that there's a chance that your baby isn't getting enough to eat – well, it just kicks that mommy guilt into high gear. A lot of moms I've known are thrown into a panic, pumping like fiends, because their doctor got them nervous that the baby wasn't gaining enough.

What to do if your baby isn't gaining "enough"

If you've been told your baby isn't gaining enough, take a step back and try to look at the whole situation, not just the numbers on a chart. A numerical weight is just one piece of the total health picture. Look for the real signs of any malnourishment.

1. Developmental milestones – this is probably the MOST important thing to look at. Is your baby alert and interactive? Is she on target for milestones like rolling over, sitting up, chattering, smiling, etc.? It's hard to develop normally if you're malnourished, so these are good signs.

2. How does the baby look? Is her skin plump and soft? Are her eyes bright? Or does she look sleepy much of the time with sunken eyes? Does she have rolls of fat on her thighs and wrists and dimples on her butt and hands? If your baby looks plump and moist, is awake and alert, she's not likely to be starving.

3. Family history – I'm a relatively large woman – good Scandinavian stock, athletic, tall (that's my personal ad...). My husband, on the other hand, is small boned and a little height-challenged and 150 pounds soaking wet. My babies were 8.5 and 9 pounds at birth, and neither hit 20 pounds by a year. They went from 90-95th percentile at birth to 10-20th percentile at 18 months. But they were both healthy, ahead of developmental milestones and speaking in sentences by 18 months. It makes sense to me that they would bounce up and down a little before settling on whose body type to have. One more story – a friend was thrown into a panic when her daughter was very small at three months – both she and her husband are big people, so the doc was concerned, but both of them had parents who were pretty small, and the baby didn't gain much even once they started supplementing with

formula. It was just her natural body type to be small, and a lot of needless worry was spent trying to get her to be bigger.

4. Understanding percentile charts – if your baby is just consistently low on the percentile charts, pay attention to the first three points above, but also remember what a percentile chart means. It's a statistical spread of all babies falling in the *normal* range – sick babies, babies with developmental disabilities, and malnourished babies are not included when the charts are made. So a baby in the 99th percentile is bigger than 99% of *normal* babies (and is still normal themselves). A baby in the 1st percentile is smaller than 99% of normal babies, but again, still normal. Some pediatricians seem to want all babies to be in the 50th percentile or higher. Just for kicks, let's play this out as a statistics problem (ugh, I know – it'll be quick). Let's say we fatten up all babies below the 50th percentile so they're 50th or above. Where is the new 1st percentile? That's right, at the old 50th percentile weight! So now even the fat babies are in the 1st percentile, and what do we do next – fatten them up more? Remember that *somebody's* got to be in the first percentile – one percent of us, to be exact.

5. Percentile charts part 2. Most percentile charts are based on formula-fed babies, who have very different growth curves and tend to be bigger. New growth charts have been developed by the CDC and WHO for breastfed babies. Links to these charts can be found in the section "Do I need to supplement" in Chapter 8?

6. Recent developmental milestones. If your baby takes a sudden drop in weight or isn't eating well, think about what they've been doing lately. Is there a new activity he's just learned? The activity can be burning a lot of calories, but also, when babies learn something new, they tend to forget everything else for a while. It may take a week or so before she can roll over AND remember to eat when she's hungry at the same time. Offer the breast frequently when your baby is learning a new skill, and watch for weight to bounce back up once the skill is mastered.

7. Offer other foods – If your baby is older than about 6 months and truly not gaining enough, see if offering a wider variety of foods more frequently makes a difference. My son would not eat baby food from a spoon, but once I cut up cooked veggies and ground meats for him, he ate a lot more.

8. Free Breast Access! As long as your baby has free access to your breasts when you're together, and as long as you're together around 12 hours per day or more, he should be able to get enough to eat, even if you're not pumping quite "enough." Free access means at night too, so don't impose any sleep schedules if you're having weight gain issues. Co-sleeping is a great way to let your baby snack all night and reverse cycling is a good way to be sure he's eating enough. See the sections on "Reverse cycling" and "Nighttime parenting" in Chapter 8 for more information on getting the rest you need when your baby feeds at night.

Doctor recommends weaning

There are several situations in which a doctor may recommend weaning. I can't think of many that are really necessary.

1. Not enough milk – if you are really, genuinely not making enough milk (this can happen with breast surgery, PCOS, thyroid problems, insufficient breast stimulation in the early postpartum period), many docs will recommend weaning and exclusive formula feeding. But why? Some breastmilk is better than none, and the health benefits of any breastmilk at all are clear. Breastmilk can be combined with formula feeding pretty easily. The best method is with a supplemental feeding system (such as a Lact-aid or SNS). With these systems, a small tube delivers formula to the nipple as the baby nurses. This way, all feedings are still at the breast, and there is no nipple confusion. If you are supplementing with a bottle, just watch for signs of the baby starting to prefer the bottle (see the handout for care providers in the Appendix for bottle-feeding recommendations). If the baby starts to prefer the bottle, consider switching to a supplemental feeder, cup or syringe to feed the supplements. And breastfeed frequently to maintain the supply that you have.

2. Medications – often weaning is recommended if you have to take a particular medication. If this is the case, ask for evidence that the drug is *not* safe, and if there are alternatives. Ask your doctor if he is relying on the manufacturer's recommendation, or if he has checked Dr. Hale's reference *Medications and Mothers' Milk* (Hale Publishing 2006). Drug manufacturers are under tremendous pressure not to approve a drug for "pregnant or lactating" women, because of the liability issues. Dr. Hale's book and website (www.iBreastfeeding.com) cite actual research about the safety of various drugs for breastfeeding, and provide information about warning signs to watch for in the infant if the drug is being used. A new resourse from the National Library of Medicine is available at http://toxnet.nlm.nih.gov and http://toxnet.nlm.nih.gov/cgi-bin/sis/htmlgen?LACT. If the drug is truly contraindicated, are there alternatives? A safer drug? Postponing the treatment until the baby is older?

Safe antidepressants are available, so treating depression does not mean you need to wean. In fact, weaning before you are ready can make depression worse, and the hormones released while nursing help to improve mood.

Chemotherapy drugs and radioactive iodine always necessitate weaning, and anti-epileptics are also problematic, although epileptic mothers can usually breastfeed under careful supervision of a physician. Other radioactive contrast materials can be used if the mother doesn't give her baby her milk until the radioactivity is mostly cleared from her system – which often takes less than 24 hours if an isotope with a short half-life is used. She'll have to pump and discard until the radioactivity is gone, but then she can start right up again.

If you only need the drug for a short time, you can often pump and dump until the medication is clear of your bloodstream. If you want to offer the breast for comfort sucking after pumping because only a small amount of the contaminated milk will be passed to your baby, this is another choice women have made when on medications.

Weaning because of baby's age

If your pediatrician tells you that you should wean because your baby is a certain age, and your child hasn't left for college yet, the best answer is "thank you for your concern" and go on and do whatever you feel like doing. There seems to be a prevalent belief that breastmilk magically turns to water at the exact moment a baby turns one year old, because that's when you'll start to hear that it has "no benefits" to the child anymore. However, even if the immune properties of breastmilk disappeared at this point (which they don't), even if the beneficial fats no longer increased brain and eye development (but they do), what is the harm in getting nutritious milk from a comforting source? I think a lot of people think that nursing a baby after a year will create a child that is overly dependant, but both psychological and anecdotal evidence show that children who feel close to their parents and secure in that unconditional love are actually *more* independent than children who feel insecure at home. Breastfeeding is not associated with bad teeth, poor eating habits, ear infections, excessive clinginess or any of the other things you may hear. There is no reason to wean because of a child reaching an arbitrary age.

In support of this, anthropological studies by Kathleen Dettwyler show that in cultures where weaning was left to happen naturally, the average age of weaning is between 2.5 and 7 – years - not months, like here in the US. Kathleen Dettwyler's book is called *Breastfeeding: Biocultural Perspectives (Foundations of Human Behavior)* and is available from Amazon if you're interested in reading more about the natural process of parenting from an anthropological viewpoint. If your child is older than 7 years old and there are concerns about continued breastfeeding, then you run out of some of your ammunition about biological norms - although there are many cases of perfectly normal healthy children continuing to nurse to as old as 10. Until then, it is my belief that all nursing pairs should follow the current recommendation of the AAP (American Academy of Pediatricics) and breastfeed "for at least a year and as long after as is *mutually desirable* for the mother and child. Note that "mutually desirable" doesn't include your doctor, your mother-in-law, or that guy on the street. It's up to you and your baby to decide what works for you.

I should add that just about no one sets out to nurse their baby for two or three years. It just sort of happens. My friend Emily is the head of an electrical contracting company; she's the consummate professional woman – speaking to the chamber of commerce, always stylish in Ann Taylor, managing million-dollar accounts without batting an eye. She's as surprised as anyone that she's still nursing her son on the eve of his third birthday – but her son only nurses once a day, she's been away from him for up to two weeks with no problems, he eats all variety of grown-up foods, and he really enjoys his nursies when mom's around. Why would they stop? He'll gradually nurse less and less often, and most moms who've nursed beyond toddlerhood report that they can't even remember the last time they nursed, they just woke up one day and realized it had been over for a while. A lovely way to move on to the next stage, I think.

Exercise, weight loss and milk supply

Breastfeeding is a great way to lose that baby weight. But after a while, that initial rapid weight loss does slow down, and you may find yourself struggling with the last few post-partum pounds. And, after several months, you might start thinking about fitting into your old clothes before they go out of style. But you may have heard that exercise will somehow spoil your milk, or that your supply can drop if you go on a diet. What's a chubby mom to do?

In a word, take it slow. Everyone's body responds differently to exercise and weight loss. Research has shown that milk output and composition did not significantly change with either calorie reduction or exercise, but in these experiments, there were mothers at the extremes who did see a reduction in milk supply when their caloric intake was a lot lower than their body's needs (Carey et al., 1997; Dewey, 1998).

I had two very different experiences with my two pregnancies. With my first, adding in some exercise starting at about eight months was all it took for me to feel great again. I didn't lose weight when I started exercising, and I just kept eating as much as I felt like, but I started to tone up, which made me feel better (and helped me fit in my clothes again). It was pretty easy to take my son for long walks (and later runs) in our jogging stroller, so baby time and exercise time could be one and the same – a perk that my husband particularly appreciated, since he also got a little time to himself.

I found that as long as I didn't overdo it, I saw no effect on my milk supply in the days after a workout. Some people say you can't breastfeed right after exercising because there will be lactic acid in your milk. Well, maybe there is, but nobody's ever found it harmful to a baby, and I found breastfeeding to be a great way to relax and bring my heart rate down after strenuous exercise. I even did a mini-triathlon when my son was about 13 months old – and have a great picture of me nursing him under a tree right after the race.

Dieting

Once my daughter was born, it was a different story. It was virtually impossible to run with both of them (we had the double jogging stroller, but between the stroller and the two kids, I was pushing over 40 pounds – not all that conducive to getting out – plus my daughter would scream the entire time), and going to the gym was a huge barrier. I had also gained more in my second pregnancy, so I was getting downright plump. In desperation, I went on my life's first diet. I chose the South Beach Diet, which I ended up really liking (and losing weight), but I did learn something from the experience. My daughter was two years old, and I wasn't as worried about milk supply since she was a great eater. I did Phase One of the diet religiously, which involves cutting out all but about 3 grams of carbohydrates for two full weeks. Even though I wasn't pumping, I noticed an almost immediate drop in my milk supply, and so did my daughter. After I started adding back some whole grains and limited carbs, my milk supply rebounded right away. Of course, after that I found out that breastfeeding moms are supposed to skip right to Phase Two – and that must be why. A carb-free diet really limited my milk production, and it was kind of amazing to watch my milk come back in as I started eating things like brown rice and plain yogurt.

Note: carb-free diets are also not recommended for breastfeeding moms because your body releases ketones when metabolizing fat in the absence of carbohydrates. Ketones are not on the recommended food list for babies. I don't know that the amounts found in breastmilk can be dangerous, but why risk it, right? A low-carb diet that emphasizes whole grains is fine – just don't do a strict Atkins regimen while you're breastfeeding.

How do you find the time?

I used to exercise religiously; I mean, I was a total gym rat. If I let more than a day go by without a workout, I was a crabby mess. This changed a lot with kids. I haven't been to a gym in months, but I have to say, I've stayed in relatively good shape. What it took for me was 1) not eating like a gym rat anymore (i.e., realizing that I don't need a half pound of pasta for dinner), and 2) accepting new forms of exercise. I used to totally scorn walking as exercise – that was for people too weak to run, right? Ha ha, joke's on me, I love to walk now. I live in town, and walk everywhere with my kids. We walk to the park, to the library, downtown for a bagel, to the waterfront. We still usually take a stroller in case anyone gets tired, which means that (at least on the way home) I can usually walk fast enough to get my heart rate up. I try to stay active with the kids – taking them swimming, skiing, ice skating, and hiking. Yes, we're an obsessively outdoorsy family, but what I've realized is that exercise doesn't have to be a formal set-aside activity to count. Just leading an active life makes up for a lot. So, pulling the kids in the bike trailer for three miles takes the place of a forty-mile solo ride. Walking them downtown takes the place of a five-mile run. Carrying them up the stairs replaces squats at the gym. Make it work for you. We have a balance board at home, and I make long phone calls into workouts by balancing on the board the whole conversation – so call me anytime – I'll make time to talk!

More organized solutions

The catch-as-catch-can approach to exercise can work in a pinch, but it does feel good to actually plan some exercise into your schedule. For me, I was not able to even think about this until my kids were at least six months old. Before that, I was doing a lot of walking with a stroller, but I was so tired from working, breastfeeding, and not sleeping that the idea of an aerobics class turned my stomach a little bit. Once I passed that six-month mark, it did get a lot easier, and working out some felt more manageable.

Scheduling

If you always used to exercise after work, you may find that this doesn't work for you anymore. You just want to be home with your baby, you're tired, and it seems ridiculous to get home at 7 at night just to put your baby to bed. If you're pumping during the day, that pretty much shoots the lunch-time trip to the gym as well. What does that leave – ah, the dreaded morning workout. But for most working moms, morning workouts are the easiest to manage.

If you've been meaning to buy a piece of exercise equipment for your home, this can be a good time to take the plunge. Taking the travel/pumping/bottle barriers away means you'll be more likely to exercise, and if you don't, at least you'll have a stylish new thing to hang your workout clothes on. Just remember, make it easy for yourself. Just like with pumping and breastfeeding, realistic goals make it seem possible. If you tell yourself on the first week that you're going to walk three miles five days a week, that may be intimidating enough that you don't start at all. If you have a treadmill, what about starting with one mile twice a week? Or walk from your house to a nearby landmark before your partner leaves for work. Or do an aerobics or yoga tape in your living room for half an hour before everyone else wakes up. Having your partner in on the plan makes morning exercise a lot easier. If they can watch the baby to give you 30 minutes to yourself, it will be possible to get a great workout.

Keeping perspective

I gained about 45 pounds with my second pregnancy. I actually lost most of the weight when I was tandem nursing, but got used to eating like a horse during that time. After my son weaned and my daughter started taking solids, I kept eating like the fate of the world depended on it, and ballooned up 25 pounds. But I was still nursing and pumping, and dealing with the time demands of two kids in diapers and a full time job. My health was not exactly at the top of my list. I didn't really care that I was fat.

But, like all things babies and parenting, nothing is forever. I had spent my life as a fit person, I knew I'd be a fit person again someday – just not that particular day. I kind of sat back and waited to start caring again. And you know what? It happened! Not until my daughter was two years old, but one day I saw a picture of myself and said "dang, I'm fat!" Not like I hadn't seen a picture of myself in two years – I was just finally ready to register it. And, I finally had the mental energy to think beyond the kids and start to think about taking care of myself again.

I didn't have much luck with exercising beyond my basic activity level because it was just so hard to justify taking more time away from the kids, so that's when I did my diet. I think because I waited until I was ready, dieting was a lot easier than I thought it was going to be, and I lost the weight in a few months.

I felt like I was at a critical juncture – if I'd let another year go by, I might have just accepted my "new" size and gone forward, but there was something about emerging from the absolute intensity of the baby period that helped me remember what it used to feel like to fit in my jeans – and make me want that feeling again.

So – give yourself some time. If you're pushing to lose weight by the time your baby is six months old, you'll probably be good at making yourself tired and stressed, and you might not be able to get the weight off as fast as you want to. Wait until you feel ready – and then, adhere to the golden rule of weight loss – find a partner! Dieting, exercise, quitting smoking – any lifestyle change is easier with a buddy. Call your old pumping buddies or breastfeeding support group – some of them might be ready to start too! In fact, as of this exact week, I just called my friend Beth and we've started going to the gym two days a week. My oldest is 5, my youngest is 3 – I think that's not too shabby to be starting to exercise again.

Getting the housework done

Housework is the bane of working mothers everywhere. I know a lot of women who are married to men who are very sensitive about sharing the housework, very willing to do laundry and dishes and cooking, and eager to be equal partners. But with few exceptions, women still feel like the overall "management" of the household is their responsibility. From scheduling the electrician to making sure there's milk in the fridge, a lot of moms take on these things as a matter of course.

Partly it's because women do tend to be better at multi-tasking – which means that even on the busiest days at the office, we're haunted by the constant prattle of our mental to-do list. "Get some eggs on the way home, when was that doctor's visit again, wonder what we'll have for dinner tonight, do I have any clean panty-hose, is our washing machine going to conk out of I don't get that maintenance check done..." – it never seems to shut up. Men (and again, this is a generalization) are better at shutting that list up when there's other stuff to be done.

Share the work

My advice – don't be a martyr. Just because you're the one who thinks of getting eggs after work, doesn't mean you have to be the one to do it. But passing these responsibilities to your partner may mean some formalizing of systems. I wasted years of frustration wishing my husband would just pay attention to the dang eggs and take the initiative to get some when we were running out. That was a huge waste of time. The market is right on his way home, and if I email him at work and say "please get eggs on the way home" he does it, and really doesn't mind – he just wouldn't think of it in his own.

My second piece of advice – formalize the job assignments. Before we had kids, my husband and I just did what needed to be done around the house, whoever saw a job did it. Seemed to work well; we did about the same amount of stuff, and nobody felt constrained or resentful. But after kids, well it all seemed to change. I had my pump to wash at night, bottles to fix and pack, I was pumping all day, and just didn't have the same energy at home, but still felt like I had to "keep up" on the housework. It took a long time for us to work things out, and we're still working on it – but it's been a worthwhile investment to figure out how to assign jobs.

For example, the garbage is his job (I know, total gender stereotype – if it helps, I installed the dishwasher and he does the kids' laundry). So, when I'm home and the garbage is full, I'll empty it if I get around to it, but I know if I don't, he'll do it. At the same time, he doesn't mind that I've ignored it – or if I tell him it needs to be emptied. It's his job, why would he mind. Packing the kids lunches has evolved into my job (from taking care of the bottles), and I just know it's something I need to do. I don't feel resentment if it's not done for me, since it's my job. If my husband does it for me, it's a nice perk that I get to feel grateful for the help, and he looks like Mister Thoughtful.

I found that the chores we fight about are the ones that aren't assigned. There's no better recipe for resentment than hoping someone else will do a job that they haven't noticed needs doing. If you're the one who notices when the cat litter needs changing, then it should probably be your job – or have a very clear arrangement that you can ask your partner to do it and they need to not complain about it.

Hire it out

Even with the best job-sharing arrangement, housework can really feel overwhelming when you're working, pumping, and taking care of a baby. If there's anything you can afford to hire out, at least for this first year, do it. Hiring a housekeeper, that's such a bourgeois luxury, isn't it? Not necessarily. We had someone who came and cleaned every other week, and it cost us $70/month. At the time, that was a lot of money for us, but the difference it made in our lives was stunning. Just to know that at least once or twice, we'd come home to a clean house saved our sanity. For $70/month, she didn't do that much – vacuumed, washed the floors, cleaned the and the grungy countertops – just the basics. But on days she'd been there, the house just *looked* so clean, in a way we could never manage, so we felt taken care of. And, when you pay someone to clean your house, you have to at least pick up a path on the floor, so it keeps the mess from getting too out of control.

And you know what? It gets easier. Our housekeeper quit this year (the kids are 3 and 5) and we were distraught. But in typical fashion, we were too lazy to replace her, and honestly, we've been fine. The kids are big enough to help with picking up, and also big enough to entertain themselves while we clean the , and we've managed to keep up with the cleaning – when only 3 years ago, it was an impossibility.

What else can you do to make your life easier? Brainstorm a bit – what would really make you feel pampered? If you have family in town, will they have you over for dinner once a week – saving you a night of shopping, cooking and cleaning up. What about take-out meals? We spend so much at the grocery store that sometimes take-out is actually cheaper. We have a great little Italian dive around the corner where you can still get a plate of pasta for $5, and eating there twice a week when our son was small felt like such a treat.

Finally – sometimes you just have to lower your standards. If you've been someone who dusts weekly, well, you might have to be someone who doesn't dust for a while. If your self-esteem is based on presenting gourmet meals every night of the week, remember, you're making gourmet meals for your baby all day long – you can let that dinner one slide a little bit. Your house won't be messy forever, but if you strive to keep it in pre-kid pristine shape, you can guarantee that you'll be miserable and exhausted. Your choice: rested and messy, or Martha-Stewart-perfect and completely devastated by stress. I think you'll enjoy your baby and your role as a parent a little more if you let some substandard housekeeping slip through. You can, instead, present a well-nourished, healthy, happy baby to the world as your public face.

What's for dinner?

This section has a selection of a few of my favorite EASY recipes. These are hand picked to take either 20 minutes or 10 hours (in a Crock-pot). Let me tell you, I never thought much of a Crock-pot till I became a working mother. Now I am a convert. There is nothing at all like having dinner ready and hot when you walk in the door at the end of the day. Since I am strangely lacking in the servant department, I have to settle for the Crock-pot. I also made an investment in a rice cooker with a 13 hour timer – this has also been a blessing, and lets us eat more healthy foods. While there's never time for brown rice if you start at 6, if it can start while you're still at work, it's easy!

One of the things I'm most looking forward to on my website is the recipe exchange. Be sure to drop by and share your favorites – you'll find a message board dedicated to quick and easy recipes at www.workandpump.com/talk.

Love that Crock-pot

OK, I know, it's technically called a "slow cooker," and there is now more than one brand on the market. Humor me, I call mine a Crock-pot. Here are my favorite (and easiest) recipes:

Barbeque Sandwiches

When I say easy, I really mean easy.

2 lbs boneless chicken of your choice OR 2 pork tenderloins, cut into 2" medallions

1 bottle barbeque sauce

Place the meat and ¼ bottle of barbeque sauce in the Crock-pot. Cover. Cook on low all day. If you have an extra minute, throw in 2-3 crushed garlic cloves and a cut up onion.

When you get home, pour off the cooking liquid, take 2 forks and pull the meat apart until it is well shredded. Mix with more barbeque sauce until it is well coated but not runny. Serve on sandwich rolls with hot sauce.

Cream of Sodium Chicken Deluxe

1 whole chicken, cut up

1 can cream of something soup – any concentrated cream soup will do – cream of chicken, mushroom, celery, etc. Make sure it's a concentrated soup (meant to be mixed with one can of water)

Veggies of your choosing – I like celery, carrots, and maybe a couple little red-skin potatoes.

Plunk it all in the Crock-pot, cook on low all day. This is great with egg noodles.

To-Die-For Roast

1 beef roast, any kind

1 package dried brown gravy mix

1 package dried Italian salad dressing mix

1 package dried ranch dressing mix

1/2 cup water

Place beef roast in Crock-pot. Mix the dried mixes together in a bowl and sprinkle over the roast. Pour the water around the roast. Cook on low for 7-9 hours.

Variations from Ann: I like to cut the meat up into small pieces. I have also added sour cream after removing it from the Crock-pot to make an easy beef stroganoff!

Chicken Chili from Liz

Skinless, boneless chicken breasts (note, Liz does not eat dark meat at all. I think this would be good with some thigh meat too)

Salsa

1 Can Fiesta (a/k/a Mexican) Corn

1 Can Pinto Beans

Put chicken in Crock-pot

Slather with salsa

Cook all day

Shred Chicken (with 2 forks, like for the barbeque sandwiches)

Add Corn & Beans

Heat through (this takes about another hour, or you can microwave if you're in a hurry)

Serve as chile, nacho topping, burrito stuffing – and it's even healthy!

Sticky Chicken from Bridget

This one takes a little more prep time up front, but is quite delicious. If you make the spice rub the night before and coat the chicken, all you have to do in the morning is start it cooking.

4 tsp salt

2 tsp paprika

1 tsp cayenne pepper (this seems like a lot, but after cooking all day, it's barely spicy)

1 tsp onion powder

1 tsp thyme

1 tsp white pepper

1/2 tsp garlic powder

1/2 tsp black pepper

1 large roasting chicken

1 cup chopped onion

In a small bowl, combine the spices. Remove giblets from chicken, clean the cavity well and pat dry with paper towels. Rub the spice mixture into the chicken, both inside and out, making sure it is evenly distributed and down deep into the skin. Place in a resealable plastic bag, seal and refrigerate overnight. When ready to cook chicken put onion in the cavity and put it in the Crock-pot and *do not add any liquid*. As the cooking process goes on it will produce it's own juices. Cook on low 8 to 10 hours and it will be falling off the bone tender. It's kind of amazing how much liquid this makes – very good with rice.

Out of the Crock-pot and onto/into the stove

Nicole's Pork Tenderloin

1/4 C. maple syrup

2 T. Dijon Mustard

1 T. Cider vinegar

1 pork tenderloin

Mix first 3 ingredients and brush/spread over pork. Let marinate for 1/2 hour to overnight. Grill or roast at 350 degrees until internal temp reaches 160 degrees Farenheight. The pork is amazingly tender and tasty!

Pesto Stove-top Chicken

1 jar pesto

2 lbs chicken – I prefer boneless skinless thighs, but breasts work OK (if a little dry)

Heat 3-4 Tbsp oil in a 12" skillet on the stove (I like a mix of vegetable and olive oil)

Slather pesto on one side of the chicken pieces. When the pan is hot, arrange the chicken in a single layer in the pan with the pesto side down. This dish does well with some benign neglect – with heat on medium, go about your business. Make a vegetable, set the table, wash your pump. If you don't disturb it, the pesto makes a delightful crust. Slather more pesto on the other side and turn after about 15 minutes. Cook until done through. Great with pasta.

Roasted Cauliflower

Note here – I don't really like cauliflower, but I love it cooked like this – it has an entirely different flavor

Cut up 1 head cauliflower into florets

Arrange in a single layer in a shallow baking dish

Drizzle liberally with olive oil

Sprinkle with coarse salt (like sea salt or kosher salt)

Bake at 400 for 25-30 minutes. Stir once ½ way through cooking time.

Soups

Weekends are soup-time at my house. I like to cook up a couple of big pots of soup over the weekend. These don't have to be quick, they can take all day. But the end result is that you have soup in your freezer and fridge to eat during the week. For soup during the week, I resort to super-easy carrot-ginger soup or the Crock-pot.

Carrot-Ginger Soup

This is the easiest soup ever, and goes from start-to-table in about 30 minutes.

Peel 1lb carrots, cut into 1" sections (can do this the night before)

Put in a 2qt saucepan, barely cover with water.

Add 1 tsp salt

Boil until carrots are tender

While carrots are boiling, peel and grate a 4" piece of ginger (don't do this the night before, it'll dry out too much)

Puree the carrots and water – don't drain! (I have an immersible hand-blender that's great for this)

Place the grated ginger in a paper towel. Hold it over the soup and squeeze hard. You'll get a surprising amount of juice! Throw out the squeezed ginger

Add ½ cup heavy cream and mix.

Ta-daah! You're done – enjoy!

Basic Bean Soup in the Crock-pot

This can be made during the week, as long as you're willing to do some chopping the night before. My standard recipe doesn't vary much, and is not very precise, but here's the basic idea. Even soup in the Crock-pot is a fair amount of work chopping, but it can all be done the night before.

Night before:

1. Chop an onion and several cloves of garlic. No matter how many layers you wrap these in, they will smell by morning. I usually leave them on the countertop with double saran wrap instead of stinking up my fridge.

2. Make a spice mixture. For a bean soup, I like about 1 tsp each of cumin, coriander, turmeric – this gives a sort of middle-eastern taste. You can also use basil, oregano, thyme (nice in a white bean soup), or bay leaves.

3. Soak beans. I start with 1lb dry beans. My favorites for soups are black beans and any kind of small white beans. Cover the beans with water and let them soak overnight.

4. Choose your meat. I like to add 1" sections of kielbasa to a soup, just because it doesn't require pre-cooking – you can just toss it into the soup right from the package. Bacon and sausage are also nice additions, but need to be cooked the night before.

5. Do you want veggies? Carrots and celery are always nice. Sometimes I add chopped kale or spinach. Chop these all the night before, or skip if it's starting to feel like too much work.

In the morning:

1. Dump everything in the Crock-pot. For a pound of beans, I find about 6 cups of broth makes a good soup.

2. Turn on low, leave the house.

Maintaining your relationship with your partner

People who know me will laugh that I'm writing about having a good marriage – mine is such a struggle sometimes. But at least we're working on it, which is the most important part. If your life before children was as carefree as ours was, it's impossible to foresee how much stress kids, jobs and responsibility can add.

I've heard people say "your kids will grow up and move out someday, and when that happens, you'd better hope you still have a relationship with your husband!" My initial response to that is "oh, shut up. You don't have to live my life, and the kids need this and that and this and that – right now! They have to be my first priority." But you know, they're right, you do have to remember that the foundation of the family is your relationship with your partner, and if that relationship is in good working order, a lot of the rest will just fall into place.

So, if your typical week revolves around baby-work-home-baby, how on earth can you find five minutes to connect with this person that, presumably, at some point, you were in love with? I think part of the secret is that five minutes can be all you need to make a difference. When you're running around frantically, if you and your partner take five minutes to sit on the couch (this can be while you're nursing) and talk to each other – you know, Ward and June style "how was your day, dear?" kind of stuff, the rest of your life will start to feel easier. It's so easy to let the rush of daily life keep us from even checking in with each other – I know my husband and I will let three days pass without any more meaningful conversation than "can you pick up some eggs on the way home." Make time to just say "hello" every day – it really works.

Sharing chores

Does the word "martyr" ever cross your mind? If you're fuming as you wash pump parts and pack bottles and make dinner while your partner watches TV, it's time for a talk. Don't let yourself get sucked into feeling like you have to do it all – this is the kiss of death for any relationship. If you need to sign up for a few couples counseling sessions to figure out a division of labor that feels equitable, it's well worth the time invested. I think in any family where there are small children, both parents feel like they are doing the lion's share of the work – because there's just a lot of work to be done. Don't let yourself become bitter – have the hard conversations about sharing work before you become entrenched in your resentment.

What about time away?

I hear a lot of moms worrying about how she and her partner are going to get some time alone, away from the baby. As if this were the magical secret to maintaining an intimate relationship. Let me start with a story. Heather emailed me, wondering how much milk she would need to pump ahead of time for an overnight at a hotel with her husband, and how often I thought she would need to wake up during the night to pump. Her husband had really wanted a "romantic" getaway, and had scheduled it for when their baby was only four months old, as if to somehow mark the end of their confinement as parents. I felt so bad for her, because she so wanted to do something to make her husband happy, but she was so stressed about pumping before the big night, pumping while she was away, and worrying about how her baby would be with her gone for the night that she was really not going to have a good time at all. It was just way too much stress for something that was supposed to be fun. I know that her husband thought he was doing something special and nice for her, but in the end, it was just making her miserable.

Try to find ways to make a special treat include the baby, and everyone will have less to worry about. Babies do sleep eventually, after all. Read on…

Where is the love?

So then, without the romantic weekend getaway your partner has been dreaming of, how do you go about re-establishing an intimate relationship? I think the first step is to recognize that most moms don't feel the need to "get away." You are biologically tied to this little person, they need you in a way you've never been needed before and there's something really special about that. So instead of getting away from the baby, what about building some special time around the baby? There are a lot of things you and your partner can do to feel connected and intimate, but a lot of times, the discussion comes down to one thing – sex.

If you're too tired for sex, let your partner know what would make you feel more well-rested. Getting up every three hours at night to pump and resenting him lying there sleeping is probably not the right answer – but maybe bringing home a nice dinner from your favorite restaurant and cleaning up all the dishes would make a difference. Or taking you out for dinner with the baby, and then putting the baby to bed after you've nursed her to sleep. Even a night in a hotel can include your baby. If you need a separate room to lose your inhibitions, a suite is usually not much more than a single room. You can put the baby to bed, enjoy some private time, watch pay-per-view, and then go to sleep with your baby. Sometimes just getting to a place where you know you don't have to make the bed in the morning is enough to help you and your partner enjoy each other.

If your baby sleeps in your bed or in your bedroom, a lot of times this makes partners feel displaced and shut out from their usual intimate space. See if you can create a new intimate space. I've read several articles written by men about how to make co-sleeping work for your family, and they all say the same thing: take sex out of the bedroom. Even the most attached baby will sleep for an hour or so in the evening or early morning, and this can be a great opportunity for a little canoodling in the guest room, TV room, or floor.

And the sad but honest truth is that you may find yourself having sex when you don't feel like it. Most new moms report feeling "touched-out" at some point, just wanting a little physical space when the baby is asleep. If you were used to jumping your partner every night in your pre-kid life, you may be wondering what's wrong with your relationship to cause you to lose that urge. The problem with your relationship is that you're exhausted, your hormones have totally changed, and you're working way too hard. Which means that what used to come naturally now may require a little more conscious effort. Making the effort to be intimate may feel really artificial, but the extra work is worth it. There are feelings of emotional closeness that are fostered by physical intimacy – it really is important. And, as my friend Liz reports, "even if I don't feel like it in the beginning, I usually find that

I relax and start enjoying myself after a few minutes (wink)."

Your partner also needs to understand that the physical demands of mothering a baby do indeed diminish your sex drive. It's a hard truth of parenting, but again, like most initial hardships, it's not forever. There are temporary solutions. Let me share a joke. A husband and wife used the euphemism "doing the laundry" for having sex. One night the wife came up to bed after her husband, and asked if he wanted to do the laundry. He replied "no, I only had a small load, so I did it by hand." Your partner may have to get by with a little more hand washing in the first six months to a year, but after that, your desire starts to creep back.

Date night

Once your baby is older, and especially if you can do it without pumping, an evening out without a baby is nice. When babies are tiny, it's actually pretty easy to take them places. The language of an R-rated movie doesn't really register with a 4-month old, and if you use a sling or put your baby in their carseat carrier to sleep, you can enjoy a lovely dinner out while your baby naps and nurses. But once they're a little older, it gets to be less fun to take them out. A walking nine-month old is not that fun in the movies, and you stop being so sure they're not learning new words. When I started teaching, I had to do a lot of prep work in the evenings, which my husband hated. We kept ourselves going by declaring every Thursday night "date night." We became the masters of the cheap date. The babysitter was an arm and a leg, so we'd get my sister-in-law to watch the kids if we wanted to eat at a nice restaurant. When we had to pay a sitter, we'd go to see a second-run movie at the cheap seats, go sit on the beach for a couple hours with a bottle of wine, or play tennis at the public courts. We had a ton of fun, and by then the kids could go to sleep without nursing, so I could just wake them for a nighttime nursing if I was feeling full before morning.

I have an acquaintance who has four kids, and has not spent so much as an evening away from them since the first was born six years ago. This is not an approach that works for me. Being able to leave my kids for the occasional evening out lets me and my husband feel like a carefree childless couple – and the truth is, we just talk about how much we miss the kids after the first five minutes or so. I also think it's important that I leave the kids with my husband and get out on my own sometimes. After an evening out with my girlfriends, I come home really appreciating my husband, and much more willing to make some special time for him.

References:

Carey G, Quinn T, et al. 1997. Breast milk composition after exercise of different intensities. *Journal of Human Lactation* **13**(2): 115-120.

Dewey K. 1998. Effects of maternal caloric restriction and exercise during lactation. *Journal of Nutrition* **128**(2): 386S-389S.

Common Concerns the Second Six Months

Troubleshooting later breastfeeding problems – part 2, the later months

Once you make it through the first two weeks, you're pretty much out of the woods as far as breastfeeding problems go. But there are issues that will tend to pop up in the later months. Dealing with them in a timely fashion keeps them from interfering with your breastfeeding.

Plugged ducts

Plugged ducts are pretty common among working moms, especially when your schedule gets disrupted. If you are not able to pump on schedule or miss a session, or are weaning from the pump, it's not uncommon for a plug to form. You will feel a hard or tender spot on your breast behind the duct that is not draining. The lump forms because milk is blocked from exiting the breast and begins to accumulate in the glandular tissue.

These plugs are usually pretty easy to get out if you can catch them early. Nurse and/or pump often on the affected side; this is the best way to work a plug loose. You can also try gently massaging from behind the lump towards the nipple while you pump or nurse. Placing a warm compress (disposable diapers run under hot water work great for this) on your breast before nursing or pumping can help the plug soften and resolve. Another method is to get into a hot shower and, after letting the hot water run on your breast for a while, gently massage from behind the lump towards the nipple. Sometimes you will even see the plug express from your nipple like a piece of spaghetti (yeah, it's gross, but you'll feel a lot better!).

Any time you are treating a plugged duct, be sure you are drinking lots of water and resting as much as you can. Your body needs good hydration and extra reserves to fight off infection when there is milk blocked in the breast. Some women seem to get more plugged ducts than others. The first thing to check is that you're nursing or pumping often enough, and that your pump flanges fit correctly. If so, taking a lecithin supplement can help keep plugs from forming. Take one dose 3-4 times each day, either 1 tablespoon of liquid or 1 capsule (1200 mg) per dose. Lecithin is a healthy nutritional supplement, so you can keep taking it every day for as long as you're nursing as long as it is helping keep the plugs at bay.

Mastitis

Mastitis is the infection that follows from a plugged duct if the milk is not drained from the breast. It gets more common in working moms as you start to work harder, rest less, and slack off in watching your nutrition. Since our breasts are one of the more vulnerable parts of our bodies, they are often the first to show signs of overwork, so mastitis can sometimes develop when you haven't even noticed a plug form. There is no mistaking mastitis, except as maybe the flu. If you start to feel tired and achy, with a fever and a sore breast, that's mastitis, and you'll need antibiotic treatment as soon as possible. And take it as a message to pamper yourself a little more – your immune system needs rest to work efficiently.

Nipple pain

Once you have successfully established breastfeeding, nipple pain works its way down the list of potential problems, since you probably have a good latch to have made it this far. If nipple pain rears its ugly head at this point, it's worth reminding yourself not to get lazy about latch, but it's also wise to look for other causes.

Thrush

The most common cause of later-onset nipple pain is the dreaded fungal infection known as thrush – a yeast infection that can colonize your nipple, the ducts of your breast, your baby's mouth and your baby's digestive system (which usually comes with a diaper rash).

Thrush often will appear after a course of antibiotics, since the yeast (Candida) that causes thrush lives in our bodies all the time, but is usually kept in check by other beneficial bacteria that live alongside it. So – getting rid of thrush is easy, right? Just tip the balance back in favor of the good guys. That's the right idea, but it's rarely that easy. Treating thrush is a royal pain, largely because of its tendency to reinfect. Get rid of thrush in your baby, but if there's any in your nipples, your baby will get it again. Get rid of thrush in your nipples, but if there's any in your baby's mouth, you will get it again. Back and forth, towards infinity. That's why it's so important that you and your baby are treated at the same time for any suspected thrush. And why it's also important to clean anything around the house that could be harboring yeast, just waiting to reinfect.

Recognizing thrush

Thrush is often confused with other things. Nipple pain can be misdiagnosed as bad latch or tongue-tie; diaper rash can be attributed to a food allergy. However, if you have nipple pain emerging after any initial discomfort has resolved, suspect thrush. If your baby cries as if in pain when nursing, suspect thrush. Thrush in your baby's mouth can look like cheese curds (the chunks in cottage cheese) that don't wipe off, and your baby will often complain when nursing, as this infection can be very painful. Sometimes the mouth looks normal, and a baby who is fussy when nursing is your only sign. Check for a yeasty diaper rash, which looks different from other diaper rash because the center is usually raised and red, with small circular dots spreading from the main area like a Jackson Pollack painting.

Treatment protocols:

Treating thrush usually starts with a drug called Nystatin. This is a topical antifungal, similar to what's found in vaginal yeast preparations. Your baby will be given nystatin drops to take orally – the drug works to kill the yeast in the baby's mouth and digestive tract. If the yeast is causing a diaper rash, a topical nystatin cream might be prescribed for your baby's bum as well. Topical nystatin cream is the first line of defense for nipple thrush, and is applied to the nipples several times a day. The cream may have carriers in it that are not suitable for your baby to ingest, so be sure to ask if you need to wipe the cream off before nursing.

Any time thrush is being treated or is suspected, I highly recommend a course of acidophilus along with it to add more good bacteria to the balance. You can take capsules orally yourself, and the infant powder can be smeared around your baby's mouth as well as on your nipples.

While treating, safeguard your house against reinfection. All toothbrushes, washcloths, towels, bras, nursing pads, bottles, nipples, and pacifiers need to be sterilized or washed in very hot water. White vinegar can be used to kill off thrush, and Grapefruit Seed Extract can be used as well. Grapefruit seed extract is sold in a very concentrated form, and 5 to 10 drops per ounce of water is strong enough to disinfect. This solution can also be used on your nipples after every feeding.

Other treatments

If thrush is not responding to the nystatin treatment, it is important to keep after it until you and your baby are pain free. An effective thrush treatment should bring about *some* improvement within two to three days, so if you're not finding any relief, it's time to re-evaluate. It can be frustrating, but keep at it, you'll be glad you did! Here are some other treatments that can be tried.

There are other nipple creams that can be used – Dr. Jack Newman's APNO (All Purpose Nipple Ointment) is often recommended by lactation consultants. This needs to be mixed by a pharmacist, but the recipe is publicly available on the kellymom. com website (ww.kellymom.com/newman/candida_protocol_12-02.html)

Gentian violet is an herbal remedy that has been used for fungal infections for ages. While this is a "natural" remedy, it is still a very strong drug, and should not be used for more than seven days. 1% Gentian Violet solution can be purchased or ordered from a health food store, or ordered online. It is not very expensive – the last time I bought a bottle, it was around $5, and it's a lifetime supply. Gentian Violet is a permanent purple dye, so be cautious when using it. The treatment protocol involves 'painting' your nipples with the solution one time a day for 4 to 7 days. The baby should also get one drop of Gentian Violet directly in the mouth once a day. More information can be found at http:// www.kellymom.com/newman/06gentian_violet.html

The pharmaceutical choice for thrush is a drug called Diflucan (fluconazole). Diflucan is usually given in doses of 100 mg twice a day, but for treating persistent ductal thrush, it requires a loading dose of 400 mg one time, then 100 mg twice a day for a full week after the mother is pain free. If symptoms are persisting, look around for how you could be reinfecting. I know one family that struggled with thrush being passed between mother and baby for months, they had tried everything. Finally, the mom took a good look in the dad's mouth and saw those little white patches – dad had been reinfecting mom, who kept passing it back to the baby. Once dad got treated (oral Nystatin did the trick) the thrush cleared up for the whole family. The cost of new toothbrushes was worth it.

http://www.kellymom.com/bf/concerns/thrush-resources.html

http://www.breastfeeding-basics.com/html/candida.htm

Normal developmental issues in the first year

Starting solids

Most pediatricians recommend starting solids when your baby is "about six months" old. What's up with "about"? Why not just a set age? Well, because most babies are ready when they're right around six months old, but it varies from baby to baby. If your baby is not showing signs of readiness, there's no reason to start solids earlier than six months.

How do you know your baby is ready? Believe me, you'll know. You'll be sitting at the table and your baby will watch every forkful as it travels from your plate to your mouth. She'll also start to drool when she watches you eat. A trusty source told me that the drooling is the maturation of salivary amylase – an enzyme that digests carbohydrates in the mouth – indicating a readiness to digest complex carbohydrates. Makes sense to me. If your baby seems ready very early, most pediatricians recommend waiting until at least four months of age, and probably even five. This is to be sure the gut is mature – which helps prevent allergies

– although I'm sure your mother will be happy to tell you that you were eating pureed broccoli with milk at three months and you turned out just fine. Actually, that's what I was fed, and I'll admit to still loving broccoli, but I've struggled with a milk allergy most of my life.

Why start solids any sooner?

If your baby is not necessarily begging for food at the table, but you're having trouble pumping enough, it is my opinion that it's perfectly OK to add a few solid foods to your baby's diet to help get through the day. This assumes that your baby is getting close to six months old, and that the vast majority of his nutrition is still coming from breastmilk. If you're going to start solids early, the whole point is to have your child care provider feed all of the solids, and provide exclusively breastmilk when you and your baby are together. This means that you can pump a little less while still maximizing the amount of breastmilk. Sometimes one meal each day that includes some rice cereal, carrots or pears is enough to keep your baby satisfied while you're at work. Talk to your doctor about what foods to start with. Start with the foods least likely to create an allergic reaction – (that's why milk, seafood and peanuts are delayed – because allergies to these foods are common). The least allergenic foods are rice, bananas, orange vegetables (carrots, squash), pears, apples, and, oddly enough, lamb.

If solids are rejected

My son, an independent soul to this day, refused any of your standard pureed baby foods. It took me a while to figure out that this was not an issue with the foods, but with the means of delivery. It was all about control – with pureed foods he was at the mercy of the spoon-wielder. Once I started giving him things he could pick up on his own, he ate just fine. So if your baby rejects the jars of foods, they may just need some home cooking for a while. My son loved cooked, cubed carrots and sweet potatoes, ground lamb, and of course, cheerios. I think we went through about ¼ of a box of rice cereal with him. My daughter would eat anything that wasn't tied down, and the only issue with her was getting the spoon to her mouth fast enough. All kids are different. If your baby doesn't like what you offer, try different foods, but also try different textures, different amounts of doneness, and different sized bites. And, if they totally reject a food, remember that their little palates are maturing every day, so try it again in a week.

No need to rush or stress

If you're pumping plenty of milk, your baby nurses well, and has no interest in solid foods, there's really no need to rush. Some babies have texture and gagging issues that make it hard for them to eat solid foods until they're a little older. This is fine. The primary function of solid foods in the first six months they're offered is just so kids can learn the physical skills of eating. Most of their nutrition still comes from breastmilk or a substitute. Let your baby set the pace. If they're still not able to manage a spoon of rice cereal at 10 months, have a chat with your doctor about any swallowing or sensory integration issues, but most babies just start eating when they're ready. You'll know.

Remember, even as adults, we all have very different attitudes about food. My five-year-old son would prefer to live on milk and crackers, while my three-year-old daughter got in trouble at Thanksgiving for stealing the black olives and grilled oysters off the table before anyone had sat down, and ate most of the sauerkraut. Personally, I can't eat okra because I think it's too slimy. So remember, as you introduce solid foods, your baby should be exposed to a variety of foods, but there will certainly be some that they don't care for, and some eaters will be more adventurous than others.

Growth spurts

You probably remember your baby's first growth spurt – it happened around 7-10 days of age. That was the day you didn't get up off the couch because you had a baby permanently attached to your breast. But, it passed, and as a result your milk supply increased to meet your growing baby's needs. When a mom and baby are together all day, this is what all of the growth spurts look like – a baby decides to nurse pretty much non-stop for a day or two, and as a result mom's milk supply is increased, and they go back to normal very quickly.

For a working mom, growth spurts are harder, there's no doubt about it. A growth spurt can start during the day, which can look like this: you get a call from the daycare that they've run out of milk, or when you pick up your baby at the end of the day, they've used up all the milk you'd left in the freezer. The problem with this is that your baby started eating more before you were able to respond by demanding more milk from your breasts. You're also left with a shortfall in the amount of milk you have for the next day. The natural response is to just grab some milk from the freezer and use it to add to the amount you pumped, but then your supply is no longer in balance with your baby's demand. If the growth spurt only lasts a day or two, this may not be a problem, but a growth spurt often leads to a baby taking a slightly larger amount, so if you just add milk from the freezer, you're the one left behind (so to speak).

How can you deal with this? The pre-emptive strike is to have your daycare call you as soon as they notice your baby taking more than usual during the day. You might be able to squeeze in an extra pumping session that day to start boosting production. Remember, you probably won't see more milk right away, but you'll be letting your body know that more will be needed in the next few days. You'll also be mimicking the frequent nursing pattern of a baby in a growth spurt. If you can't pump more at work, you might be able to squeeze in one extra session at home. Or, just pump 5 minutes longer each pumping session.

If you don't find out until the end of the day that your baby has taken a lot more than usual, pay special attention to letting your baby nurse as frequently as possible when you're home. This will boost your supply, while also letting your baby get more "from the tap" – meaning you may not have to increase your pumping.

The other way you'll see a growth spurt start is your baby will nurse a lot more during the night – to the degree that you notice a reduced output when you have your first pumping session the next day. The solutions are the same – increase pumping if you can, pump before or after work, and focus on frequent nursing. Some babies hold out during the day so that the only sign of the growth spurt is increased nursing at night – but it can make it hard to pump even your normal amount. Just remember the basics – the more milk you take out of your breasts, the more milk you will make.

A growth spurt can also be a useful reminder that your body is still doing a lot of work making milk for your baby. Rest as much as you can, turn your attention back to good eating, and let any extra commitments go for a couple of days. Let someone cook dinner for you or splurge on take-out and veg on the couch with a nursing baby as much as you can. These are basic things, but ones we all tend to forget as the busy life of a working mom takes over.

The key thing to remember about growth spurts is that they only last a day or two. If you can keep up with your baby during this time, you'll stay in balance once it's over. Some moms who have responded very quickly to a growth spurt by pumping more find that they have a pleasant little stash of extra milk once it's over and the baby goes back to their usual amount of nursing and bottles.

Biting

I hate to even think of the number of moms I know who quit nursing when their baby started teething. I doubt there's a nursing mom alive who hasn't been bitten at one point, but if you address it quickly, you can keep it from happening more than once or twice.

Biting in babies is pretty predictable. When they are teething, they will want to chomp on anything in their mouth – it just makes the gums feel better. But, they won't chomp when they're hungry. If you suspect teething or have been bitten already, watch your baby carefully when she's nursing. She'll wind down to the end of a feeding, then usually start to look around or wiggle – this is when the bite will happen. With a chronic biter, just end the feeding or switch sides when this restlessness starts. My friend Laura swore that her baby would never give up biting – but once she started watching her more carefully, she did find that it was pretty predictable.

There are a few other tricks to deal with biting. The one that worked for me was to press my baby's head *in* when he bit. This is totally counterintuitive because all you want to do is get those teeth *off* your breast, not further on. But it works because as you press in, your baby's nose is blocked by breast, and he has to open his mouth (thus releasing your nipple) to get a breath of air. I only had to do this once – babies do not like having their nose blocked, as you may have noticed.

Another method is to end the feeding at the first bite. Take your baby from the breast, place her on the floor, and say "No" in a stern voice. Try not to scream – you don't want to scare your baby, and you don't want it to become a game. Just be firm. No biting.

You'll need to know your baby's personality to know what will work for you, but babies will learn quickly not to do what gets their food taken away from them.

What not to try: Don't numb your baby's gums with anbesol or ice before nursing – if they can't feel their gums, they may not realize if they're biting. It's OK to give some Tylenol for teething pain, which may reduce biting. Give your baby something cool to chew on between feedings. My mother likes to freeze a wet washcloth (the center of the washcloth is twisted up into a point) and let them suck on it – this worked better than all of the teething toys I'd gone out and bought at no small expense.

Nursing strikes

Sometimes a baby will refuse to nurse for no apparent reason. This can be heartbreaking for a mom who has worked so hard pumping so that her baby will keep nursing. The nursing strike is a bit of a mystery. It is a different thing than a baby who starts to prefer the bottle, because some babies who never have bottles will still go on nursing strikes.

Sometimes a strike can happen when a baby notices the world around them is more interesting – often this happens around four months, and again around nine months. With a distractible baby, sometimes nursing in a quiet or dark room is all that is needed to get her nursing again. Sometimes you will need to focus on nursing when the baby is sleepy or very relaxed, like you do for a baby showing a bottle preference (see the section "Breast refusal" in Chapter 8 for more suggestions).

Some babies will stop nursing around a stressful event in their lives. Lili and her husband were desperately trying to get Ariel to sleep longer at night, and had resorted to letting her cry alone in her crib a couple of times. At the same time, Ariel bit Lili while she was nursing, and Lili spoke to her sternly and put her on the floor to end the nursing session – just like you're supposed to. Somehow the combination of these two stresses was enough to convince Ariel that she was not willing to nurse anymore. I will say in Lili's defense, she didn't do anything wrong. Ariel (to this day) is an incredibly strong-willed child and always very particular about feedings. She just happened to respond to stressful events by taking charge of one of the only things she could control – whether she would nurse or not.

Most babies will go back to the breast after a strike within a few days. If they are old enough, try to feed them from a cup during the strike so that they do not come to expect a bottle. In my opinion, it is OK to withhold bottles for a few days as your baby works through a strike. However, you need to let your baby be your guide. If your baby is not nursing within a day or two, and is not taking any other foods, then you must feed them somehow.

Is this self-weaning? A lot of moms mistake a nursing strike for self-weaning, and stop offering the breast. However, baby-led weaning looks a lot different from a nursing strike. If a baby self-weans, you will see them gradually reduce the amount they are nursing over time. A nursing strike tends to come on suddenly, and can usually be traced to a stressful event or period of increased distractibility. And after a few days, a nursing strike usually ends, and the baby resumes nursing as usual.

Sometimes a nursing strike does lead to weaning, even with the most conscientious mom. This is very difficult emotionally – and is what happened to Ariel and Lili. After Ariel began her strike, Lili tells the story of what happened next:

I took 2 days off from work and spent a ton of time with her. I tried every day for a month to nurse her – it wasn't working, and was not helping my sanity or her sleep. I figured I'd at least out-stubborn her by continuing to pump and not buy formula. I would pump in the morning when I got up, twice at work, and once before bed. She still drank breastmilk out of sippy cups, so I just pumped until close to her first birthday, then weaned off the pump and finished up the milk in the stash.

Lili continued to pump and provide breastmilk for Ariel well past her first birthday, and while she was upset that Ariel stopped nursing, she was proud that she'd been able to nurse her for so long and provide her with such good nutrition.

Normal sleep patterns

Babies are born without any sleep habits, but most get into something of a pattern by the time you go back to work.

> You may even have a baby who sleeps most of the night – but realize that this is not typical. Babies need to eat frequently, especially in the first six months, and need to get a lot of their nutrition during the night. In my mind, the lucky working moms are the ones whose babies wake often to feed at night, but then go right back to sleep! This way you don't have to pump as much, but you still get a good nights rest.

In any case, your baby has a pattern of how they sleep, and it's something you get used to. And then, just as you start to feel comfortable with the pattern, it changes. Are you doing something wrong? Did you ruin your baby's sleep by keeping him out past bedtime that one night? Will he ever sleep normally again after that trip to grandmas where he cried until 2 AM? Short answer, no. You didn't do anything wrong, you can't "ruin" your baby's sleep. The longer answer, though, is that baby's sleep patterns are very sensitive to disruption. While most babies return to their typical sleep patterns after a disruption has passed, the change can last several days.

What causes changes in sleep patterns? What doesn't? A few things off the top of my head: taking a trip, staying home too much, spending the night in a different bed, a long car ride, learning a new skill, trying a new food, changes at daycare, meeting new people, having a busy day, having a less-than-busy day, being around loud noises, being where it's too quiet, mom and dad fighting, and being in a bad mood because the stars are not properly aligned.

I think a frequently overlooked but common cause of sleep pattern changes is learning a new skill. If your baby slept five hours at a stretch and is now up every two, take a look at what he's doing during the day. Is he about to roll over? Did he just start sitting up? Is he using a spoon by himself? Often when a baby learns a new skill, he'll regress in other areas for a while – and sleeping is a skill. The good news is that once the new skill is mastered, the old ones come back, including the old sleeping patterns. By being aware of what you're baby is doing developmentally, you can start to anticipate and accept the changes in sleep. While you'll still lose some sleep, I find I adapt better if I at least understand what's going on.

Getting a baby to sleep through the night

First, let's be clear that "sleeping through the night" means sleeping for 5 hours. That's the medical definition. While we'd like it to be going to bed at 7:30 and waking at 6, this is not a realistic possibility for most babies. But if your baby is over six months old and still waking every two hours, you can probably start to do a few things to encourage him or her to sleep longer.

The No-Cry Sleep Solution by Elizabeth Pantley has a lot of good ideas for getting your baby to sleep longer without using the "cry it out" technique. The basic principle of helping a baby sleep longer is that they need to be able to reproduce the conditions in which they fell asleep on their own. Nobody can keep a baby from waking up during the night, but what we can do is give them tools to help them fall back asleep.

Personally, I am not at all in favor of letting babies "cry it out." I mean, think about it. They learn to stay quiet at night because they learn that nobody's going to meet their needs, so why even bother crying. They've been abandoned, might as well conserve energy. I want my kids to know that I'm there for them, that their needs will be met. Which is why I think it's cruel to wait quietly nearby as your baby screams her head off.

However, that said, I have a few words in defense of Dr. Ferber, because I think his method actually has merit. When we talk about "Ferberizing" a baby, most people think this means just leaving a baby alone to cry for as long as it takes them to fall asleep. This is not what Dr. Ferber says in his book. If you're going to try it – buy the book. First of all, he says that no sleep training at all should happen before a baby is six months old – which I agree with. Then he gives pretty reasonable solutions for helping an older baby or young child sleep longer – none of which involve abandonment. The baby always knows that a parent is nearby, and parents are encouraged to talk to their babies, rub their backs, and let them know that they are safe. Yes, there is some crying involved, but I think Dr. Ferber actually encourages parents to help their children feel safe in their sleep environment. We used his method with great success to get our 2 year old to stay in his room at night. And, when we got tired of getting up at night to nurse a younger baby, we just brought them into our bed.

And, just like there are good eaters and picky eaters, there are people who will grow up to with the ability to sleep through mortar rounds, and those who wake up when a mouse runs across the kitchen floor three stories down. I don't think we, as parents, have much influence over whether our child will be a sound or light sleeper. Respect what genetics has provided, and work with what you've got. So if your best friend's baby sleeps 8 hours at night, be gracious. Say "how nice for you." And then enjoy the extra time you get with your baby during the late hours. It won't last forever. Soon you'll be up all night waiting for them to come home from a party and banging on the door for them to get out of bed at noon.

12 | The End of the Line

Deciding to quit or cut back

If you do decide that working and pumping is just not working out for you, I have a few suggestions.

1. First ask yourself "is there something else going on?" Is having to deal with pumping that last straw breaking your back? Would it be easier if you had more help with other things? (This is a good self-examination process for any new mom anyway.) Conditioned to be supermoms, we hate to say "it's too much, I can't do it all," but saying these exact words is very liberating! Sometimes something as simple as having your partner agree to wash your pump parts each night can make the difference between continuing and quitting. Or finding the right technique or dietary improvement or new pump to allow you to pump more. Figure out the changes you want to try (see #2 and #3 below) before you throw in the towel – then proceed to step #4 if it's still not working out for you.

2. See if partial supplementation is the right answer. Sometimes taking away the pressure to provide every drop of breastmilk for your baby is enough to make the pumping feel totally manageable. Any breastmilk is better than none, and while breastmilk is the best food, infant formula really is a reasonable substitute, especially in the older baby.

3. Set a timeline for things to get better. When things are hard, the natural inclination is to quit right then and there, at this very instant! But a rash decision is rarely a good one. Set a timeline for yourself. Tell yourself that if it doesn't get better by Sunday, or by the end of the month, or by your birthday, then you'll stop. While pumping another 3 months may have become too unwieldy of a goal, pumping until the end of the week is usually something we can manage. And the best decisions are generally made on a Sunday, after a weekend of rest, rather than on Friday afternoon when you've absolutely had it up to here.

4. Don't beat yourself up. If you have to completely give up pumping, look at what you have achieved! Make a note of each milestone or goal that you did meet – whether that was just breastfeeding for the first month of your baby's life, or providing breastmilk for several months. You have given your baby the best start to a lifetime of good health, and if pumping is causing you so much stress that it's cutting into your ability to be a good mom, it's not worth it. This is a decision only you can make, so revisit steps 1, 2 and 3 above, and then once you make an informed and well thought-out decision, let yourself off the hook. You really are a good mom, and we all do the best we can for our children – if that means a mom who's less stressed out when she stops pumping, then so be it.

My friend Beth pumped for six months, then decided to quit pumping and start some formula. Here's her story:

I breastfed exclusively for six months, and went back to work when my second baby was two months old. I packed my pump supplies every night at the same time I made my 4 year old's lunch for the next day. The first week back to work was an adjustment but as my body acclimated to needing to pump at work, I just knew that twice a day at the same time each day I needed to take 10 minutes and basically get the milk out! My body and I got into a predictable routine. I kept the pumped milk in a cooler in a fridge at work. It was a black cooler and no one asked what was inside (and I didn't tell because I knew not everyone I worked with could handle it). Once I got to 6 months, which was the goal I had set for myself, I allowed myself to reevaluate. I was really ready to be done pumping and so I brought formula to daycare shortly after that milestone. Looking back, I recognize that there is a "bottle culture" in many daycares. I knew that George was eating enough food that he didn't really need bottles during the day, and he certainly could have had some water, but not having "milk" in a bottle is odd for the infant caregiver. They often time bottle-feed right before nap and it becomes part of the routine. I felt OK with formula being another "new food" we were introducing (vs. formula being the sole source of nutrition), since George was still getting mostly breastmilk since I was nursing at home and during the night. It became a concession I was willing to make.

I wasn't willing to continue pumping and I knew daycare expected a bottle to be part of the day; so two 4 oz bottles per day became part of my baby's ever expanding food choices. George is almost a year old now, and still nursing often when we're together. I nursed his brother until he was two and a half, so I don't see any reason George won't do the same thing.

Weaning from the pump

When you decide it's time to stop pumping, this is a big milestone in your life as a mother. Celebrate your success! If you google "hanging up the horns" you will find many poignant message board posts in which moms celebrate their time pumping, giving the best to their babies. Many of these posts talk about the hardships encountered along the way, but all celebrate the accomplishment of being a working and pumping mom.

Not pumping doesn't mean not breastfeeding

You can stop pumping during the day and keep breastfeeding for as long as you want to. This is easier if your baby is older than about 10 months, since you can substitute other foods for most of the breastmilk you will no longer be providing and may not need to use formula. With your doctor's approval, you can start to offer your baby cow's milk, soy milk or water to drink, while adding in more sources of protein and food with nutritious fats.

Keep offering the breast when you and your baby are together, and you'll find that breastfeeding can continue for some time after you stop pumping. See the section "Breastfeeding beyond a year "for more information on extended nursing.

Take it slow

Just like weaning a baby, you want to wean from the pump gradually. If you just show up at work without your pump one Monday, you'll probably find yourself engorged by lunch, a plugged duct by five, and a breast infection by Wednesday. Try to give yourself at least two weeks to completely wean from daytime pumping.

For me, the easiest thing to do was to gradually push my pumping sessions back until they effectively "fell off" the end of the day. For example, if you're pumping three times a day, at 10, 12:30 and 3, you can change each session by 15-30 minutes per day (depending on your comfort level), until your sessions are (for example) at 11:30, 2 and 4:30. At that point, you can probably skip the 4:30 and just wait till you pick up your baby to nurse. If you feel full at the end of the day, your baby will have a satisfying nursing session – this will encourage them to keep breastfeeding even as you cut out pumping. If your schedule is very flexible, you can decide to just pump when you feel full. You can also gradually decrease your milk production by pumping for a shorter duration each time while keeping the sessions at the same time. Only you can decide what will work best for you – but just remember – gradual!!

Remember from the "Demand and Supply" Chapter, your storage capacity determines how long you can go between pumping sessions without feeling full, so if you have a large storage capacity, you may be able to stretch out your pumping times a lot faster than someone with a smaller storage capacity (who will feel full sooner).

A gradual approach to pump-weaning also lets you see the effect that not pumping has on your milk supply. You may find that you need to offer more foods to your baby during the day on days you are home, or you may find that your baby is still satisfied nursing – it depends on the individual. You can also keep nursing at night for as long or as short a time as you want to. My kids gave up nursing to bed before any of the other sessions, but were very attached to nursing at the end of the work day until they were about 18 months old. Then they kept nursing in the morning for years after I stopped pumping – it was a great way for all of us to wake up, snuggled in the "big bed."

What about your milk supply?

You may find that weaning entirely from the pump decreases your milk supply more than you want it to – in that case, you can always add back one midday session. There's no law that says you have to stop pumping at any particular time, although many moms end up stopping pumping around the 12-month mark – just because they've gotten tired of it.

If you decide to stop pumping when your baby is younger than about 9 or 10 months, you may find that you have to supplement with some formula on the days you are home. Weaning from the pump with a very young baby (younger than six months) can make it challenging to keep breastfeeding – but it's not impossible. You may see a drop in your milk supply over the course of the whole day, so you should keep a careful eye on your baby to ensure she's getting enough to eat. If you need to supplement with formula when you and your baby are together, you can feed the formula from a cup, sippy cup, or mixed with rice cereal to avoid the nipple confusion that can happen – especially when mom is giving the bottles. Even if you are supplementing, I think babies are more likely to keep breastfeeding if mom never gives them a bottle. Sleeping with or near your baby can encourage your baby to nurse frequently at night, maximizing the amount of breastmilk she gets in her diet. Please check out the section on "Nighttime parenting" and "Reverse cycling" in Chapter 8 for more information on how you can safely keep your baby receiving breastmilk at night.

If your baby is older (like more than 10 months or so), you can stop pumping and just provide more nutritious foods during the day to make up for the breastmilk they are not getting. Dairy foods like yogurt and cheese are easy sources of calcium and calories – but are by no means necessary for a healthy diet. Formula is also a healthy supplemental food, and can be mixed with infant cereal and fed from a spoon if you don't want to offer it in bottles. Just keep a close eye on your baby's energy level and developmental milestones any time you make a significant change in how you are feeding them.

Hanging up the horns

For a lot of women, "hanging up the horns" is a significant milestone as a mother. My Working and Pumping message board always brought me to tears when someone would post their "hanging up the horns" message. A poignant reflection on the transition to motherhood, the sacrifices we make to provide our babies with the best, the joys of breastfeeding, the pride we feel in meeting our goals, and our child's transition out of babyhood. I get a little choked up just thinking about it now.

Breastfeeding beyond a year

My friend Emily, who is breastfeeding her son on the eve of his third birthday summed it up so well for me: "Nobody starts breastfeeding thinking they'll be nursing a toddler who can talk!" Most of the moms I pumped with started out wanting to breastfeed for a year. But then, with few exceptions, we got to a year and said "now what?" One by one we stopped pumping at work, but breastfeeding before and after work was so easy and enjoyable – why would we give it up? And so thirteen months stretched to eighteen and on to age two and sometimes three. Who would have figured, a bunch of working women becoming extended breastfeeders! But why on earth not? What could be easier?

You don't often see older babies and toddlers nursing, but believe me, it's going on all around you. Most mothers of babies older than a year become "closet nursers." When you don't see other moms nursing these "big kids" out and about, you just figure it's not something that's done. But once you start asking around, people will sheepishly admit to nursing for years – as if it's some big embarrassing secret!

Instead of asking "why breastfeed beyond a year?," I just thought of it as "why stop?" Some pediatricians and books recommend weaning at a year, and one book I particularly dislike even says "if you don't wean your baby by a year, they may never stop." What does that mean? *Never?* They'll be unwilling to look at out-of-state colleges because they're still nursing? Somehow I doubt it. Biologically, we're programmed for weaning between the ages of 2 and 7, and most kids, if left to their own devices, will wean by about three and a half. Breastmilk stays a nutritious food for your child, and still provides immunity, so again, "why stop?"

If you talk to new moms about breastfeeding beyond a year, they'll often start to get a really glazed look, thinking about nursing 10 times a day for another week is usually about all they can manage.

But after a year, breastfeeding is a totally different thing. Your baby is eating a variety of solid foods, can drink from a cup, and can be dissuaded with a toy or snack if you don't feel like feeding at that exact second. They can tell you when they want to nurse, instead of having to watch for feeding cues, and if you're not immediately available, they can usually find something else to do for a few minutes.

Here's what nursing my three year old looks like: most mornings she asks to come lie down in bed with me when she wakes up. She gets out of her own bed, walks to my room, climbs in bed and says "may I have some mee-mees please?" She'll lie with me, nurse for about five minutes, then say "all done," and get up and on with her day. And that's it. No nursing to bed, for naps, or after school, we're down to just that once. Sometimes when she's feeling under the weather, she'll ask for more – which is great. She's getting a little liquid in, some antibodies, and comfort, all in one easily portable package.

Watch your language

Given that you don't know how long your child will nurse, I recommend giving nursing a name you're comfortable with in public. My friend Anna used to offer her daughter "a little tit" when she was a baby – but I'm not sure how she'd feel about a two year old calling out for that in a crowded room. My friend Lauren's baby Tenaya said "Naya nurse!" which was usually fine, except during the swearing-in ceremony of her grandmother as a federal judge – but it got a good laugh from the bench.

Your child will come up with a name that you like, but you do have the power to edit their selection. Mee-mees, nursies, num-nums, nummies, nursies, mama milk, milkies, nu-nus, you and your child can pick what works for you. Calling nursing by your chosen name from an early age, even if you don't plan to breastfeed after they learn to talk, can help you be ready just in case you don't end up stopping when you thought you would.

The last word

It is only fitting that my friend Emily, who started this project with me five (!!) years ago, should have the last word. Here is the email she sent me today:

Here is a great quote for your book - on looking back at the nursing relationship with your child. It's from Housekeeping by Marilynne Robinson. The set up is that the father has died, and the 3 teenaged girls are spending all of their time hovering near their mother. "Never since they were small children had they clustered about her so, and never since then had she been so aware of the smell of their hair, their softness, breathiness, abruptness. It filled her with a strange elation, the same pleasure she had felt when any one of them, as a sucking child, had fastened her eyes on her face and reached for her other breast, her hair, her lips, hungry to touch, eager to be filled for a while and sleep." When I read that I realized in my head what I know in my heart - I keep nursing Charlie to keep that little bit of baby in him. He has always had lovely wandering hands, not that pinching, pulling type, but a soft stroking touch. When he nurses, he becomes that baby and touches me with those baby hands. That is what I don't want to give up.

APPENDIX

"The Baby Friendly Hospital"
Ten Steps to Successful Breastfeeding

Every facility providing maternity services and care for newborn infants should:

1.   Have a written breastfeeding policy that is routinely communicated to all health care staff.

2.   Train all health care staff in skills necessary to implement this policy.

3.   Inform all pregnant women about the benefits and management of breastfeeding.

4.   Help mothers initiate breastfeeding within half an hour of birth.

5.   Show mothers how to breastfeed, and how to maintain lactation even if they should be separated from their infants.

6.   Give newborn infants no food or drink other than breast milk, unless medically indicated.

7.   Practice rooming-in - that is, allow mothers and infants to remain together - 24 hours a day.

8.   Encourage breastfeeding on demand.

9.   Give no artificial teats or pacifiers (also called dummies or soothers) to breastfeeding infants.

10. Foster the establishment of breastfeeding support groups and refer mothers to them on discharge from the hospital or clinic.

Source: *Protecting, Promoting and Supporting Breastfeeding: The Special Role of Maternity Services,* a joint WHO/UNICEF statement published by the <u>World Health Organization</u>.

Feeding Log

Circle a number each time you feed or change a diaper.

Day 1
Feedings 1 2 3 4 5 6 7 8 9 10 11 12 + + + + +
Wet diapers   1 + + +
Dirty diapers 1 + +

Day 2
Feedings 1 2 3 4 5 6 7 8 9 10 11 12 + + + + +
Wet diapers   1 2 + + +
Dirty diapers 1 2 + +

Day 3
Feedings 1 2 3 4 5 6 7 8 9 10 11 12 + + + + +
Wet diapers   1 2 3 + + + +
Dirty diapers 1 2 3 + +

Day 4
Feedings 1 2 3 4 5 6 7 8 9 10 11 12 + + + + +
Wet diapers   1 2 3 4 + + +
Dirty diapers 1 2 3 + +

Day 5
Feedings 1 2 3 4 5 6 7 8 9 10 11 12 + + + + +
Wet diapers   1 2 3 4 5 + + +
Dirty diapers 1 2 3 + +

Day 6
Feedings 1 2 3 4 5 6 7 8 9 10 11 12 + + + + +
Wet diapers   1 2 3 4 5 6 + +
Dirty diapers 1 2 3 + +

Day 7
Feedings 1 2 3 4 5 6 7 8 9 10 11 12 + + + + +
Wet diapers   1 2 3 4 5 6 + +
Dirty diapers 1 2 3 + +

Day 8
Feedings 1 2 3 4 5 6 7 8 9 10 11 12 + + + + +
Wet diapers   1 2 3 4 5 6 + +
Dirty diapers 1 2 3 + +

Day 9
Feedings 1 2 3 4 5 6 7 8 9 10 11 12 + + + + +
Wet diapers   1 2 3 4 5 6 + +
Dirty diapers 1 2 3 + +

Day 10
Feedings 1 2 3 4 5 6 7 8 9 10 11 12 + + + + +
Wet diapers   1 2 3 4 5 6 + +
Dirty diapers 1 2 3 + +

Day 11
Feedings 1 2 3 4 5 6 7 8 9 10 11 12 + + + + +
Wet diapers   1 2 3 4 5 6 + +
Dirty diapers 1 2 3 + +

Day 12
Feedings 1 2 3 4 5 6 7 8 9 10 11 12 + + + + +
Wet diapers   1 2 3 4 5 6 + +
Dirty diapers 1 2 3 + +

Day 13
Feedings 1 2 3 4 5 6 7 8 9 10 11 12 + + + + +
Wet diapers   1 2 3 4 5 6 + +
Dirty diapers 1 2 3 + +

Day 14
Feedings 1 2 3 4 5 6 7 8 9 10 11 12 + + + + +
Wet diapers   1 2 3 4 5 6 + +
Dirty diapers 1 2 3 + +

Birthweight   _____

Weight at 3 day checkup   _____

Weight at 2 week checkup   _____

Excerpted with permission from *My Pregnancy and Breastfeeding Calendar*
Available from www.iBreastfeeding.com

Caring for Breastfed Babies

Many mothers want to continue breastfeeding after they return to work or school. They feel good knowing their milk helps keep their babies healthy, and they savor the special closeness they feel with their babies, especially when they must be away all day. You can help!

- Encourage mothers to breastfeed at their convenience at your facility.

- Help the day begin and end calmly by offering the mother a place to rock and breastfeed her baby (this space can also be used for pumping). This quiet time can help baby transition peacefully to other caregivers, and helps make the drive home easier for mom.

- Put mothers in touch with other women who have successfully combined breastfeeding and working, and post a list of community breastfeeding resources.

Helping Breastfed Babies Adjust to the Childcare Setting

- Being separated from "Mommy" can be a difficult adjustment for any child or infant. Holding and cuddling is important for baby's development and can be the secret to a peaceful and enriching childcare experience.

- Realize that breastfed babies are used to being held closely and often. If you are busy with many children, "wearing" an infant in a sling or carrier can provide the infant with the close contact she needs, while leaving your hands free to care for older children.

- Giving baby a blanket that has been in contact with the mother's skin may also comfort the breastfed baby.

Handling Human Milk

According to the American Academy of Pediatrics (AAP) and Centers for Disease Control (CDC), breastmilk should be stored and handled the same as other foods and nutritional supplements. The milk can be stored in the refrigerator or freezer along with other foods. Universal precautions are not necessary when handling expressed breastmilk.

- ✗ Post **Human Milk Storage Guidelines** where bottles are heated and on the refrigerator.

- ✗ Mothers work hard to express their milk, and care should be taken so it is not wasted.

- ✗ It may be helpful to store a small amount of frozen milk in case a baby finishes all of his bottles. Ask mothers if they would like to provide you with a few "backup" ounces.

Human milk can be stored:

- At room temperature (66-72°F, 19-22°C) for up to 10 hours

- In a refrigerator (32-39°F, 0-4°C) for up to 8 days. Do not store in the door, as it is not as cold.

- In a freezer compartment inside a refrigerator for up to 2 weeks

- In a freezer compartment with a separate door for up to 3 to 4 months.

- In a separate deep freeze (0°F, -19°C) for up to 6 months.

Warming:

- Thaw and/or heat under warm, running water.

- Gently swirl milk before testing the temperature. Swirling will also redistribute the cream into the milk. (It is normal for stored milk to separate into a cream and milk layer.) Do not shake.

- Do not use a microwave oven to heat human milk or bring it to the boiling point.

- Discuss with the mother if she wants milk left in the bottle after a feeding saved and used for a later feeding. It is considered safe to do this if the milk has not been frozen.

Thawed (previously frozen) milk:

- If milk has been frozen and thawed, it can be kept in the refrigerator for up to 24 hours. It should not be refrozen. It is not known whether previously frozen milk that is left in the bottle after a feeding can be safely kept until the next feeding.

Feeding the breastfed baby

- ⚥ *Breastmilk is digested more easily than formula*, so breastfed babies usually get hungry more often than formula-fed babies, about every 1½ to 3 hours. Feed the breastfed baby when their cues indicate hunger, not on a schedule. Early hunger cues include mouth movements, rooting, sucking on hands, and restlessness (crying is a late sign of hunger).

- ⚥ *Feed the baby in a way that mimics breastfeeding.* Hold the baby in an upright position, and never put a baby to bed with a bottle. Switch from one side to another midway through a feeding – this provides for eye stimulation and brain development, helps pace feedings, and keeps the baby from developing a preference for one side.

- ⚥ *Begin feeds gently*, allowing the infant to draw nipple into mouth rather than pushing it in, so that baby controls when the feed begins. Stroke baby's lips with the nipple to illicit a rooting response with a wide-open mouth, and then allow the baby to "accept" or draw in the nipple.

- ⚥ *Feed Slowly.* An infant's system needs time to recognize that they are full – rapid feedings can lead to overfeeding, which can cause discomfort in the baby, and can put the mother's milk supply at risk. Pause frequently during feedings to burp, switch sides, or talk to the baby. Keeping the bottle close to horizontal allows a baby to control the pace of feeding better than if the bottle is vertical and gravity drives the milk flow.

- ⚥ *Stop feeding when the baby is ready.* Do not encourage a baby to finish "just the last bit" of a bottle. If baby is drowsing off and releases the bottle nipple before the bottle is empty, that means baby is done; don't reawaken the baby to finish. If bottles are often left unfinished, ask the mother to send the milk in smaller amounts to reduce waste.

- Because breastmilk is completely digested, breastfed babies often do not need to eat as much as babies who are exclusively formula-fed. The amount of breastmilk consumed may or may not increase with the age of the baby.

Advantages of feeding in this manner:

The infant will consume a volume appropriate to their size and age, rather than over- or under-eating. This supports the working and pumping mom who will be more likely to pump a daily volume that matches the baby's demand. This can minimize colic-like symptoms seen in the baby whose stomach is too full. It also supports the breastfeeding relationship, leading to increased success at breastfeeding for mothers who are separated from their nurslings.

Other Ways to Offer Support to breastfeeding mothers

Breastfeeding is natural, but not always easy. Your support can make the difference.

- Ask the mother what to feed her baby. Many mothers want their babies to be fed only breastmilk; while others provide a combination of breastmilk and formula.

- Talk with the mother about her special requests if difficulties arise. For instance, if baby gets hungry before mother arrives at the end of the day, does she want you to provide a pacifier, some water, a small amount of breastmilk, solid foods, or formula?

- Tell her you are proud of her efforts to provide her milk for her baby!

INDEX

295

Ordering Information

Hale Publishing

1712 N. Forest St.
Amarillo, Texas 79106 USA

8:00 am to 5:00 pm CST

☒

Call...806-376-9900
Sales...800-378-1317
FAX...806-376-9901

☒

Online Web Orders...
http://www.iBreastfeeding.com